D0849515

Putin's
Energy Agenda

PUTIN'S

ENERGY

AGENDA

The Contradictions of Russia's Resource Wealth

Stefan Hedlund

LYNNE
RIENNER
PUBLISHERS

BOULDER
LONDON

Published in the United States of America in 2014 by
Lynne Rienner Publishers, Inc.
1800 30th Street, Boulder, Colorado 80301
www.rienner.com

and in the United Kingdom by
Lynne Rienner Publishers, Inc.
3 Henrietta Street, Covent Garden, London WC2E 8LU

© 2014 by Lynne Rienner Publishers, Inc. All rights reserved

Library of Congress Cataloging-in-Publication Data
Hedlund, Stefan, 1953–
  Putin's energy agenda : the contradictions of Russia's resource wealth /
Stefan Hedlund.
      pages cm
  Includes bibliographical references and index.
  ISBN 978-1-62637-069-2 (hc : alk. paper) 1. Energy policy—Russia
(Federation) I. Title.
  HD9502.R82H43 2014
  333.790947—dc23

                                                    2013048221

British Cataloguing in Publication Data
A Cataloguing in Publication record for this book
is available from the British Library.

Printed and bound in the United States of America

      The paper used in this publication meets the requirements
  ∞   of the American National Standard for Permanence of
      Paper for Printed Library Materials Z39.48-1992.

  5 4 3 2 1

What is happening in Russia?
They are stealing.
—Nikolai Karamzin

Contents

Preface

Since Vladimir Putin came to power, news regarding Russia's energy sector has tended to be strikingly polarized. The positive side has been dominated by stories about the effects of a massive influx of petro-dollars, about how persistent deficits in the state budget were suddenly turned into surpluses, how wages and pensions were increasingly paid on time, how a crippling sovereign foreign debt was more or less eliminated, and how large reserves of foreign currency were accumulated that would come in handy when the global financial crisis struck.

The negative side, in contrast, has featured stories about how the Kremlin began throwing its weight around in foreign energy relations, highlighting how Tokyo and Beijing were drawn into a frustrating bidding war for an oil pipeline to the Pacific, how countries in Central Asia were transformed into a game board for a new great contest over that region's energy resources, how other countries in Russia's near abroad were drawn into repeated pricing disputes, leading to periodic interruptions of gas flows, and how even some of the new European Union member states experienced supply shutoffs, causing their populations to freeze in the dead of winter.

When I began work on the book in 2009, the latter imagery dominated. It was a time when outside observers began to worry about reemerging Russian great power or even superpower ambitions, linked to the building of an ersatz "energy superpower." Attention was focused on how Vladimir Putin's "authoritarian restoration" was combined with the wielding of a newfound "energy weapon." The presumed aim of the latter was to restore Russian power and influence by putting political pressure on countries that were dependent, or were becoming dependent, on Russian energy. Alleged bullying by the Kremlin not only attracted substantial media attention, but also became an important foreign policy issue.

As subsequent events would show, much of this imagery was too simplistic and sometimes widely missed the mark. It is true that the sudden accumulation of petrowealth was used in Russia's ambition to make itself great again, and it is true that there were elements of bullying in foreign energy relations. But more important, it is also true that behind the façade of a resurgent authoritarian Russia, a more complex reality may be identified, one in which the Kremlin would itself become the main victim of its growing "resource nationalism."

* * *

Work on the book profited greatly from my month-long stay, in the spring of 2011, at George Washington University's Institute for Russian, European, and Eurasian Studies. Thanks are due in particular to its director, Henry Hale, for hosting me, and to Robert Orttung for generously sharing his time in discussions on Russian energy issues.

Valuable insights into the Chinese angle on Russian energy policy have been derived from several visits to the Russian Research Center at East China Normal University in Shanghai. I am grateful in particular to its director, Feng Shaolei, for generously receiving me, and to Yang Cheng for numerous enlightening conversations, as well as for having several articles of mine translated and published in the center's Chinese-language journal, *Russian Studies*.

Aside from Shanghai, various bits and pieces of the account have been presented at seminars in places ranging from the Freeman Spogli Institute at Stanford University to the Davis Center at Harvard University and the Higher School of Economics in Moscow. Helpful comments on early drafts have been provided by Stephen Blank, Philip Hanson, and Robert Orttung, as well as by two anonymous reviewers. The final draft benefited additionally from extensive comments by a third anonymous reviewer. Sincere thanks are due to them all.

A final set of thanks go to my editor at Lynne Rienner Publishers, Jessica Gribble, for her patience with my repeated rewrites; to my research assistant, Ausra Padskocimaite, for her valuable assistance in a host of different matters; and to my dear wife, Lilian, for putting up with my protracted insistence that weekends are best spent reading about Russian energy policy. Responsibility for remaining errors and omissions remains mine alone.

1

Russia Emerges out of Chaos

The collapse of the Soviet order in Europe was a momentous event. It had been predicted by some, but such predictions had been made for the wrong reasons, such as armed conflict or rebellion by national minorities.[1] The way in which it finally did unravel was both highly unexpected and deeply revealing of the inherent fragility of the system. Mikhail Gorbachev's policies of glasnost, perestroika, and new political thinking were designed to rejuvenate the Soviet Union. But in the end, they brought about its dissolution. The outcome could not fail to bring to mind Alexis de Tocqueville's classic dictum that the most dangerous moment for a bad government is when it begins to reform.[2]

The sudden breakdown of a deeply ingrained bipolar world order was bound to have far-reaching consequences. And so it did. At the outset, most could entertain only positive visions. The end of the Cold War would allow states to cash in on a peace dividend through substantial restructuring and downsizing of their standing military forces. The envisioned transition to a rules-based market economy would open up tantalizing business opportunities, as long-deprived populations would scramble for Western consumer goods. And the transition to democracy and the rule of law would herald a new era of peace and fruitful international cooperation.

The Europeans in particular were prone to see a radiant future ahead. At a meeting in Maastricht in December 1991, only two weeks before the formal dissolution of the Soviet Union, European leaders agreed to transform the European Community into a European Union with a common constitution, a common currency, and eventually a common foreign and security policy. Europe, it was believed, had finally come of age and would now

1

stand ready to assume the responsibilities of a global player. The days when Henry Kissinger could quip about the lack of telephone contact with Europe were finally over.

It did seem very promising. But reality would not live up to the rosy expectations. The transition to a market economy resulted, at best, in what came to be known as a transformational recession. Even in the best-performing countries, such as Poland, production went into years of decline, causing hardship and raising questions about the wisdom of marketizing reform. Countries even less fortunate would experience deep and protracted depression, with severe implications both for the poor and for the pursuit of reform. In Russia, it would not be until 2007 that the level of gross domestic product (GDP) achieved in 1990 was once again attained.

The transition to democracy was similarly marred by setbacks. Although countries in the Baltic and in Central Europe would eventually pass the test of democratic consolidation, reform-minded parties as a rule lost ground to nationalists and to right- and left-wing extremists. Many countries experienced regime interventions that included vote-rigging and other, more blatant forms of electoral fraud. Some even relapsed into clan-based politics and what Max Weber would have referred to as sultanic rule.

The new world order was put to an early test when bloody civil wars broke out in the Balkans, and the Europeans eventually had to turn to the United States for help. The controversy over how to deal with the crisis drove home to Moscow that Russia was still not considered a reliable partner by the West. It was a dismal lesson. Though the Cold War might have been over, the centuries-old tradition of distrust and divergent interests between Russia and the West had not been laid to rest. Slowly but surely, new lines of division—not to mention confrontation—began to emerge.

As an increasingly resentful Russia began to ratchet up its rhetoric, other former socialist states began to strive for integration into Western structures such as the North Atlantic Treaty Organization (NATO) and the European Union (EU). Following much debate, public as well as internal, over how to proceed, in 1999 NATO made a "Big Bang" decision, granting membership to four Central European states (Poland, Hungary, Slovakia, and the Czech Republic), together with three Baltic states (Estonia, Latvia, and Lithuania). In 2004, Bulgaria and Romania followed, and in 2009 Albania was admitted. In a parallel, albeit slower, process, the EU followed suit with a similar enlargement. In 2004, the very same Baltic and Central European states were admitted, together with Slovenia, Malta, and Cyprus. Bulgaria and Romania followed in 2007, and Croatia in 2013.

Although Moscow did grudgingly accept the membership of the Baltic and Central European states in the Western alliances, countries such as Ukraine and Georgia called for lines to be drawn in the sand. Following the Revolution of Roses in Georgia in 2003, President Mikheil Saakashvili pursued a strongly pro-Western policy that included inviting US military advisers to train Georgian troops and sending some of those troops to join US coalition forces in both Iraq and Afghanistan. Following the Orange Revolution in Ukraine in 2004–2005, President Viktor Yushchenko was even allowed to address a joint session of the US Congress, where he received a standing ovation. The doors to NATO for a free and democratic Ukraine appeared to be wide open.

While the desire to join the EU may have been conditioned by a combination of hopes for economic benefit and for the security membership in a Western alliance, that of joining NATO was clearly driven by apprehension over a resurgent Russia. And the haste in undertaking the controversial "Big Bang" enlargement was equally clearly motivated by a fear that the window of opportunity for eastward expansion might soon be shut. From Moscow's perspective, it was becoming clear that Russia was an outcast, not to be considered for membership in either of the two Western alliances. Consequently, some prominent Russian observers became increasingly insistent that enlargement represented a breach of a promise once allegedly made to Gorbachev, that acceptance of German (re)unification would not be followed by one inch of eastward expansion by NATO.[3]

By the time Putin handed over the presidency to Dmitry Medvedev, who was duly elected in March 2008, the process was about to stabilize. The EU was headed for a deep fiscal crisis that would delay any ambitions for further additions to its membership. And the brief war that was fought between Russia and Georgia in August 2008 was viewed on the Russian side as having put a conclusive halt to plans for further NATO expansion. The victory of Viktor Yanukovich in Ukraine's 2010 presidential election signaled the demise of the former heroes of the Orange Revolution, with Viktor Yushchenko completely marginalized and Yulia Tymoshenko headed for prison. The victory, finally, of Bidzina Ivanishvili in Georgia's 2012 parliamentary elections pointed to the pending demise of Mikheil Saakashvili, thus removing a very personal thorn from Putin's side.

It may have looked as though Russia was now well on its way toward recapturing its old position as a great power. The resurgence entailed a customs union formed with Belarus and Kazakhstan in 2010, a common economic space launched with the same members in 2012, and visions of a fully fledged Eurasian Union to be formed in 2015. To Putin, all of this was most satisfactory. In April 2011, he hailed the customs union as "the most important geopolitical and integration event in the post-Soviet space since the break-up of the Soviet Union,"[4] and in February 2013 he said that post-Soviet integration was "unstoppable."[5] Whether these projects will in the end succeed in attracting sufficient membership to overcome the Russian trauma of lost superpower stature remains to be seen. Even if they were to do so, which is highly doubtful, much damage has already been done.

While Americans and Europeans found plenty of reasons for disappointment, not to mention disgruntlement, Russians in general considered themselves the main losers. Their state had been fragmented, their social and economic life had been thrown into turmoil, and their nation's standing on the global scene had been vastly diminished. From the Russian perspective, there were numerous reasons for resentment.

First and foremost was the sense of loss and humiliation associated with the collapse of the Soviet Union. In the words of Marie Mendras: "Twenty years on, the Russians still cannot comprehend how such rapid destruction was possible, and they blame it on Gorbachev and the Communist reformers. Mikhail Gorbachev's political destiny was heroic and tragic."[6] But it was not just Gorbachev who was held culpable. The general chaos that marked the 1990s would be firmly blamed on Boris Yeltsin. To historically conscious Russians, his time in power would come to be known as a "time of trouble," a *smutnoe vremya,* recalling the period of utter chaos that followed in the wake of the collapse of Muscovy, toward the end of the sixteenth century. In addition to the general resentment against Western-inspired reform that emerged during the Yeltsin era, hard-line circles would also and more seriously find reason to view Western policies as a stab in the back, aimed at dismembering Russia in a time of weakness.

Looking back, the first decade after the dissolution of the Soviet Union seems an amorphous period in Russian development. It began with great hopes for a rapid rise in consumer welfare, for global integration, and for a constructive partnership with the West—on equal terms. What followed instead was economic depression, political fragmentation, and a severe identity crisis. The sense of bewilderment about what had happened was manifested in a search for a new Russian identity, most notably so in a special commission established by Yeltsin in 1996 for this very purpose.[7] Although none of this was anticipated at the outset, at least not by any of the leading international actors, with the benefit of hindsight we may see rather clearly why the process evolved the way it did.

The ambition to undertake a transition to democracy and a rules-based market economy was certainly laudable. If reform really could have been implemented with a tabula rasa—without consideration of historical and cultural legacies—then it all might have turned out very differently. Democratization could have ensured accountability in government and thus laid the foundations for credible government enforcement of contractual rights. Marketizing reform could have been based on secure property rights, ensuring improved corporate governance and enhanced efficiency and consequently allowing Russian companies to compete favorably in global markets. And transition to a reasonably sized and structured defense force could have been combined with conversion of military to civilian production. The latter would have allowed the resources and brain power that was housed in military industries and research facilities to ensure a place for

Russia in the global market for civilian high technology. But as events would show, the challenges that were placed before the reformers were much greater than commonly anticipated.

There were good reasons why economics in particular failed to conceptualize the problems ahead. Standard neoclassical economic theory does well when faced with marginal change under conditions of reasonable certainty, all else being equal. The ambition to undertake sweeping systemic change represented something very far removed from the textbook ideal. It was a case of simultaneous change on multiple margins, under conditions of extreme uncertainty and pursued by hosts of actors with multiple agendas, often under the influence of conflicting advice.

theory (dream)

reality

The striking diversity in outcomes in the nearly thirty transition economies at that time drives home an important lesson. Instead of believing that simple deregulation would be sufficient to ensure a successful transition, the great disparity in initial conditions should have been taken into account. Included, here were differences in historical and cultural legacies, and the associated fact that different regimes had very different agendas. What today may look to outside observers as cases of failed reforms may to some regimes represent quite successful outcomes.

What unfolded may be viewed, from a more theoretical perspective, as a major confrontation between the formal and informal dimensions of the institutional matrices of these countries. Agency-based policy formulation aimed to introduce sets of formal institutions that in the case of Russia had been repeatedly attempted before but had never taken root. The counterforce was powerful institutional inertia in systems of informal norms. These norms had emerged in response to the seven decades of market repression that was the reality of central planning, and they were arguably rooted in deeper Russian history.

Recalling Nobel Prize laureate Douglass North's central insight that it is the norms that provide legitimacy for the rules, we may understand why systemic change resulted in so many unintended and often negative consequences.[8] When self-interested actors are faced with opportunity, the core question to ask is whether they will prefer a value-adding or a value-redistributing or even a value-detracting strategy. In plain language, one should ask whether the majority of economic actors will use opportunity to form new ventures that are in accordance with given rules and add to GDP, or will prefer rent-seeking and outright predatory options that enhance their own wealth at the expense of others and in the process detract from GDP.

options

Much of the answer to this core question rests in the third part of North's institutional triad, that of enforcement mechanisms. Under a stable market order that is characterized by the rule of law, actors emulate the norms of the Golden Rule, exercising self-restraint when faced with the temptation to defraud others. Such voluntary rule-abiding behavior is the avenue to a high-performance economy. The alternative is that economic actions are constrained by rules upheld not by internalized informal norms but by government supervision and powerful sanctions.

The Soviet economy was a classic case of the latter. It was marked by a grossly inefficient formal sector, surrounded by an extensive informal sector in which actors attempted to compensate for poor remuneration from formal-sector work with private semilegal or even illegal ventures at the fringes. Although such ventures were often hyped by Westerners as evidence that private production is superior to public, this was largely ideological wishful thinking. As evidenced by many third world countries, the true hallmark of informal-sector activity is that much effort is expended producing little value added.[9] Even more important, in the Soviet case informal-sector activity generated distinctive norms regarding the morality of rule evasion and of defrauding the state, norms that would survive well into the post-Soviet period.[10]

The collapse of the Soviet Union was associated with, and actually preceded by, a weakening of the authority of the Communist Party in restraining private informal sector activities. The initial result was a proliferation of cooperatives, soon to be followed by a process of spontaneous privatization and eventually by a highly targeted process of insider privatization that transferred substantial wealth into the hands of cronies of the regime. Most if not all of this took place in a void, marked by the absence of adequate legislation and supervisory agencies. The discipline of the party was gone, and the discipline of the market had not yet taken hold. Pursuing a market-based economy without adequate legislation on bankruptcy, for example, was destined to produce poor results.

Adam Smith, although his thinking has been enlisted as support for neoliberal policies of extreme deregulation, was eminently aware of the dangers involved in allowing free rein for the pursuit of self-interest. His fabled "invisible hand" was used, in *The Wealth of Nations,* more as metaphor than as an argument in favor of unconstrained pursuit of self-interest.[11] Viewed as a whole, the process of Russian economic reform provided ample support for Lionel Robbins's classic dictum that "the pursuit of self-interest, unrestrained by suitable institutions, carries no guarantee of anything but chaos."[12]

The "wild capitalism" of Russia in the 1990s was marked by ad hoc policymaking, initially known as "shock therapy," that entailed little effective coordination and little operational vision, beyond an emphasis on deregulation and speedy privatization. One might be tempted here to recall Lenin's frequent reference to Napoleon's classic maxim *On s'engage, et puis on voit.*[13] The outcome was marked by uncertainty, widespread distrust in authorities, a short time horizon for decisionmaking—and mass looting.

The conclusion of this first phase in Russian post-Soviet adjustment arrived in August 1998, when the ruble was devalued and the country's financial markets suffered a meltdown, wiping out some $40 billion in short-term treasury bills (the notorious GKOs).[14] The calamity had the combined effect of further entrenching already deep Russian resentment of Western-inspired reform and of provoking resentment from Western investors, consultants, and politicians. The latter would now blame the Russians for losses both of financial capital and of political prestige that had been vested in the wisdom of reforming Russia.[15]

At the time, it was widely believed that Russia was simply finished and would not be able to stage a comeback within a foreseeable future. But such gloomy predictions would soon be proved wrong. Buoyed by devaluation and by a rapid rise in hydrocarbon prices, the Russian economy staged a remarkable recovery, recording average annual growth during Putin's first two terms in office of about 7 percent.

The coming to power of Vladimir Putin represented a seemingly new and illuminating stage in Russian development. The way in which Russia emerged out of the "time of trouble" under Yeltsin provided fundamental insights into the scope and prospects for transforming institutional arrangements that for centuries had set Russia apart from other European states.

The sudden spike in the price of oil that marked Putin's first term in office produced a massive windfall of revenue from hydrocarbon exports. During the Yeltsin era, the main sources of rent-seeking had been rigged privatization deals, manipulation of quotas and licenses to exploit the substantial differences between domestic and foreign prices, and the rapid buildup of both domestic and foreign debt. The bonanza of hydrocarbon revenue added a new dimension to the ongoing games for power and profit. It created substantial new opportunities, and the response was a mixed bag of various ambitions and agendas.

On the positive side, it is true that much of the influx of petrodollars was put to prudent use in paying down the country's foreign debt and in building cautionary reserves that would come in handy when the global financial crisis erupted. While this was to the great credit of Aleksei Kudrin, Putin's long-serving minister of finance, it had little impact on the fundamental determinants of how the game was played. The dark side of the hydrocarbon bonanza was that it also ratcheted up the temptation to loot, to the point even that corruption would become the linchpin of the system.

During the Yeltsin era, great scandal erupted when it was revealed that leading "reform economists" had received an advance royalty of $90,000 for a book that would never be written, and presumably was never intended to be written. During the Putin era, corruption rose to such levels that bribes of $100,000 would be viewed by leading kleptocrats as simply laughable.

The magnitude of the difference is reflected in allegations by Moscow political analyst Stanislav Belkovsky, made in a 2007 interview with the

German newspaper *Die Welt,* that by then Putin had succeed in accumulating a private fortune of $40 billion, making him the richest man in Europe.[16] By 2012, Belkovsky would have raised the estimate to $70 billion, making Putin the wealthiest man in the world.[17] Not bad for a rather junior operative in the service of the Soviet KGB.

The main thrust of my argument is that struggles over access to resource rents emerged as the true defining feature of the Putin era. Entailed here were a host of varying objectives. Temptations ranged from using the energy wealth to restore national pride, to using threats of price hikes and supply disruptions as punishment for neighboring states that refused to comply with Russian interests, to simply diverting hydrocarbon revenues for personal enrichment. Needless to say, there was a price to be paid. As will be detailed in subsequent chapters, the associated absence of a coordinated policy on how to develop rather than simply loot the country's energy resources would have seriously negative consequences.

By the time that Boris Yeltsin opted to step down, prematurely in the eyes of many if not most Russians, both market economy and democracy had been thoroughly discredited. It was symptomatic of Russia's incomplete transition to a constitutional order that Yeltsin's time in power would end in an elaborate inside operation to resolve a pending crisis of succession. Stephen Blank maintains that Vladimir Putin's ascent from obscurity to supreme power was the "key to the resolution of a succession and state-building crisis on the part of a coalition of elites which, it turned out, held rather disparate views of what the future would bring."[18]

When Putin assumed power, having been duly elected president in March 2000, he was clearly expected to restore order. The experience of hardship and dislocations that had marked the "time of trouble" would be used to rationalize and legitimate harsh policies devised for this purpose. Deliberately recalling the lengthy and increasingly fossilized leadership of Leonid Brezhnev, Yeltsin's time in power would be referred to as a "period of stagnation," a *period zastoia.*

During his first term in office, from 2000 until 2004, Putin was still viewed as a promising reformer. He struck a deal with the Communist Party in the Duma, allowing long-delayed and much-needed reforms on matters such as land use and taxation to be rapidly enacted. Even when his increasingly authoritarian stance began to cause what some referred to, euphemistically, as "democratic backsliding," he still retained his credentials as market reformer.

But the early hopes for a new world order, marked by friendship and cooperation between Russia and the United States, would soon fade. Though Putin was among the first to offer condolences to the American people after the terrorist attacks of September 11, 2001, and promised to assist the United States in the "war on terror," he would soon begin to feel that there was little reciprocity and that the United States was not to be trusted as a friend or even as a partner. Although accusations that the United States contributed to the demise of the Soviet Union may not have been seriously believed, the fact remained that the Soviet empire had fallen apart and that NATO had made big inroads into the periphery of the former Soviet Union itself. The latter was not to be taken lightly.

When President Putin delivered his televised 2005 "state of the federation" address, he may have felt genuinely justified in claiming that "the collapse of the Soviet Union was a major geopolitical disaster of the century."[19] His own personal background would clearly also play into the formulation of a policy on how to make Russia great again. During his time as KGB operative in the German Democratic Republic (East Germany), he had the opportunity to watch up-close what power from below could achieve. And it is not a far-fetched guess that he harbored a deep sense of distrust, not to mention resentment, of the West in general.

Although Russia has arguably never been more secure from foreign invasion than during Putin's time in power, the rhetoric from hard-line circles would become infused with virulent projections of NATO as an enemy, and with a growing sense of hostility toward the West in general. Sentiments of this kind came to a head at a security conference in Munich in February 2007, where Putin accused the United States of "an almost uncontained use of military force" and made it clear that Moscow would no longer accept being treated without respect.[20]

It was a heady brew. Russia might have lost a battle, but the war was still on. And it was a war in which Moscow would have to stand its ground. In military circles, the ensuing urge to overcome "superpower hangover" was fueled by feelings of gross conspiratorial injustice and by a belief in the temporary nature of the weakness. NATO generals would report frequent cases of conversation with Russian counterparts whose message was to wait and see, that "we shall be back."[21]

With the election of Barack Obama as president of the United States, there was a brief interlude, framed as a "reset" of relations between Russia and the United States. As Dmitry Medvedev, the equally newly elected Russian president, proved to be responsive, hopes were rising that the increasingly confrontational Putin era was over. Consequently, diplomatic efforts were made to persuade Medvedev to run for a second term. As it turned out, however, that possibility had never been real. When Putin returned to the Kremlin following his turbulent election in March 2012, there was general agreement that the reset was dead.

The negative reactions that followed brought into focus the question of whether Putin had a deliberate and premeditated authoritarian strategy for

Russia that he would now return to. Given how dramatically different the Putin era did seem to be, if compared to that of Yeltsin, it was tempting to believe that there had indeed been a master plan of sorts, perhaps even one that incorporated the building of an energy superpower.

There is a clear danger of overinterpretation here. With the benefit of hindsight, it is always tempting to assume that deliberate policies have been pursued and to see causality where none may have existed. In countries with strong leaders, it becomes all the more tempting to suggest that what evolved was in accordance with the ruler's preferences.

The plethora of distinctive slogans that accompanied Putin's first term in office did support such a view, ranging from the introduction of a "dictatorship of the law" and a "power vertical" to threats of eradicating the oligarchs "as a class." His characteristically foul language added to the worries that some felt about a pending police state, about a return to autocracy, and about the rebirth of imperial ambitions. But we must be wary of assuming that what did happen was in line with some more detailed vision. It would simply ascribe to the ruler far too much capacity in achieving institutional transformation by intervening directly and deliberately.

There can be little doubt that Putin did have certain overriding ambitions. He was clearly committed to putting an end to the chaos of the Yeltsin era, to restoring the pride and dignity of Russia, and to standing up against the West. But these were very general ambitions concerning desired outcomes. They did not really touch on the fundamental institutional characteristics of the system. As Robert Orttung puts it, the main driver of early political events was simply that of Putin "reacting to his perception of the 1990s and working to correct what he considered to be some of the mistakes of that era."[22]

What happened during Russia's first two decades of post-Soviet existence was not so much the result of deliberate policy. Rather, it was a case of ongoing, endogenous, systemic readjustment, mainly in the form of old, established institutional patterns responding to massive systemic shock by reestablishing themselves. Agency-based interventions were obviously important, but they did not always have the intended consequences.

The initial trigger was the erosion and eventual collapse of Communist Party command and control, which implied that state property was suddenly up for grabs. Faced with massive opportunity, and with equally massive uncertainty, self-interested actors formulated strategies for gain that wrought serious havoc on the prospects for an orderly transition to democracy and a rules-based market economy. With Putin's ascent to power, the nature of the game appeared to be transformed. New cronies of the regime were promoted, and the role of hydrocarbon revenues became paramount. But the nature of the game remained that of multiple actors responding to multiple changes in multiple ways. The frequent views of Putin as a strong and decisive leader bent on remaking Russia in his image grossly underestimate the power of institutional inertia, notably the dependency that follows from investments made in playing opaque influence games.

Against the prevailing imagery of a radical break between the Yeltsin and Putin regimes, replacing ambitions toward democracy with ambitions toward authoritarianism, Stephen Holmes suggests that closer consideration will instead reveal substantial continuity and systemic inertia. Below the turbulent surface, the bureaucracy simply muddled on. Enjoying a vast expansion in its numbers, which had begun already under Yeltsin, under Putin it persisted with impunity in tending to its own interests and in simply ignoring directives from above.[23]

The point of departure for this book shall be that as Russia emerged from the "time of trouble," Russian elites were permeated by an increasingly powerful drive to restore lost greatness. I agree with Pavel Baev's argument that these elites are possessed by a "mental scheme" of great power, of Russia as an "indispensable power" that is "objectively destined to come out as an independent player, a separate center of force not to be dissolved in any international amalgamations."[24]

Public opinion polls have also demonstrated firm support from the general population for such an agenda.[25] The trauma over the loss of the Soviet Union had been compounded by a sense of shame over the sometimes rather odd forms of behavior that were displayed by President Yeltsin in front of foreign audiences. President Putin's promise to restore the country's dignity was consequently well received.

Although there may have been broad agreement on the need to restore Russian greatness, that still left unanswered the question of how to achieve it. There was, above all, a distinct risk here of overestimating the ability of the ruler to ensure implementation of whatever plans he might have nourished. Posturing as a fearsome authoritarian leader is one thing. Making sure that underlings actually do what they are told is something very different. In the words of Holmes, the predicament of the Putin regime provides an important insight, namely, that "an authoritarian regime is almost as difficult to create and consolidate as a democratic regime."[26] It is against this background that we must view the entry onto center stage of the Russian energy complex and the ensuing ambitions to build an energy superpower.

When Putin embarked on his program of "authoritarian restoration," the military was in such a sorry state that reclaiming greatness by way of restoring a military superpower was clearly not an option. Proudly proclaiming that it was promoting conversion of military to civilian production, the Yegor Gaidar government undertook sweeping cancellations of state orders to the country's formerly mighty military-industrial complex,

military industrial complex

which then ground to a halt. From 1991 to 1998, the output of this crucial sector dropped by more than 80 percent.[27] Given that military production had accounted for perhaps 30 percent of Soviet GDP, this was an important reason why the country was thrown into depression.[28]

The Kremlin, having divested itself of the option of placing a wager on the military complex, instead logically focused its ambition to restore greatness on the energy complex, which offered a very different set of opportunities. To Baev, the shift of focus from the military to the energy complex occurred simply by default: "As the more traditional characteristics that justified Russia's claim for this status, like military might or cutting edge natural science, have been eroding, energy has become the default option that appeared infallible."[29]

It is true that by the time of the collapse of the Soviet Union the Russian energy sector was beset by numerous problems. It suffered from a dilapidated infrastructure, and it was faced with the fact that traditional oil and gas fields in Western Siberia were being depleted. Maintaining a high rate of output would require moving into new areas, into Eastern Siberia and into the Arctic offshore. Meeting the challenges of adverse climate and geology that mark these regions would in turn require access to foreign technology. But in theory, as in the case of the attempted transitions to democracy and market economy, none of this was beyond the realm of the possible.

A considered policy of restructuring and privatization could have resulted in better corporate governance. Targeted investment into upgrading pipelines and compressor stations could have paid off handsomely. A wager on exploration combined with foreign partnerships to acquire technology could have ensured new field development. A policy of energy conservation and of increased energy efficiency could have freed up larger volumes of exportable resources. And a rational business model could have been formulated to integrate pipelines, tankers, and liquefied natural gas (LNG) plants into a viable marketing strategy.

The outcome could have been an energy superpower in a positive commercial sense, with energy companies assuming the role as drivers of high-technology development. It might even have been supportive of the vision of Anatoly Chubais, espoused in 2003, that "Russia's ideology in the 21st century should be liberal capitalism with the aim of creating a liberal empire."[30]

Although there has been much talk about a presumed need to diversify the Russian economy, which essentially means attempting to escape from the dependence on hydrocarbons, there is little actual substance in such talk. It is, on the contrary, easy enough to agree with Clifford Gaddy and Barry Ickes that "even under optimal conditions for investment, any dream of creating a 'non-oil' Russia that could perform as well as today's commodity-based economy is unrealistic. The proportion of GDP that would have to be invested in non-oil sectors is impossibly high."[31]

Thane Gustafson makes much the same point: "Oil, together with natural gas, remains Russia's chief comparative advantage in the modern world." And he calls for a realization by Russian leaders of where their efforts need to be aimed: "But Russia can make better use of the opportunities that oil offers as a high-tech sector and as a catalyst for home-grown innovation."[32]

The conclusion reached by Gaddy and Ickes is twofold. First, that the only realistic future for Russia is one that continues to be based on the commodity sectors, and second, that true modernization of Russia is not possible without modernization of its oil and gas sectors. This would be the way in which a wager on the energy complex could be construed as a sensible choice, if not the only rational choice. If only a way could be found to achieve modernization of the energy complex, Russia would be home free: "With the oil and gas companies in the lead for modernization, Russia would become a genuine energy superpower, an 'energy superpower in depth.'"[33]

What followed instead was a scramble by hosts of differently motivated actors to secure their own short-term interests, often with little regard to collateral damage. Writing about developments in the military sector, Stephen Blank presents the image of "a game played concurrently on multiple boards with multiple interrelated players all jockeying for power and assets." And he argues that "this game has gone on, relatively uninterrupted, for decades if not centuries," conditioned by "the unending legacy of how to overcome backwardness."[34]

Much the same can be said about the games that have been played around the country's energy assets. I agree, for example, with Markku Kivinen's suggestion that what is good for the Russian natural gas giant Gazprom may not necessarily be good also for Russia. Rather than view Russia as a monolithic actor in the energy field, we should note the presence of numerous competing agendas and conflicting interests. Gazprom has suffered from being at the same time a commercial operation and a residual ministry. Tax and pricing policies have been held hostage to competition between various resource lobbies. The relative fortunes of major actors such as Gazprom and Rosneft are determined by key political appointments at the peak of power. Even the "energy superpower" agenda, in Kivinen's words, is more likely driven by domestic than by foreign policy agendas.[35]

The process as a whole resulted not just in a massive redistribution of both assets and revenue streams, allowing some to build up substantial private wealth. More seriously, it also had a clearly detrimental influence on the prospects for reforming the country's energy sector. On the domestic scene, competing agendas and outright turf battles wrought havoc on the prospect for exploration and development of new oil and gas fields as the old went into decline. In the foreign policy field, blurred lines of division between commercial and foreign policy objectives of major energy companies such as Gazprom caused a plethora of problems, ranging from conflicts with neighboring governments to damage to Russia's reputation as a secure provider of energy, and massive outlays on the construction of commercially dubious pipelines. While it was all seriously debilitating to a sound commercial development of the energy sector, to the Kremlin it presented an irresistible temptation.

President Putin, in the lead-up to Russia's chairing of the Group of Eight (G8) in 2006, was "clearly excited about this perspective for maximizing the returns on his political investments and converting gas earnings into political dividends," in the words of Baev.[36] This was the essence of the country's new status as a great energy power, and the challenge was to convince the European partners that Moscow could be trusted as a benevolent provider of energy. It was thus that the vision of building an "energy superpower" was born. But the vision would fall far short of being realized.

The much publicized ambition to transform the defunct Soviet military superpower into an ersatz Russian "energy superpower" would be marked by three core features, to be explored in subsequent chapters. It would further entrench path dependent patterns of unaccountable government, rent-granting, and dependency. It would be seriously detrimental to the prospects for a rational commercial development of the country's energy resources. And it would ultimately be supplanted by an ambition to funnel energy rents into rebuilding the traditional military superpower.

Outline of the Book

This book tours the various games that have been played around Russian energy assets, with emphasis on the Putin era. It identifies the main actors, inside as well as outside Russia, and details how the prospects for conflict and cooperation have evolved. The main argument is that privatization and an open field for foreign investment represented a temporary interlude in a long-term tradition of state control over resources, and of an economic policy that rests on resource extraction as a means to support the country's capacity for military defense.

Chapter 2 sets the stage. It aims to place the notion of a Russian "energy superpower" into a sobering context by emphasizing what it meant to be a true Cold War superpower. It discusses the meaning of the wielding of an "energy weapon," detailing the case against Russia as an energy bully. This chapter presents the argument that Russia, rather than suffering from a "resource curse," is suffering from an institutional curse rooted in old patterns.

Chapter 3 provides added background on the energy assets that have been at the Kremlin's disposal. It discusses the legacy of Soviet oil and gas, the looting of Russian oil during the Yeltsin era, the emergence of new energy powers to the south, and the mounting complications of relations between the Soviet Union and the European Union.

Chapter 4 looks at the ways in which Putin set out to assemble the powerhouse of his envisioned energy superpower: by restoring state control over the country's energy assets, by cutting domestic oligarchs down to size, by rolling back the influence of foreign oil majors, and by seeking to ensure that energy-producing republics in the Caspian Basin would remain locked into the Russian sphere of interest.

Chapter 5 takes a special look at the Russian natural gas giant Gazprom, which emerged as the core of the energy powerhouse. Placed in the awkward position of serving as a combination foreign policy tool and cash cow for Kremlin-affiliated interests, it seriously neglected its core business of extracting and exploring for natural gas. Its mixed roles instead bred corruption and poor corporate governance, consequently eroding the very foundations of the energy complex.

Chapter 6 looks at reactions to Russian foreign energy policy, which emerged from a variety of directions, beginning with countries in Central Asia and the South Caucasus, notably Turkmenistan and Azerbaijan; proceeding to Ukraine and Belarus, with serious spillover effects for the European Union; and in the end also encompassing China, which must be viewed as the ultimate challenge to Russian energy policy.

Chapter 7 looks at the impact of the global financial crisis, at the revealed wisdom of accumulating reserves while the going was good, at just how vulnerable the Russian economy proved to be to a serious drop in hydrocarbon revenues, and at how all such experience would be conveniently forgotten once the economy emerged from the crisis.

Chapter 8 looks more broadly at how the Kremlin went about picking up the pieces after the crisis, demonstrating that Russian energy policy had long been in disarray. It looks at the prospects for sustaining output growth and for developing foreign markets, and suggests that pipeline politics have been driven by objectives that go beyond the commercial.

Finally, Chapter 9 looks at challenges and prospects for Russia, which presently may be characterized as moving backward into the future. This chapter questions the sustainability of its energy policy, presents the obstacles faced by its ambitions to modernize, and outlines how the burden of history is again being manifested.

Notes

1. For example, Amalrik, *Will the Soviet Union Survive Until 1984?;* and Carrère d'Encausse, *L'Empire éclaté.*
2. Tocqueville, *The Old Regime and the Revolution,* p. 214.
3. Exactly what was said at the time, and whether any firm promise was issued, has long been an issue of contention. For an update that expresses some sympathy for the Russian position, see Uwe Klussmann, Matthias Schepp, and Klaus Wiegrefe, "NATO's Eastward Expansion: Did the West Break Its Promise to Moscow?" *Spiegel Online International,* November 26, 2009, http://www.spiegel.de /international/world/0,1518,663315,00.html.
4. "Putin Praises Post-Soviet Integration," *RIA Novosti,* April 11, 2012, http://en.ria.ru/russia/20120411/172746585.html.
5. "Post-Soviet Integration Is Unstoppable," *RIA Novosti,* February 14, 2013, http://en.ria.ru/russia/20130214/179465611.html.
6. Mendras, *Russian Politics,* pp. 39–40.
7. The notion of a "Russian Idea" has important historical roots that stretch back to Fyodor Dostoyevsky. In the 1990s it became a prominent part of Communist Party rhetoric, and following Yeltsin's defeat of Communist challenger Gennady Zyuganov in the 1996 presidential election, he appointed a commission to find a more precise definition. Although the commission failed to reach a consensus opinion, Yeltsin incorporated much of its agenda. Vladimir Putin would, symptomatically, be fond of calling for a "new Russian Idea."
8. In his Nobel Prize speech, North emphasized that deregulation alone would not do the trick, that "transferring the formal political and economic rules of successful Western market economies to third world and Eastern European economies is not a sufficient condition for good economic performance." North, "Economic Performance Through Time," p. 366.
9. Soto, *The Mystery of Capital.*
10. Rose, "Living in an Anti-Modern Society."
11. See further Hedlund, *Invisible Hands, Russian Experience, and Social Science,* chap. 2.
12. Robbins, *The Theory of Economic Policy,* p. 56.
13. The literal meaning is "engage, and then see what happens." It was one of Napoleon's favorite expressions, reflecting his emphasis on decisiveness. Lenin was similarly fond of repeating it, when describing the challenges faced by the young Soviet state.
14. Hedlund, *Russia's "Market" Economy,* chap. 7.
15. This would become a political issue even in the United States, in the 2000 electoral race for the presidency, with an all-Republican congressional committee producing a massive report titled "Russia's Road to Corruption" that purported to detail "how the Clinton administration exported government instead of free enterprise and failed the Russian people." Text available at http://www.globalsecurity.org /wmd/library/news/russia/2000/russia/index.html.
16. Luke Harding, "Putin, the Kremlin Power Struggle, and the $40bn Fortune," *The Guardian,* December 21, 2007, http://www.guardian.co.uk/world /2007/dec/21/russia.topstories3.
17. "Vladimir Putin Could Secretly Be the Richest Person in the World," *Business Insider,* April 19, 2012, http://www.businessinsider.com/is-vladimir-putin -secretly-the-richest-person-in-the-world-2012-4.
18. Blank, "The 18th Brumaire of Vladimir Putin," p. 133.

19. President of Russia, "Annual Address to the Federal Assembly of the Russian Federation," April 25, 2005, http://archive.kremlin.ru/eng/speeches/2005/04/25/2031_type70029type82912_87086.shtml.

20. Andrew Tully, "Russia: Washington Reacts to Putin's Munich Speech," *Radio Free Europe/Radio Liberty,* February 13, 2007, http://www.rferl.org/content/article/1074671.html.

21. Personal information from multiple sources.

22. Orttung, "Energy and State-Society Relations," p. 54.

23. Holmes, "Never Show Weakness."

24. Baev, *Russian Energy Policy and Military Power,* p. 119.

25. Pipes, "Flight from Freedom."

26. Holmes, "Fragments of a Defunct State," p. 28.

27. Cooper, "The Russian Military-Industrial Complex," p. 43.

28. Problems relating to the role of the military-industrial complex in the Soviet economy, and the prospects for relying on remilitarization as a means to kick-start renewed economic growth, are analyzed in Rosefielde, *Russia in the 21st Century.*

29. Baev, *Russian Energy Policy and Military Power,* p. 119.

30. "Anatoly Chubais: Russia Should Aim to Create Liberal Empire in CIS," *Pravda,* September 25, 2003, http://english.pravda.ru/news/russia/25-09-2003/52757-0.

31. Gaddy and Ickes, "Bear Traps," p. 119.

32. Gustafson, *Wheel of Fortune,* p. 29.

33. Gaddy and Ickes, "Bear Traps," p. 119.

34. Blank, "Voodoo Economics," p. 48.

35. Kivinen, "Public and Business Actors in Russia's Energy Policy."

36. Baev, *Russian Energy Policy and Military Power,* p. 124.

2

An Energy
Superpower?

The public discussion about Russia's resurgence, and about the role of energy in this process, has at times been highly emotional. Strong language has been used, reflecting the presence of deep distrust and resentment on both sides. Westerners have expressed concern about an increasingly assertive Russian foreign energy policy. Russians in contrast have displayed frustration over being denied access to European downstream assets, and over being held hostage by transit states like Ukraine that are traversed by its export pipelines.

An important consequence of this war of words has been to blur the vision of what is really happening, suggesting the presence of a more coherent agenda than may actually be the case. As outlined in the previous chapter, multiple and at times conflicting agendas have been pursued. The purpose of this chapter is to provide some conceptual support for this understanding. Moving beyond the rhetoric, it takes a closer look at some of the key concepts that have been placed in focus.

Given the central role that has been played by reference to a renewed Cold War, and to an emerging ersatz Russian "energy superpower," the chapter begins by recalling the true nature of what it meant to be a Cold War superpower. This has the salutary effect of placing the discussion into a more realistic context, one in which grand Russian ambitions can be gauged against seriously degraded Russian capabilities, and in which worries about how Russia may throw its weight around are scaled back accordingly.

Next the chapter proceeds to accusations of Russia wielding a newfound "energy weapon." It considers prior evidence from other countries on the use of resource wealth as a weapon, suggesting that although conflicts over Russian energy have been important, they are but part of the broader patterns of conflict with other former republics of the Soviet Union. There is little substance—beyond the rhetoric—in allegations that Russia has a master plan to use energy in lieu of weaponry as a means to return itself to its former status as a great power.

The chapter also explores the often repeated claim that Russia suffers from a "resource curse"—the rather counterintuitive view that abundance of natural resources constitutes a problem rather than an asset. But a look at the broader academic discussion on this topic suggests that its applicability to Russia is questionable, as the core of the problem for Russia rests in its historical, institutional legacy, in place long before the arrival of energy wealth.

In this regard, Russia's projects of transition, of devising a sustainable energy policy, and indeed of modernization have all been bogged down in historically rooted conflicts. The latter stem from institutional problems relating to lack of accountability in governance, to the conditional nature of property rights, and to the associated patterns of corruption, dependency, and poor transparency, notably so in the management of rents from the energy complex.

On Being a Superpower

There was a time when discussions of international politics, and of international security, would revolve around the respective roles and activities of sets of regional great powers. Determined to pursue their own clearly defined national interests, these heavyweight contenders were locked in struggles for control over trade as well as over territory. This essentially was the story of colonial expansion by a handful of European powers into broad reaches of Africa, Asia, and the Americas.

One of the most epic of such cases was the great game for supremacy over Central Asia that was played out between the British and Russian empires during the course of the nineteenth century.[1] I mention this here because the historical parallel will appear repeatedly throughout subsequent chapters. The reason is that the struggles for control over the region that were played out during the Putin era would be cast as a renewed great game, only now it would be energy resources that were placed in focus.

The golden age of the old-style great powers came to an end with the conclusion of World War I, which saw the collapse of the Russian, Austro-Hungarian, and Ottoman empires. Following the end of World War II, the process of decolonization completed the process, causing the British empire to mutate into a commonwealth and the other European colonial powers to be shorn of their respective overseas possessions—with varying degrees of violence.

It was the introduction of nuclear weapons, however, and the ensuing Cold War between the United States and the Soviet Union, that fundamentally transformed the game board. With the European continent divided by an Iron Curtain, famously portrayed by Winston Churchill as having descended across the continent "from Stettin in the Baltic to Trieste in the Adriatic,"[2] the world as a whole, separated into two mutually hostile blocs, was drawn into the contest. Although it was true that in Europe the Cold War was indeed cold, in the sense of an absence of live-fire exchanges, on other continents this was an era of devastating proxy warfare that laid waste to large parts of Africa and Southeast Asia and forced poor countries into a spiral of military spending.

The essence of the balance of power that was achieved between the two adversarial blocs was captured in the phrase "mutual assured destruction," which reflected the fact that both sides possessed sufficient nuclear weapons to destroy the world several times over. Although few if any believed that nuclear war could or would be initiated by a sane government, fears abounded that mistake, misperception, or simple malfunction could ignite a third world war.[3]

The Cuban missile crisis, in 1962, provided the first live illustration of just how dangerous the situation was. Although it would remain by far the most spectacular, it was not an isolated case. As late as 1983, in the midst of Ronald Reagan's arms buildup and the associated rhetoric about the Soviet Union as an "evil empire," a NATO exercise called Able Archer came very close to convincing Moscow that a US surprise attack was imminent. Consequently, some think that the Soviet Union seriously contemplated a preventive first strike with nuclear weapons. The crisis was averted only following urgent warnings from Oleg Gordievsky, a high-level Western intelligence source in Moscow, which convinced NATO to stand down and regroup.[4]

Exactly what it was that put an end to this spiral of madness has remained controversial and is not of much consequence for the present argument. However, we cannot ignore the coincidence in positions of power of two world leaders who were bent on achieving true détente. Although the reforms undertaken by Mikhail Gorbachev have been subjected to scathing criticism, by outside observers as well as by his former Soviet insiders, it was his personal ambition to put an end to the Cold War that made the final difference, and that won him the Nobel Peace Prize. While Ronald Reagan did play a vital role as partner in the process, it was Gorbachev who took the first and most decisive steps.[5] In the wake of the opening of the Berlin Wall, and of the subsequent collapse of the Soviet order in Europe, the former adversaries in East and West proceeded to enjoy a decade or so of warm and for a time potentially promising relations.

But relations between Moscow and Washington began to sour again toward the end of the administration of George W. Bush, when talk of a new Cold War began to proliferate. And now it was energy that was placed in focus. In the words of Angela Stent, "For some in the West, Russia now seeks to achieve with oil and gas what it once sought to achieve with nuclear weapons during the Cold War, namely increased political influence over Europe and over its neighbors."[6] The rhetoric was catchy and well-suited to the increasing chill in relations. But it also had negative consequences.

To begin with, it was simply ludicrous to compare tensions between Moscow and Washington in the latter part of the Bush-Putin era to the very real dangers of the superpower standoff during the dark decades of the Cold War. It conveniently neglected both the military downsizing that had taken place on both sides and the fact that areas of substantial mutual interest and continuing fruitful cooperation remained. There was no single incident during the Bush-Putin era that came even remotely close to the Cold War standoff in divided Berlin, where a devastating third world war at times may have been only minutes away.

Second, the rhetoric of a renewed Cold War also neglected the fact that the prior stability between the two hostile blocs had given way to a much less predictable world. The old system of client states and proxy wars had morphed into an order dominated by hosts of nonstate actors that presented fundamentally different dangers. From a NATO point of view, the role of Russia under this new world order would be ambivalent, ranging from cooperation in the war against terrorism to acquiescence in dealing with the crisis in Libya and to obstruction in the case of Syria. From the opposite, Russian, point of view, it all provided evidence on how the role of world policeman had been unilaterally and unacceptably usurped by the United States.

The third and arguably most important problem with the rhetoric of a renewed Cold War, and an emerging Russian superpower of any kind, is that it seriously neglects the greatly diminished capabilities of Russia as compared to the old Soviet Union. Once we move beyond the flamboyant rhetoric of some of the more notorious Russian hard-liners, we at once discover that a reconstitution of Moscow as the center of a superpower with global reach has simply not been in the cards—with or without the addition of the energy dimension. The best possible case from a Russian nationalist perspective would be for the country to emerge as a regional great power, with influence over countries that once formed part of the Soviet Union. And even that seems ambitious.

Yet we cannot completely disregard reference to notions of "superpower" status. The reason is that the main symbols of the Cold War, such as nuclear weapons and massed tank armies, no longer play the role that they once did. Notions of great or superpower status must consequently be differently understood. This is not to deny that the nuclear powers, whose numbers keep expanding, still wield sufficient destructive potential to end civilization. The very fact of ongoing proliferation into areas of the world that are highly prone to conflict also does increase the risk of something actually going terribly wrong. This said, it remains equally true that in the today's globalized world, true power is economic and commercial in nature.

While there has been some disagreement as to whether China could or should rightly be viewed as a fully fledged military superpower during the Cold War, it is on a trajectory to become the largest economy in the world, with substantial consequences for world trade and for the distribution of global economic power.[7] Faced with the combined prospects of the United States as the sole remaining military superpower and of China as an emerging economic superpower, we are left wondering where all of this leaves Russia in its aspirations to become an energy superpower. The answer must be sought in its greatly diminished capabilities since the end of the Cold War, and in the associated illusions that the sudden inflow of hydrocarbon wealth would offer a way toward curing "superpower hangover."

Following the political turmoil and economic depression of the Yeltsin years, under Vladimir Putin's authoritarian leadership Moscow entered an era of political stability and economic rebound. The transformation was striking, mainly in the sense that the Russian economy underwent a rapid transition from basket case to star performer. Bolstered by its growing economic strength, the Kremlin began exuding the confidence of a superpower reborn. In the words of Dmitry Trenin, uttered in 2007: "Anyone listening to Russian officials is impressed by their self-confidence, and even triumphalism. As the Russians see it, Russia is up, the United States is down, and Europe is out."[8]

The driving force behind the transformation was the sharp increase in oil prices that began during Putin's first term in office. Enjoying a rare combination of prices and output rising in tandem, Russia found its fiscal position strengthening daily. The Kremlin also discovered the potential of regaining lost political respect and influence by wielding its "energy weapon." The outward manifestations of the latter would include but not be limited to recurrent low-profile pricing disputes between Moscow and capitals in Russia's "near abroad"—countries regarded by the Kremlin as belonging to its own sphere of "privileged interest." More high-profile supply shutoffs would also occur, leaving some of the new European Union member states freezing in the dead of winter.[9]

The highly controversial issue of an emerging Russian "energy superpower" must be viewed against precisely this background. The mounting apprehension about growing Russian energy influence that may be found in some circles must be contrasted against the observations of inherent contradictions between military power and commercial energy relations that are considered by others as having the most relevance.[10] The balance of the argument will vary greatly between countries, depending on the nature of previous relations to Moscow and on degrees of current dependence on Russian energy.

In looking more closely at the argument that Moscow has been wielding an alleged "energy weapon," we must maintain a distinction between visions of recreating a superpower with global reach, and more modest ambitions of building a regional great power. In line with this distinction, we must also differentiate between countries in the former Soviet Union and countries belonging to the greatly expanded European Union.

As enlargement of the latter proceeded to absorb former Soviet satellite states in Central Europe, not to mention former Soviet republics in the Baltic, this not only increased Russian resentment of NATO expansion but also greatly increased internal frictions within the EU and thus complicated the formulation of a common policy on relations with Russia.

Wielding the Energy Weapon

Fears of the presence of a Russian "energy weapon" date back to the times of Ronald Reagan and the height of the Cold War, when the US administration tried to caution Europe against becoming dependent on Soviet energy supply. Moscow was bent on combining its wager on a vast expansion of its gas industry with a system of major pipelines that would carry gas to Europe. Washington's fear was that in a time of crisis Moscow might be able to elicit concessions from the European members of NATO, simply by threatening to shut down the gas supply. Substantial pressure in consequence was applied on Western companies not to supply advanced technology for the pipeline project.[11]

In the end, such ambitions would come up short. The Europeans remained committed to energy cooperation with the Soviet Union, and some companies defied the embargo against providing high technology. The pipelines were built, and gas started flowing. Then the Soviet Union collapsed, and for some time there seemed to be little reason for apprehension over dependence on energy from Russia. The return of such apprehension was fueled yet again by US caution against enhancing Europe's dependence on Russian energy by way of getting involved in further pipeline projects.

The Oil Weapon

Can the possession of substantial energy resources really can be construed as having effective power over others? The prime illustration is the so-called oil crisis that erupted in October 1973. When the United States agreed to resupply the Israeli military during the Yom Kippur War, the Arab members of the Organization of Petroleum Exporting Countries (OPEC) responded by proclaiming an oil embargo that caused prices to skyrocket. Ever since, OPEC has been in a position to throttle all prospects for growth and prosperity in the "developed" world. It has rationally abstained from doing so, preferring instead to strive for price stability at a level that is consistent with its own long-term interest in discouraging shifts to conservation and to renewable energy sources.

The original purpose of wielding what was then known as an "oil weapon" was to extract political concessions from oil-consuming nations that were viewed as being supportive of Israel. The main reason why it failed to achieve the desired goal was that the targeted countries responded with effective countermeasures. These included the establishment of the International Energy Agency, which allows oil-importing nations to coordinate and contain supply shocks; the creation of ninety-day strategic oil reserves; significant ambitions to reduce the energy intensity of oil-dependent economies; and a strategic alliance between the United States and Saudi Arabia, which began to operate as a "swing producer."[12] Iran and Venezuela provide further and more recent illustrations of how resource-rich countries have resorted to explicit threats to disrupt oil deliveries, in futile ambitions to elicit political concessions.

In June 2006, Iran's supreme leader, Ayatollah Ali Khamenei, threatened that in case of further escalation of the conflict with the United States, Iran would block the flow of oil via the Strait of Hormuz. As this narrow passageway accounts for two-fifths of all globally traded oil, the threat was a potent one. The United States promptly pledged that its military would stand ready to secure the shipping lanes. Although it did not enact its pledge, the threat remained. And it was, predictably, brought back onto center stage during the peak of the standoff regarding Iran's nuclear ambitions, in 2011 and 2012.

What makes the situation so problematic is that Tehran is likely aware that if the United States does follow through on its threat, seriously negative consequences will result. Tehran would be drawn into military conflict with the United States. It would suffer crippling damage to its economy, and it would ultimately be unable to keep the passageway closed for very long. The bottom line is that the threat from Iran against the Strait of Hormuz cannot be construed as an "energy weapon," in the sense of applying pressure to elicit concessions. Wielding it would be viewed as an act of war.

The case of Venezuela is even less suited to support the presence of such a weapon in its own right, regardless of Venezuelan president Hugo Chávez's repeated threats to halt all exports of oil to the United States. A case in point was marked in July 2010, when an escalating conflict with neighboring Colombia seemed to be on the verge of spilling over into open war. Claiming that his country was under threat of military aggression, which allegedly would be supported by the United States, Chávez told a political rally that "the Yankee Empire has no limit to its manipulation."[13] Given that the United States is the top customer of its oil, halting the trade would deal the Venezuelan economy a powerful blow. Consequently, most observers viewed Chávez's flamboyant threats as no more than simple posturing, and ineffectual at that.

The worries that have been expressed about how Russia might use threats of disruption in the energy flow to elicit concessions from the European Union must be viewed against the background of these three cases. Pressuring small neighboring states into concessions is one thing. And this is something that Moscow has been repeatedly guilty of, albeit with varying degrees of success.[14] But engaging the European Union, or for that matter China, in energy-based blackmail, would be a very different story.

Russia as an Energy Bully

There is little evidence indeed that Russia has been ready to use any form of energy weapon against the "old" members of the European Union. Moscow has, on the contrary, been quite insistent and indeed also long successful in projecting an image of itself as a reliable source of energy security for Europe. Both commercial and political interests within the old member states have been quite happy to play along in this game. At least that was the case until 2006. It is in looking at the "new" EU member states that we may find more serious concern being voiced about Russian intentions. The reason is linked to observations of how Moscow has acted in relation to a number of former Soviet republics that are heavily dependent on Russian energy.

There has been a consistent pattern whereby countries viewed as friendly to Moscow have been charged lower prices for gas than those that have opted for a more pro-Western policy. As late as 2007, for example, Belarus, Armenia, and Ukraine were charged $100, $110, and $130 per thousand cubic meters of gas. This stands in contrast to the price received on the European market at the time, which was $235 per thousand cubic meters. Georgia and Azerbaijan were paying prices in line with the latter.[15]

To this we may add a long series of supply disruptions that have been explained ad hoc by Moscow as conditioned by technical malfunctions and pricing disputes. Those at the receiving end, meanwhile, have been prone to view such incidents as parts of a pattern of deliberate attempts to use threats of energy shutoff as a means of extending political influence and forcing concession to Russia's demands to assume control over national energy transport infrastructure.[16]

The prime illustration is the recurrent crises in relations between Russia and Ukraine, which have brought serious collateral damage also to some of the new EU member states. Much more will be said about this in later chapters, but suffice it to say here that Ukraine has been far from alone in being drawn into disputes of this kind.

The first substantial case of Russia being accused of using its hydrocarbon exports as a political tool was marked at the outset of the 1990s, when supply disruptions became part of the ever more complex relations between Moscow and capitals in the Baltic Soviet republics. It began in 1990, toward the very end of Soviet power, when Moscow cut energy supply in what was viewed as a futile attempt to stifle the Baltic independence movement. The same was repeated in 1992 and 1993, now in retaliation for demands by newly independent governments in the region that Moscow withdraw its remaining military forces, and define Russian-speaking minorities more broadly as foreigners for purposes of repatriatation.[17]

It is true that pricing disputes were ongoing and that supply disruptions may be viewed as part of those commercial disputes. But it is equally true that in 1992 the Russian Duma made a connection between commercial and political relations by threatening sanctions in retaliation for alleged discrimination of ethnic Russians living in Estonia. And, in a 2005 review of Russian gas conflicts, even the state-owned news agency *RIA Novosti* linked a June 1993 gas supply cutoff to Estonia with a decision by that country to define Russian-speakers as foreigners.[18]

In a second, parallel process, Moscow was also accused of using energy cutoffs as a tactic in its dispute with Ukraine over the Black Sea Fleet. In the wake of the dissolution of the Soviet Union, Kiev had claimed ownership to the bulk of that fleet, and in April 1992 it was unilaterally placed under Ukrainian jurisdiction. In August 1992 an agreement was reached to divide the assets, with final settlement to be reached in 1995. In July 1993, however, Russia upped the ante by claiming Sevastopol, the Crimean home port for the Ukrainian part of the fleet, as a Russian city. A decision was reached to resolve the issue at a summit to be held in the Crimean townlet of Massandra in September 1993. A week prior to that summit, Moscow reduced gas flow to Ukraine by 25 percent, and at the summit it offered to cancel Ukraine's multibillion-dollar energy debt—in return for Russian control over the Black Sea Fleet.[19]

Although it could again be argued that the supply reduction was part of a pricing conflict, it is hard not to see the strategic linkage to the conflict over fleet ownership and over naval basing rights. Subsequent Russian-Ukrainian relations would also remain heavily marked by linkage between Ukrainian energy debts and Russian demands that such debts be written off against concessions in the form of increased Russian control over Ukraine's energy transport infrastructure.

A third and rather similar case of alleged energy blackmail may be found in Russia's complicated relations with Georgia. Ever since the breakup of the Soviet Union, Moscow and Tbilisi had been at odds over the status of the independence-minded Georgian provinces South Ossetia and Abkhazia, a conflict that in August 2008 would lead to an open shooting war. In addition to this mounting friction, Moscow was also bent on assuming control over Georgian energy transport infrastructure. At stake here was a perceived risk that these pipelines might be used to transport gas from Iran and the Caspian Basin to Europe—without involving Russia.

In January 2006, two large explosions damaged the main and reserve pipelines that supplied Georgia with Russian gas. Nine hours later, an attack was made also on the main electricity line into Georgia. Both incidents took place on Russian territory. Georgia accused Russia of sabotage, and Russia blamed insurgents, none of whom ever claimed responsibility. According to Georgian president Mikheil Saakashvili, "officials at several levels of the Russian government had been issuing veiled threats in recent weeks."[20]

A fourth and more distinctly commercial case was played out in 2006, in connection with a decision by the Lithuanian government to sell its only oil refinery to a Polish rather than a Russian company. Shortly after the decision was announced, Russia shut down its Druzhba oil pipeline to Lithuania, citing technical reasons. This could of course be viewed as mere coincidence, but it could also be viewed against the background of prior conflict. From 1998 until 2000, Russian oil supplies to Lithuania were cut off nine times, as Moscow sought to ensure that a Russian company would benefit from the privatization policies of the Lithuanian government. In 2004, oil shipments again were stopped, allegedly in order to force Lithuania to privatize its oil port to a Russian company. And in 2006, oil flow through the Druzhba pipeline was terminated permanently.[21]

Until 2006, energy-related conflicts were limited to countries that had a prior history of membership in the Soviet Union. The conflict that erupted between Russia and Ukraine in January 2006 was different, in the sense that it had a direct impact also on countries within the European Union. The background was a demand from natural gas giant Gazprom, made in March 2005, that Ukraine pay "market prices" for gas. Following lengthy bargaining over the substantial price hike, Gazprom also began to accuse the Ukrainian side of illegally diverting gas intended for European customers for its own use. On January 1, 2006, the conflict came to a head, as Gazprom shut down gas flow to, and via, Ukraine. Those that were the hardest hit by the supply disruption included new EU member states such as Slovakia and Bulgaria that already had a troubled relation to Russia.[22] It was consequently to be expected that strong demands would emerge for diversification away from Russia.

What is reflected here is that Russia and the EU have fundamentally different interpretations of the very notion of "energy security." While Russia is bent on achieving security on the demand side, entailing a desire for control over the entire chain, from extraction to transport and to distribution of energy, the EU is playing for supply security—to ensure that it will not suffer disputes or other incidents that can lead to disruptions in energy supply.

Removing politics from the equation, to the point even of ignoring the presence of sentiments of fundamental distrust on both sides, this would have been a purely commercial matter of contracting. Assume, for example, that the Nord Stream gas pipeline had been built by Finland rather than by Russia and Germany in cooperation. It would then surely have been inconceivable for it to have attracted the high levels of political animosity that have surrounded this project. But politics, quite obviously, cannot be removed. On the contrary, as we shall see, political differences have been at the forefront of energy relations between Russia and Europe.

Facing the European Union

The core of the difficulties that Russia and the EU have encountered in seeking to place their energy dialogue on a purely commercial footing may be found in different perceptions of what the dialogue should concern. While Moscow has been playing for hard economic gains, Brussels has introduced soft ambitions to transform Russia into a liberal democracy and a rules-based market economy. The two sides have in consequence simply not been playing the same game. The implied conflict between their respective strategies has been formulated pointedly by Alexander Rahr: "Russia offers the EU a community based on interest, instead of values, economic pragmatism instead of civil dialogue, a modernization partnership instead of democratic partnership."[23]

As it seems unlikely indeed that Russia will be soon inclined toward a full adoption of Western values, however these may or should be defined, it does appear that Brussels has been trying to keep score in the wrong game. This, moreover, is far from the only problem facing an increasingly beleaguered European Commission. Although the account here is not much concerned with internal EU politics, it will be impossible to understand the evolution of its Russia policy without keeping this dimension in mind.

In line with this understanding of the energy game as being marked by multiple actors pursuing multiple agendas, the root cause of the problems that have marred Russian-European energy relations is reflected in the pronounced difficulties that the two sides have had in formulating coherent strategies to overcome conflicting agendas on their own respective sides. While the European side has suffered from differences in national interests, causing some member states to prefer separate dealings with Gazprom over adhering to common EU principles, for example, the Russian position has been marked by conflicts between different sectoral interests. There can be little doubt that conflicts of these kinds have been seriously detrimental to prospects for efficiency and mutual gain, especially so with respect to energy transport infrastructure. But, and this is the important point, there is little to be gained by presenting the Russian side as being committed to wielding an "energy weapon."

The point may be illustrated with the help of Karen Smith Stegen, who sets out to deconstruct the common understanding of the latter concept. Her argument is that the regime in a resource-rich country that is faced with temptation to use the export of oil and gas for purposes that go beyond commerce will have to meet a list of four conditions. First, it must be able to consolidate the country's energy resources; second, it must acquire control over transit routes; third, it must be willing to use its energy resources for political objectives; and fourth, it must ensure that the targeted country adjusts its policy in the desired direction.[24]

In retrospect, as detailed in Chapter 4, it may appear that in the Putin era the Kremlin was clearly focused on meeting the first two counts—securing and maintaining control both over the sources of energy production and over the means of transport, mainly pipelines. But again, we must be wary of finding causality where none may have existed. The parallel drives to reimpose state control over the oil industry and to build new sets of export pipelines, may, as suggested by Markku Kivinen, be more credibly explained by domestic than by foreign policy agendas.[25] On Smith Stegen's third count, the issue is even more complex. The alleged willingness to use energy for political purposes has not only conflicted with powerful commercial interests on the side of the energy companies but also been much easier to document in Russia's relations with countries of the former Soviet Union than in Russia's relations with countries outside the former Soviet bloc.

The real crux, however, which is also at the focus of Smith Stegen's argument, concerns her fourth count—whether Moscow has also been successful in achieving desired adjustments in policy from the side of targeted countries. Even where the presence of nefarious ambitions can be credibly documented, which again concerns countries of the former Soviet Union, the rate of success has not corresponded to the costs involved in terms of damage to reputation. If the wielding of an energy weapon really was a deliberate strategy, then it has not been very successful. Perhaps it is again more fruitful to view energy conflicts as the result of conflicting agendas and of ad hoc interventions.

The main reason why the Kremlin was able for so long to play such a successful game of divide and conquer against the European Union, which remains by far the dominant market for its energy exports, rests in the fact, alluded to earlier, that the EU member states have been so divided in their attitudes toward Russia. An effective common policy to counter mounting Russian influence over energy supply to the EU has consequently been difficult to formulate. The moves that were made against Gazprom by the EU's antitrust watchdog, the DG Competition, in 2011–2012 could be viewed as a sign of emerging consensus, with potentially far-reaching consequences for Russia.[26] We shall have reason to return to this argument in Chapter 8.

In retrospect, there can be no denying that the European Union has willfully placed itself in a situation of enhanced dependence on Russian energy. In some quarters (namely Germany under former chancellor Gerhard Schröder), this was the result of deliberate policy. The Kremlin was consequently placed in a position where, by halting the flow of energy, it could inflict substantial harm on receiving countries. Recalling what was said earlier about the days of Ronald Reagan and the Cold War, many voices have warned that if push comes to shove, Moscow will not hesitate to use this option. The underlying presumption has been that in case of rising tension between Russia and the United States, the European Union would be prone to be more accommodating to Moscow than would otherwise be the case. But is this really a reasonable presumption?

The core of the question concerns whether the threat of cutting off energy supply to Europe is in any sense credible. By way of illustration, we may note that by simply selling off its vast holdings of US securities, China could wreak substantial havoc on the US economy. Yet in so doing it would cause such harm to the global economy that the negative consequences for its own economic performance would surely outweigh any potential pleasure derived from seeing the US Treasury Department thrown into serious trouble over the refinancing of US foreign debt.

Moscow arguably finds itself in a similar position. It could in theory deal a crippling blow to European industries and communal central-heating systems. But the boomerang effect would likely be equally devastating. On balance, it is probably correct to say that Russia is more dependent on its trade with countries in the European Union than the latter are on being able to purchase Russian energy. Finding options to compensate for cutbacks in energy supply seems easier than developing new markets for nonenergy exports. It may be useful here to conclude with Stacy Closson's argument, based on observations of actual interdependency, that "the portrayal of Russia as the aggressor and Europe as the dependent actor, may be more the result of semantics than of facts."[27]

The Resource Curse

Leaving the highly politicized and media-driven questions of superpowers and energy weapons, we turn now to the more complex issue of whether the abundance of natural resources should be viewed as a blessing or perhaps as a curse. This represents a general problem that has produced a substantial scholarly literature on the implications of resource-based economic growth. It has been alternately known as the "resource curse" and as the "paradox of plenty."[28]

In the 1950s and the 1960s, there was general agreement, as part of the staples theory of economic growth, that possession of abundant natural resource endowments was clearly supportive of rapid economic development. The intuitive logic was that a resource boom in an underdeveloped area would attract labor and capital and by way of reinvestment of profits set in motion a process of diversified growth. It is only in the past couple decades that economists have begun to investigate and test econometrically the presence of a counterintuitive "resource curse."

In a broad and well-documented overview of the general case, Michael Ross finds that since the late 1980s, "economists and political scientists have produced a flood of new research that bears on this question. There is now strong evidence that states with abundant resource wealth perform less well than their resource-poor counterparts, but there is little agreement on why this occurs."[29] As Russia has often been held up as a classic example of such a curse, it may be useful to revisit briefly what the argument is all about.[30]

The most immediate way in which Russia's dependence on hydrocarbon exports may be construed as a problem proceeds via price volatility. At times of a resource boom, a sharp rise in exports will cause a country's real exchange rate to appreciate. This reduces the cost of imports, makes nonresource exports less competitive, and raises production costs in the manufacturing and agricultural sectors by pulling resources into the booming sector. Inspired by events that followed in the wake of the discovery, in 1959, of the Dutch Groningen gas field, this scenario has been generally known as the "Dutch Disease."[31]

In the Russian case, it has been common to associate developments in the 1990s with a bad case of this disease. From the mid-1990s, when the real exchange rate of the ruble began to appreciate, the nonenergy sectors suffered clear and substantial damage.[32] Several factors, however, combined to make it questionable whether the Dutch Disease really did offer a good frame of reference. One such factor was that government regulation kept energy prices for domestic users much lower than export prices. This was true for gas in particular, which in effect meant that Gazprom was forced to subsidize domestic energy-intensive producers.[33] The simple fact that the oil sector failed to exhibit any signs of a boom also caused some to speak of a peculiar "Russian Disease."[34]

The only sure ways of countering influences that might cause the Dutch Disease must proceed via slowing the appreciation of the real exchange rate or boosting the competitiveness of the manufacturing sector. In the Putin era, Moscow was highly successful in the former but failed abysmally in the latter. The success was due to the generally praised introduction, in 2004, of a stabilization fund that absorbed all oil export revenue above a certain cutoff price. This consequently relieved some of the potential upward pressure on the currency.[35]

Turning to the more general case of a possible resource curse, the literature may be divided into three different types of argument. The first holds that resource wealth will impact negatively on economic growth, the second that it will be the cause of civil wars, and the third that it will impair the quality of institutions and erode the prospects for democracy. By far the most important of these, at least in terms of attention, has been the presumption of an inverse link between growth and resources.

The first installment in a subsequently large number of contributions on this topic was made in 1995, by Jeffrey Sachs and Andrew Warner. They claimed to have found a "statistically significant, inverse, and robust association between natural resource intensity and growth over the past twenty years."[36] A few years later, the same authors found reason to conclude that while empirical support for the existence of a resource curse was not "bullet proof," repeated regressions based on growth data from the postwar period had shown quite strong evidence that high resource intensity tends to correlate with slow growth.[37]

In a scathing critique of this literature, Michael Alexeev and Robert Conrad point at several shortcomings related in the main to misinterpretation of available data. Their own claims, based on extensive econometric work, are that oil and mineral resources have enhanced rather than inhibited long-term growth, and that oil and minerals are largely neutral with respect to institutions.[38]

The first and most controversial of these claims is supported by running regressions based on GDP per capita levels rather than employing the standard comparison of growth rates over given periods of time. The argument is that measuring growth rates over a period of no more than thirty years, often beginning in 1965 or 1970, fails to capture the whole picture. As many of the studied countries began exploiting their oil wealth well before 1950, they may have enjoyed high rates of growth in the early stages and slower rates as deposits matured. The existing literature on the "curse" may thus be correct but incomplete.[39]

The second of Alexeev and Conrad's claims, concerning the impact of resource wealth on institutions, is largely derived from the first—that resource wealth has a positive impact on growth. Arguing that resource wealth represents "manna from heaven" that increases per capita GDP without affecting other important variables, the authors conclude that countries that are rich because of resource endowments may exhibit slower growth over time but will still remain richer than they would have been in the absence of such endowments. The potential downside is that while resource endowments cannot be shown to have a negative impact on institutions, nor does resource-based growth lead to better institutions.[40]

Leaving the link between resource wealth and civil war aside, as empirically irrelevant to the Russian case, we may proceed to look at the more complex argument on damage to institutions and impediments to the building of democracy. While the argument for an inverse relationship between resource wealth and growth is clearly counterintuitive, and may not hold water after all, the argument for a negative impact on institutions is more readily acceptable. It is, after all, a fact that with the exception of Norway (and possibly the United States), there are no democracies in existence that have a dominant resource sector. In the exceptional case or cases, moreover, democracy had been firmly established well before the discovery of oil and gas. All the other big oil- and gas-exporting nations in the world represent variations on the themes of authoritarianism, autocracy, and kleptocracy, some with the addition of civil war.

In the case of Russia, there has been no shortage of arguments linking oil wealth with obstacles to democratic institution building. The question concerns which of these arguments may actually hold water. Setting out to probe whether Russia really may be viewed as being "cursed by oil," Daniel Treisman begins by citing a couple of representative voices.[41] One belongs to Moisés Naím, the editor-in-chief of *Foreign Policy* magazine and former trade and industry minister of oil-rich Venezuela: "Russia's future will be defined as much by the geology of its subsoil as by the ideology of its leaders."[42] To Naím's argument, that lots of oil in combination with weak public institutions produces poverty, inequality, and corruption, Treisman adds an argument made by *New York Times* columnist Thomas Friedman, that commodity prices will reduce the extent of liberty in resource-rich states: "Russia, from Gorbachev to Putin, fits this relationship perfectly."[43] While such views are indeed "immediately plausible," and while oil and gas have indeed been at the core of Russia's political economy in recent decades, Treisman has a serious point when he suggests that "arguments that seem to fit so well . . . deserve particular scrutiny."[44]

Beginning with the general case of a link between democracy and resource wealth, he undertakes to plot the political regimes of the thirty-two largest oil and gas producers in the world, classified by scores from the Polity IV dataset, against average national income per capita derived from oil and gas. While the results confirm the absence of a resource curse in countries that are liberal democracies, they also indicate, in line with the argument by Alexeev and Conrad, that countries in Latin America appear to have enjoyed an intuitively plausible resource blessing. Most striking, Russia is found to be clustered with these latter countries.[45]

Arguing that "the pattern of evidence from around the world suggests that the ups and downs in Russia's oil and gas income in recent decades have only had a minor influence on its regime," Treisman then goes on to investigate the various ways in which scholars have argued that resource wealth may impact negatively on democracy, claiming that it is "hard to find much evidence of these mechanisms at work in Russia."[46] The most important of such mechanisms concerns "fiscal bargains"—the need for rulers to bargain with their subjects over taxes. This, however, also is where it gets a bit complicated.

From a historical perspective, this is indeed suggestive of this argument. Bargaining between king and subjects was at the very heart of the Glorious Revolution that set England on the path toward a rules-based market economy. Yet in the Russian case a long tradition of autocracy has implied the absence of any need to even discuss a link between taxation and representation. From tsars and emperors up through Communist Party general secretaries, rulers have reserved the right to command and extract, without seeking approval from below.

Treisman's argument on Russia maintains that in contrast to states in the Persian Gulf that have sufficient incomes from oil to avoid the need to raise taxes, the Russian government's income from oil and gas has been in no way sufficient to secure such independence.[47] The implication is that the government will be forced to enter into bargaining with the private sector. While such bargaining has indeed been a prominent part of Russian economic policy since the collapse of the Soviet Union, the core question is whether it has also been conducive to the building of democracy.

An important part of the answer to this question, which Treisman does not address, concerns the role of private property within the energy complex. Russia is in this respect fundamentally different from the general pattern of other petrostates. While Gazprom has remained a de facto monopoly with close links to the Kremlin, the oil industry was both privatized and broken up into competing entities. As pointed out by Peter Rutland, for example, this pluralism led to intense political bargaining, both vertically and horizontally.[48] But again it remains questionable whether the nature of this bargaining has been conducive or detrimental to the building of institutions in support of democracy and a rules-based market economy.

The core of the matter concerns the contrast between such clearly defined and transparently enforceable rules that emerged out of England's Glorious Revolution and the fuzzy unwritten rules, generating opaque influence games, that for so long have been a hallmark of Russian political economy. Pursuing their thesis on Russia's "virtual economy," Clifford Gaddy and Barry Ickes have emphasized the particular role played in post-Soviet Russia by what they refer to as "informal taxes"—demands for contributions that are made by the Kremlin outside the formal system of taxation and other rules-based obligations.[49]

Accepting that the practice of imposing such demands from above will impact negatively both the quality of corporate governance and the prospects for securing accountability in government, we may find good reason to agree with Rutland that on this vital count, specificity in the Russian case trumps efforts to find general patterns: "The 'Russian curse' of statism overlaps and supplants the 'resource curse,' in complex and unpredictable ways that may diverge from predictions based on the experiences of other countries."[50]

The Heavy Burden of History

When Soviet power suddenly imploded, and sweeping deregulation did away with the multitude of restrictions associated with central economic planning, there emerged a general *faiblesse* for thinking in terms of a window of opportunity. For a limited time, there would be scope for "extraordinary politics," aimed at achieving a broad systemic transformation. As mentioned in Chapter 1, hopes were high and many were prone to belief in the possibility of launching reforms based on a tabula rasa, a clean slate by which marketizing reform was bound to produce gains in efficiency.[51]

As suggested earlier, the main cause of the failure of such visions may be derived from a conflict between a new set of radically different formal rules seeking to promote market economy and a set of highly resilient informal norms that had emerged in response to the old system. It is in this dimension of longer-term historical progression that the core of arguments for Russian distinctiveness may be found, to the point even of suggesting that Russia is a sui generis, a kind of its own.[52]

It should be immediately recognized that long-term historical perspectives will always harbor the danger of succumbing to determinism, of believing that simply because matters developed the way they did, this was somehow in the cards from the outset. This is clearly not acceptable, and Russian history does indeed provide a wealth of illustration of fateful points in time where the course of history could have taken a very different turn. Suggestions on historical continuity must contend with the presence of forces for change, and in the case of Russia the latter have at times been powerful indeed. Yet it is imperative that we also seek to understand what has driven the highly distinctive Russian pendulum movement between reform and repression, at times interspersed by seriously disruptive "times of trouble."

This discussion will refrain from delving too deep into history, resting content with a few stylized facts about the Russian institutional matrix that over the centuries has remained so strikingly resilient to change.[53] The origins may be dated to the fifteenth and sixteenth centuries, the formative era of what came to be known as Muscovy. Faced with a combination of weak resources and an ever present danger of being overrun by hostile neighbors, the Muscovite rulers opted for what turned out to be an enduring and for some time highly rational solution.

By agreeing that one of the leading families should serve as first among equals, it was possible to ensure effective command and control in the face of enemy threats. By making rights to property conditional on service to the ruler, it was possible to ensure that all available resources could be harnessed for defensive purposes. And by allowing officials to "feed" off the land—to extract freely from the peasantry—resource-constrained rulers could ensure that they would still be able to remunerate loyal agents of the regime. The success of these institutional arrangements may be measured in the fact that in lieu of succumbing, Moscow would over time evolve into the center of a superpower with global reach. While there is undeniable achievement here, it is also an achievement that has come at a price.

Institutional solutions that may have been highly rational to early Muscovy would over time evolve into obstacles against modernization, producing a strong urge over the centuries for Russia to escape backwardness and to "catch up"—first with Europe and then with the United States. Perhaps the most striking feature of Russian history is that long after the time when effective security against destruction by foreign invasion had been ensured, a feat that may be associated with Peter the Great and the rise of the Russian empire, institutions that had been designed for defense rather than for development would remain intact, and become increasingly troublesome.

An autocratic mode of government, more properly defined as unaccountable government, would remain the defining character of Russia, arguably into the present day. The associated refusal to ensure credible property rights protection, known somewhat misleadingly as conditional property rights, would go hand in hand with that mode of governance. The early practice of allowing officials to "feed" off the peasants, known as *kormlenie,* would remain a key feature of relations between principals and their agents, amply illustrated by the corruption and looting of state property that marked both the Yeltsin and Putin eras.

While the Soviet order was publicly touted as modernizing, it in effect represented a full reversal of the important ambitions to reform that had marked the latter part of the nineteenth century, and a return to the distinctive patterns of old Muscovy. The Communist Party provided a perfect illustration of unaccountable government. The introduction of the notion of "people's property" was an extreme case of conditional rights to the usufruct of the means of production. And remuneration of state and party officials would have strong elements of *kormlenie,* of officials being allowed to help themselves to assets and revenue streams rightly belonging to the people.

By far the most important feature was that the basic legitimacy of the system remained so strongly linked to providing defense rather than economic development. The economic logic of the Soviet system was firmly rooted in forced extraction of resources from above. The purpose was to ensure that although the Soviet Union had a GDP that was much inferior to that of the United States, it could still keep up in the arms race. During the Cold War it was sometimes jokingly said that the Soviet Union did not *have* a military-industrial complex, but that it *was* a military-industrial complex.

Again, however, there was a price to be paid. As in the deeper past, the lack of institutional adaptation to the needs of modernization caused increasing technological backwardness, resulting in perceived needs to catch up. Fluctuating revenues from hydrocarbon exports meanwhile proved to be both an essential life-support system and a highly destabilizing influence.

The window of opportunity that was opened up by the collapse of the Soviet Union was transformed under Boris Yeltsin, if not by Boris Yeltsin, into a free-for-all in which state and party officials feathered their own nests, largely unconstrained by the norms of self-restraint associated with the Golden Rule of a high-performance market economy. Emerging out of the "time of trouble," the Putin era at first seemed to offer yet another window of opportunity. But it would soon transpire that the emphasis was more on order than on law, and more on control over resources than on development of those resources.

As evidenced by the mass outpouring of discontent during the winter of 2011–2012, governance in Russia has remained unaccountable. As evidenced both by the fate of Yukos Oil and by the diverse fates of a number of major foreign energy giants, rights to contracts and to property have remained conditional on a good relationship with the Kremlin. And as evidenced, again, by the outpouring of massive anger against United Russia, the regime's "party of power," forever branded by Aleksei Navalnyi as a "party of swindlers and thieves" (*partiya zhulikov i vorov*), corruption has remained the essential feature of politics.[54]

The various and at times conflicting roles that were played by components of the country's energy complex during the Putin era would be deeply revealing of the nature of the systems of informal norms that kept the system going.

Economic actors saw little reason to develop trust in the kinds of formal rules, and in the associated credible enforcement by impartial public agencies, that constitute the lifeblood of a high-performance rules-based market economy. They instead would invest heavily in honing their skill in playing influence games, in securing preferential access to resources and protection against "enemies." The outcome was the very same maze of dense, deeply personal, and highly opaque relations that for so long had been so distinctive of Russian tradition.

Before addressing the nature and consequences of these games, let us first turn to the energy assets that have been at the disposal of the Kremlin and, by implication, its cronies.

Notes

1. The term "great game" was invented in British military circles, and was popularized by British writer Rudyard Kipling in his 1901 novel *Kim*.

2. Winston Churchill delivered his classic speech, formally titled "Sinews of Peace," at Westminster College in Fulton, Missouri, on March 5, 1946. The full text may be found at http://www.historyguide.org/europe/churchill.html.

3. Director Stanley Kubrick's darkly funny motion picture *Dr. Strangelove* provided one such scenario, disturbingly possible to the point even of anticipating fears, prevalent among American "hawks," that détente under Gorbachev was a mere Soviet ruse. Following a paring down of US weapons capability, the Soviet side would emerge with even bigger bombs.

4. The full story of what (may have) happened is told in Fischer, *A Cold War Conundrum*.

5. This argument is made with great force by Archie Brown, for example in *Seven Years That Changed the World* and *The Rise and Fall of Communism,* pt. 5.

6. Stent, "An Energy Superpower?" p. 78. See also Lucas, *The New Cold War.*

7. In mid-August 2010 it was reported that the Chinese economy had surpassed that of Japan, to occupy the position as second-largest economy in the world. Linda Stern, "China Gaining on U.S., Now World's Second Largest Economy," *CBS News,* August 16, 2010, http://moneywatch.bnet.com/economic-news/blog/daily-money /china-gaining-on-us-now-worlds-second-largest-economy/1194.

8. Trenin, *Russia's Strategic Choices,* p. 1.

9. The notion of spheres of "privileged interest" has replaced the discredited prior notion of a "near abroad," consisting of former Soviet republics that, implicitly, were not regarded as truly foreign and independent countries. The replacement was introduced by President Dmitry Medvedev in the wake of the 2008 war between Russia and Georgia. His stated rationale was that Russia would defend "the life and dignity" of Russian citizens "no matter where they are located." Charles Clover, "Russia Announces 'Spheres of Interest,'" *Financial Times,* August 31, 2008, http://www.ft.com/intl/cms/s/0/e9469744-7784-11dd-be24-0000779fd18c .html#axzz1wKapo3EE.

10. For example, Rutland, "Russia as an Energy Superpower."

11. For a background on how the United States formulated its response, based on a Central Intelligence Agency national intelligence estimate titled "The Soviet Gas

Pipeline in Perspective," see Roman Kupchinsky, "Analysis: The Recurring Fear of Russian Gas Dependency," *Radio Free Europe/Radio Liberty,* September 11, 2013, http://www.rferl.org/content/article/1068318.html.

12. See further Smith Stegen, "Deconstructing the 'Energy Weapon,'" p. 6511.

13. "Chavez Threatens to Cut Off Oil to U.S.," *CNN,* July 25, 2010, http://articles.cnn.com/2010-07-25/world/venezuela.chavez.us_1_farc-venezuela-and-colombia-revolutionary-armed-forces?_s=PM:WORLD.

14. For a broad country-by-country overview of Russia's foreign energy policy, see Larsson, *Russia's Energy Policy.*

15. Nies, *Oil and Gas Delivery to Europe,* p. 19.

16. A powerful case against Russia for using its energy resources as an "energy weapon" is made by Keith Smith, who from 1997 to 2000 was US ambassador to Lithuania; see Smith, *Russian Energy Politics* and *Security Implications of Russian Energy Policies.* Seeking to alert Western politicians to the perceived dangers in Russian energy assertiveness, he also cites a warning issued in 2008 by Andrei Illarionov, Putin's former chief economic adviser, suggesting that Russia's increasing tendency to use its energy weapon must be taken as a wake-up call to Western governments; Smith, *Security Implications of Russian Energy Policies,* p. 1.

17. Smith, *Security Implications of Russian Energy Policies,* p. 1.

18. Celestine Bohlen, "Why Are Russians Still Here? The Free Baltics Ask," *New York Times,* August 7, 1992, http://www.nytimes.com/1992/08/07/world/why-are-russians-still-here-the-free-baltics-ask.html?pagewanted=all&src=pm; and Smith Stegen, "Deconstructing the 'Energy Weapon,'" p. 6508.

19. Smith Stegen, "Deconstructing the 'Energy Weapon,'" p. 6509.

20. C. J. Chivers, "Explosions in Southern Russia Sever Gas Lines to Georgia," *New York Times,* January 23, 2006, http://www.nytimes.com/2006/01/23/international/europe/23georgia.html; and Smith Stegen, "Deconstructing the 'Energy Weapon,'" pp. 6508–6509.

21. Smith, *Russia and European Energy Security,* pp. 5–6.

22. For a detailed account of differences in degrees of friendliness toward Russia, see Braghiroli and Carta, "An Index of Friendliness Toward Russia," pp. 12–20.

23. Rahr, "Strategic Neighbourhood."

24. Smith Stegen, "Deconstructing the 'Energy Weapon,'" pp. 6506–6507.

25. Kivinen, "Public and Business Actors in Russia's Energy Policy."

26. "Antitrust: Commission Opens Proceedings Against Gazprom," *EU Press Releases Database,* September 4, 2012, http://europa.eu/rapid/press-release_IP-12-937_en.htm.

27. Closson, "Russia's Key Customer: Europe," p. 90.

28. The notion of a "resource curse" was first introduced in Auty, *Sustaining Development in Mineral Economies.* See also Karl, *The Paradox of Plenty.*

29. Ross, "The Political Economy of the Resource Curse," p. 297.

30. On the Russian case of hydrocarbon dependence, see also a broad collection of papers in Ellman, *Russia's Oil and Natural Gas;* and Tabata, *Dependent on Oil and Gas.*

31. The term was coined in "The Dutch Disease," *The Economist,* November 26, 1977. What has come to be known as the "core model" in economics was introduced in Corden and Neary, "Booming Sector and De-Industrialisation." The subsequent literature is nothing short of massive.

32. Tabata, "The Great Russian Depression of the 1990s."

33. Tabata, "Price Differences, Taxes, and the Stabilization Fund."

34. Goldman, "The 'Russian Disease.'"

35. Tabata, "The Russian Stabilization Fund and Its Successor."

36. Sachs and Warner, *Natural Resource Abundance and Economic Growth*, p. 21.

37. Sachs and Warner, "The Curse of Natural Resources," p. 828.

38. Alexeev and Conrad, "The Elusive Curse of Oil," p. 586. See also Jones Luong and Weinthal, *Oil Is Not a Curse*.

39. Alexeev and Conrad, "The Elusive Curse of Oil," pp. 587–592.

40. Ibid., pp. 592–595.

41. Treisman, "Is Russia Cursed by Oil?"

42. Naím, "Russia's Oily Future," p. 96

43. Friedman, "The First Law of Petropolitics."

44. Treisman, "Is Russia Cursed by Oil?" p. 85.

45. Ibid., pp. 86–89.

46. Ibid., p. 93.

47. Ibid., pp. 94–95.

48. Rutland, "Putin's Economic Record," pp. 1061–1062. See also Hanson, "The Resistible Rise of State Control in the Russian Oil Industry."

49. For example, Gaddy and Ickes, "Resource Rents and the Russian Economy."

50. Rutland, "Putin's Economic Record," p. 1063.

51. For a detailed analysis of the role of economics, and of economists, in the Russian transition, see Roland, *Transition and Economics*.

52. The point about Russia as a sui generis is made, for example, in Pipes, *Russia Under the Old Regime*, p. 23.

53. A fuller story is told in Hedlund, *Russian Path Dependence*.

54. The event took place during a radio talk show in which Navalnyi engaged in debate with United Russia Duma member Yevgeny Federov. The debate may be viewed on YouTube at http://www.youtube.com/watch?v=ccE-zCR1ej4.

3

Energy Assets

Energy and energy-related issues have been at the forefront of reporting from and about Russia ever since the dissolution of the Soviet Union. Given the dominant role that has been played by such issues, in economic as well as political developments, there is nothing at all strange in this. We must, however, not be led into believing that the current dependence of the Russian Federation on revenues from exports of oil and gas in and of itself constitutes something new. Even a cursory glance at the substantial literature that emerged on Soviet oil and gas will indicate that both the economic performance and the configuration of power politics in the Soviet Union could be tightly linked to the energy sector.[1]

The most obvious dimension concerns the notorious volatility of global hydrocarbon prices. Swings in export prices for Soviet oil and gas impacted not just the inflow of hard currency, which in turn translated into fluctuations in the ability to import sorely needed machinery and technology. Related to such disruptive influence was the fact that volatility in export prices also translated into variation in the size of resource rents, which in turn would influence ongoing struggles between such industry lobbies that were later to be known as political elites.

We may usefully return here to the case of the oil crisis in 1973. As mentioned in Chapter 2, the Arab members of OPEC responded to the US decision to resupply Israel in the Yom Kippur War by introducing an oil embargo that caused prices to skyrocket. The result was an unprecedented shift of income from oil-consuming to oil-producing nations. Over the period 1973–1985, energy exports accounted for 80 percent of the Soviet

Union's expanding hard currency earnings, and other oil-exporting countries were equally fortunate. Because many of the suddenly enriched Arab
oil states were also big customers of the Soviet arms industry, Moscow was
able to reap a double benefit. All told, the oil crisis provided what historian
Stephen Kotkin has called "the greatest economic boon the Soviet Union
ever experienced."[2]

The Soviet Union found numerous uses for the sudden windfall of oil
revenue, ranging from support for a massive Soviet military buildup, and
help in defraying the costs of the war in Afghanistan that was begun in
1979, to handouts that cushioned the impact of the oil shock on Soviet
satellite states in Eastern Europe.[3] Domestically, oil money financed imports that helped spur technological change, improving the lot of Soviet
consumers. And oil money was of course channeled into higher pay and
perks for members of the elite.[4]

The downside, however, was that the inflow of petrodollars also served
to breed complacency, which in turn would pave the way toward economic
stagnation. It was symptomatic that in retrospect, as mentioned in Chapter
1, the Brezhnev era would come to be known as the "period of stagnation,"
the *period zastoia*. As oil prices began to decline, it became apparent that
little if any of the sudden windfall had been put to good use. Both Mikhail
Gorbachev and even more so Boris Yeltsin would have to contend with the
consequences of shrinking revenues that plunged Moscow into an escalating and politically sensitive dependence on foreign creditors.

While it may be argued that fluctuations in the price of hydrocarbons
were largely beyond the control of Moscow, price volatility was only part
of the picture. Due to a fundamental geographical dilemma, the Kremlin
also had to face a parallel process of falling production as volume began to
decline. The scope of this account must thus be broadened from price
movements to include aspects of energy extraction and transport, which, in
contrast to fluctuations in the price of hydrocarbons, were very much
within the control of Moscow, and badly mismanaged.

The main purpose of this chapter is to provide a historical perspective
on the changing nature and location of the energy assets that the Kremlin
has had at its disposal. (Appendixes 2 and 3 add an international perspective on the relative importance of Russian oil and gas, with respect to production as well as proven reserves, from 1991 onward.) The chapter begins
by looking at the role of hydrocarbons during the Soviet era, with particular emphasis on the constraints inherent in the geographical dilemma. It
then explores the looting of the Russian oil and gas sectors that followed
during the Yeltsin era, and the emergence of a set of new energy powers in
former Soviet republics to the south. Finally, the chapter provides a brief
account of the severity of the economic depression of the 1990s, mainly to
provide a backdrop for the subsequent turnaround of the Russian economy.

Soviet Oil and Gas

The history of Russian oil antedates that of the Soviet Union. One of the first oil wells ever drilled in the world, and by far the most important, was the Drake Well, discovered in the middle of quiet farm country in northwestern Pennsylvania in 1859. Triggering an international search for petroleum, the discovery would in many respects change the world.[5] The Russians, however, were not far behind. It might even be argued that they were a bit ahead of the Americans in the search for petroleum.

The original center of what would eventually become a mighty Soviet oil and gas complex was located at and around Baku, the capital of present-day Azerbaijan.[6] The first oil well in this region was drilled in 1846, more than a decade before the Drake Well in Pennsylvania. Despite this early start, it was not until 1873 that a genuine gusher was struck.[7] That year also saw the arrival on the scene of the Swedish Nobel family, who went on to found the company Nobel Brothers Petroleum Producing.[8] Over the coming decades, Baku would constitute the hub of an oil boom that entailed introduction of the world's first oil tanker and the world's first oil pipeline. It was significant that precisely these oil fields would be an important objective of the Nazi German offensive that began in 1941.

In the post–World War II era, Soviet oil production was marked by a shift in geographical focus. An important reason was that producers failed to overcome the damage done to oil installations in Azerbaijan during the war. Efforts were consequently aimed instead at fields in the Volga Basin and the Ural Mountains, where output continued to increase until about 1970.

Given the overwhelming role that would be played by oil fields in Western Siberia, it is of some importance to note that in sharp contrast to the major international oil companies, in Moscow decisionmakers were slow to realize what a treasure trove of oil and gas they had beneath their own feet. In the years immediately following the end of World War II, planners remained insistent that oil and gas represented a considerably more risky source of energy than traditional coal, peat, and wood.[9]

Development of oil fields in Western Siberia proceeded during the 1960s, and with the discovery in 1969 of the supergiant Samotlor field, the region was poised for a spectacular takeoff. From 1970 until 1977, annual oil output increased sevenfold, from 31 to about 210 million tons.[10] Kotkin may well be right in stating that "without the discovery of Siberian oil, the Soviet Union might have collapsed decades earlier."[11] This success, however, was a fragile one: "By 1975 the Tiumen oil industry remained dependent on the largest two or three fields, and especially Samotlor."[12]

Given that oil production in the Volga-Ural region declined after 1970, the lack of emphasis on exploration and development of new fields would prove to be a recipe for disaster. In 1977, the US Central Intelligence Agency produced a set of three reports predicting that Soviet oil and gas output would peak in 1980 and decline sharply thereafter. Suggesting that the Soviet bloc would thus be transformed from a net exporter to net importer, these reports received massive attention.[13] As we now know, they turned out to be seriously wrong. To what extent they actually had an impact on the Kremlin is hard to say, but they did coincide with a rude awakening on the Soviet side.

By coincidence or not, in that same year, 1977, Leonid Brezhnev introduced a set of emergency measures that were fully consistent with Soviet standard operating procedure, ordering a massive increase in resource inputs. This took the form, above all, of an ambitious boost in investment. Over the five-year period from 1977 until 1982, the latter being Brezhnev's last year in office, Soviet investment in oil nearly doubled.[14] The immediate effect was a boost in output that more than made up for the decline in older oil fields. This would be no more than a quick fix, however. At the core of the crisis was a combination of faulty exploration, escalating costs of drilling, and complete neglect of energy conservation. The stage was set for a new round of crisis.

By 1980 the Kremlin finally decided to make an all-out wager on natural gas. The Soviet gas industry had been developing since the mid-1960s, and in the second half of the 1970s it had been a star performer. In 1980, gas was the only source of energy that actually succeeded in meeting set targets. Although exploration had shown that massive reserves were available, the Kremlin again had been slow in responding. An important reason may have been successful lobbying by the coal industry, which claimed that transmission of coal-generated power by high-voltage cable would be preferable to the building of expensive gas pipelines.[15]

The decision point arrived at the twenty-sixth Party Congress, held in 1980. In his speech, General Secretary Brezhnev announced that the output of gas would be increased by nearly half over the coming five years, from 435 billion cubic meters in 1980 to 630–640 billion cubic meters in 1985. The bulk of this increase would come from Western Siberia. More than two-thirds of the associated boost in investment would be devoted to the construction of six huge trunk lines containing 20,000 kilometers of 56-inch pipe that would connect Western Siberia with the European parts of the Soviet Union. One of these lines, the previously mentioned Druzhba (Friendship) pipeline, would extend all the way to Western Europe, with a capacity to supply up to 40 billion cubic meters of gas in return for badly needed hard currency.[16] It is still the longest pipeline in the world.

By this time, Soviet economic development had become intimately linked with development of the country's energy complex. From 1981 to

1985, energy absorbed 90 percent of total industrial investment growth, leaving little for other sectors.[17] At first sight, this did appear to be a successful wager. From 1970 to 1988, the volume of net energy exports increased by 270 percent, and in the early 1980s, energy export brought in 80 percent of hard currency earnings.[18] But as mentioned, this success was built on shaky foundations.

The campaign mode of developing West Siberian oil and gas rested on forced production techniques, such as aggressive water-flooding, that were highly detrimental. A lack of coordination between the oil and gas sectors also resulted in excessive flaring in the oil fields, wasting huge volumes of gas, and an overwhelming emphasis on supply caused energy demand to skyrocket. Absent metering devices to record volume flared, and with absurdly low prices for end users, there was nothing to constrain demand. All of these would constitute important parts of the energy legacy left for post-Soviet Russia.

By the mid-1980s, Western Siberia was no longer a star performer. By 1985, the depletion rate for oil (the share of new oil that simply offsets decline in older fields) had risen to 85 percent.[19] Over and above the escalating costs of extraction, the Kremlin now also had to contend with falling export prices and a weakening dollar. From 1983 to 1986, Soviet terms of trade, measured as crude oil for West German manufactures, dropped by 60 percent.[20] It was at this inauspicious time that Mikhail Gorbachev succeeded to power, as the last general secretary of the Communist Party of the Soviet Union. The prospects were not good. The huge windfall that was triggered by the oil crisis in 1973 had been squandered.[21]

The challenge that was placed before the Kremlin was related to the inherent geographical dilemma. Being forced to witness increasing depletion of its West Siberian oil fields, Moscow now also had to contend with a set of additional problems. New finds of oil and gas were located in areas that required development of infrastructure as well as technology, neither of which was readily available without foreign assistance. These latter problems would constitute much of the core of the subsequent story.

The Looting of Russian Oil

When Mikhail Gorbachev assumed power, Soviet energy resources were still firmly under state control. This applied across the board, from production facilities to pipeline grids, export terminals, and foreign trade organizations. Although beset with multiple problems, this was still a mighty complex, accounting for substantial shares of GDP, foreign trade turnover, and government revenue. The three main bureaucracies that were in charge of maintaining and developing this complex were the Ministry of Oil, the

Ministry of Gas, and the Ministry of Geology, the latter being responsible for exploration.

As the Soviet Union lapsed into terminal decline, actors within these bureaucracies responded very differently to the problems and prospects that suddenly materialized. As it was becoming ever more apparent that state ownership and central control over production assets was slipping, and that even the state itself might collapse, it was up to well-placed insiders to make hay while the sun was shining.

By far the most proficient in responding to these challenges was the last Soviet minister of gas, Viktor Chernomyrdin. Sensing the general drift toward an increasing role for cooperatives, joint ventures, and various leasing arrangements that marked the policy of perestroika under Gorbachev, he made his play. The key was to win approval from the Kremlin for a set of measures that would secure the integrity of the gas sector as a Kremlin-controlled monolith. Given the important role of Gazprom in these events, we shall return to this story at great length in Chapter 5.

Chernomyrdin's first step, taken already in August 1989, was to transform his ministry into a joint stock company, RAO Gazprom, which he placed under his own leadership. When he was subsequently appointed prime minister under Yeltsin in December 1992, Chernomyrdin handed over the reins of power to his close associate Rem Vyakhirev. Throughout the Yeltsin era, the two would achieve such success in tandem that many began to question whether it was Gazprom that controlled the Kremlin rather than the other way around.

This in a sense was typical of the times. As Angela Stent puts it, "the symbiotic relationship between political and business elites makes it difficult to determine where politics end and business begins." Yet the links between the Kremlin and the Gazprom management became so tight that it was "sometimes difficult to determine whether Gazprom's policies [were] those of the Kremlin or of the company."[22]

Turning to the side of oil, the demise of the Soviet Union would be associated also with a demise of the oil industry as a centrally controlled entity. In sharp contrast to the case of gas, the assets controlled by the Ministry of Oil were subjected to a stepwise process of breakup and transfer into private hands. Whereas Chernomyrdin succeeded in transitioning effortlessly from his role as minister of gas into chief executive officer of Gazprom, in the case of oil, movers and shakers would come from a variety of directions, representing insiders as well as (initial) outsiders. The reasons were not wholly due to Chernomyrdin's greater political experience and dexterity. Predators would find oil more attractive than gas for the simple reason that oil is easier to transport and sell. In further vital contrast to the case of gas, which would remain firmly in Russian hands, the oil industry would also be opened up to participation by foreign oil majors, in a process rife with controversy.

At the time of the breakup of the Soviet Union, the Ministry of Oil was transformed into a joint stock company, following the example of the Ministry of Gas. This took place in September 1991, in the wake of the failed coup against Gorbachev. The new entity at first was known as Rosneftegaz. In stark contrast to Gazprom, however, which would successfully resist all subsequent attempts at subdivision, Rosneftegaz was to be broken up into a near dozen formally independent companies.[23]

The first spin-off was created, in November 1991, when the acting minister of oil, Vagit Alekperov, succeeded in carving out three oil fields— Langepaz, Urengoi, and Kogalym—and packaging them into a new entity that he named LUKoil and placed under his own control as chief executive officer. In November 1992, Rosneftegaz was renamed Rosneft (a name that will loom large later in the story), and in 1993, two more private companies of subsequent renown—Yukos and Surgutneftegaz—were spun off. Surgutneftegaz was taken over by another prominent insider, Vladimir Bogdanov, whose role at the Ministry of Oil had been to supervise precisely that entity.[24]

As a result of these spin-offs, Rosneft was greatly diminished in both size and importance, but still accounted for more than 60 percent of Russian oil output. That was set to change. By way of further spin-offs and shady auctions, Rosneft would be reduced to a mere shadow of its former might. In 1998, it came very close to being auctioned off by the government of Sergei Kiriyenko. Given the prominent role that would be played by Rosneft in Vladimir Putin's subsequent "authoritarian restoration," it is intriguing to note how close it also came to being thrown to the wolves, along with the rest of the assets of the former Ministry of Oil.[25]

The truly fundamental transformation of the Russian oil industry as a whole arrived in 1995, when a small set of well-connected operators were allowed to acquire major stakes in the country's oil and minerals giants. The general background was that the government was in serious need of funds to cover gaping holes in the budget. In a technical deal that came to be known, infamously, as the "loans for shares" scheme, a group of private bankers offered to advance credits against collateral in the form of government-held blocks of shares in strategic industries.

On the face of it, this was somewhat unorthodox but not by necessity against the law. If the government had succeeded in raising sufficient taxes in order to repay the credits, all would have been fine. The trick, however, was that nobody expected this to happen. Instead, when it transpired that the credits would not be repaid, it was up to the banks to recover their money by auctioning off the collateral. This they did among themselves, in closed and rigged proceedings that rarely involved more than one bidder. The end result was that the government allowed a group of cronies to acquire substantial stakes in the country's most valuable industries, at rock-bottom prices.[26]

This represented the creation of what would come to be known as the Russian oligarchy. Private financial fortunes that had been amassed via short-term speculation on currency markets and in government securities could now be transformed into substantial holdings of real assets with significant worth. This was the time, for example, when Mikhail Khodorkovsky won control over Yukos for a mere $309 million, when Vladimir Potanin paid out $170 million to acquire Norilsk Nickel, when Boris Berezovsky put up no more than $100 million for 51 percent of Sibneft, and when both Alekperov and Bogdanov succeeded in enhancing their personal stock holdings.[27] By the fall of 1996, these men would reach the peak of their fame and fortune, allowing Berezovsky, for example, to claim in an interview with the *Financial Times* that he and six others jointly controlled half of the Russian economy.[28]

Proceeding to the parallel involvement of foreign oil, we turn first to Sakhalin Island, located off the east coast of the Russian mainland. The presence of substantial hydrocarbon reserves in this region had been known since the late nineteenth century, and oil production dates back to 1928, when a Russian-Japanese joint venture discovered oil onshore. Due to the severity of the climate and the need to engage in technologically challenging offshore drilling, however, no serious operation was undertaken in the Soviet era. The only exception was begun in 1973–1974, when Moscow entered into a joint venture with Japan to develop the Sakhalin continental shelf. Although funding was provided and significant finds were made, a host of political problems, notably but not exclusively the war in Afghanistan, caused the effort to peter out.[29] Following the breakup of the Soviet Union, matters were considerably different. Being in desperate need of foreign investment and technology, the Russian government decided to change tack and allow the entry of foreign partners.

In order to understand the conflicts that would follow between the Kremlin and these foreign partners, we must begin by noting that discussions on foreign involvement began when oil prices were very low and the Russian side was in a financially weak position. The outcome was that Moscow accepted production-sharing agreements, meaning that before the sharing of proceeds could begin, the foreign partner would be allowed to recoup all costs. Common in other parts of the world since the 1950s, production-sharing agreements are favored by investors for the added and simple reason that they provide protection against changes in tax laws and license regulation.[30]

The arrangement also carries a risk of being inherently biased against the host country, because cost overruns by the foreign partner will postpone the time when the sharing of proceeds begins. As the latter aspect will be critically dependent on how the contract is written, superior legal skills on the investor side may tilt the balance against the host. In the case of Russia, there also was the added factor of Russians feeling that they were being treated as a third world country.[31]

In retrospect, both foreign and Russian observers have agreed that the initial production-sharing agreements signed by the Russian government were overly favorable to the foreign partners.[32] While not alone, Vladimir Putin has been one of the most vocal in expressing such critique. At a meeting with foreign journalists at the 2007 G8 summit in St. Petersburg, he denounced the Sakhalin II production-sharing agreement as a "colonial project that had nothing to do with the interests of the Russian Federation."[33] Driving the point home, he also expressed regret that the Russian officials who authorized such arrangements had not been put in prison.[34]

The first production-sharing agreement to be signed in Russia was completed in 1994, for Royal Dutch Shell to explore the giant Sakhalin II gas field.[35] Based on exploration that had begun already in 1986, the first phase of the project involved a giant offshore production platform, named Molikpaq, that began delivering Russia's first offshore oil in 1999. In December 2000, Shell officially assumed the operatorship of the Sakhalin Energy company. Having acquired a 37.5 percent stake from Marathon Oil, and having sold a 7.5 percent stake to Mitsui, it was left with 55 percent and—importantly—with no Russian participation. The much more ambitious second phase involved additional offshore platforms, onshore processing plants, a 500-mile onshore pipeline system for oil and gas, a liquefied natural gas plant, and an oil export terminal. The LNG plant was inaugurated in February 2009 and reached full capacity by the end of 2010. Representing one of the world's biggest integrated oil and gas projects, total project costs in the end came to $22 billion, or more than twice the original estimate of $10 billion.[36] Given that the production-sharing agreement allowed the foreign partner to recoup cost before revenue sharing could begin, the latter overdraft would become a major cause of subsequent conflict.

The 1994 production-sharing agreement for Shell to develop Sakhalin II was followed in 1996 by a similar agreement for ExxonMobil to develop the Sakhalin I oil and gas field, representing "one of the largest single international direct investments in Russia and an excellent example of how advanced technologies are being applied to meet the challenges of the world's growing energy demand."[37] Compared to the Shell venture, the ExxonMobil venture took longer to come online. The initial exploration phase was completed only in September 2000, and the project was declared commercial in October 2001. The ExxonMobil venture was different also in the important sense of having significant Russian participation; although it assumed operating responsibility, ExxonMobil had no more than a 30 percent share. The venture began producing in October 2005, with gas deliveries being made to Russia's Khabarovsk region and oil being exported via the mainland De-Kastri oil terminal. Peak production of 250,000 barrels of oil per day was reached in the first quarter of 2007.[38] Again in contrast to Sakhalin II, Sakhalin I achieved cost recovery after only three years of operation, and has proven to be very lucrative for all concerned. The main problem here has been that there is more gas than can be absorbed by the local market. While ExxonMobil sought early on to contract with China for an export pipeline, which would make a lot of sense, the Kremlin and Gazprom had different plans.[39]

The high-water mark of foreign involvement in Russian oil may be dated to June 26, 2003, when a ceremony was held to mark the deal of the century—a joint venture between British Petroleum (BP) and the Russian group Alfa, Access, Renova (AAR). Held during a state visit by Putin to the United Kingdom, the event was jointly presided over by the Russian president and the British prime minister Tony Blair. It was not just the size of the deal—$14 billion—that resulted in banner headlines. Even more important was the fact that BP would enter into the new venture with AAR—to be known as TNK-BP—as an equal partner.

The merger called for the two sides to contribute their respective assets in Russian oil and gas, creating the country's third-largest oil company, with an output of 1.2 million barrels per day.[40] Those who may have felt apprehension about the wisdom of BP's commitment could have pointed to the fact that one of the assets it brought to the table—Sidanco oil—had been at the focus of a previous hostile takeover attack from TNK, causing BP substantial losses.[41]

Firmly convinced to let bygones be bygones, markets hailed what was then generally viewed as the start of a new era of strategic energy cooperation between Russia and the West. The anticipated next step was a deal between ExxonMobil and Yukos, at the time Russia's flagship oil company. That deal would have created a privately owned—and thus privately controlled—route for export of Russian oil via Murmansk to the United States.

Expectations for the latter to happen had been given a strong boost already in July 2002, when a Yukos-chartered supertanker delivered 2 million barrels of oil to a refinery in Houston. Although Khodorkovsky, then still chief executive officer of Yukos, himself noted that the delivery was "merely experimental," it was taken as a firm sign of progress in the US-Russian "energy dialogue" that was initiated during a visit by President George W. Bush to Moscow in May of that year.[42]

The context of international politics is important here. By quickly showing his support for the United States at the time of the terrorist attacks of September 11, 2001, Putin had skillfully deflected criticism against the war in Chechnya. Grateful for Russian cooperation in its attack on the Taliban in Afghanistan, the Bush administration accepted that Russian operations in Chechnya formed part of the global "war on terror." During a summit meeting at President Bush's ranch in Crawford, Texas, in November 2001, Putin sensed that he could deflect rising criticism against Russian "democratic backsliding" by adding an energy dimension to the counterterrorism alliance with the United States. The proposal was made at the summit meeting in Moscow, and the grand launch took place at the US-Russian Commercial Energy Summit in Houston, Texas, in November 2002.[43]

Given the strategic importance not only to the United States but also to the West in general of having an alternative source of energy that might reduce dependence on the troubled Middle East, it was not surprising that the proposal went down so well. As we shall see in subsequent chapters, however, the Kremlin would again prove to have an altogether different agenda.

Emerging New Energy Powers

While domestic oligarchs and foreign oilmen were busy carving up the Russian oil patch, Moscow was forced also to witness the parallel emergence of a set of aspiring new energy powers in Central Asia and in the South Caucasus. As background to this process, it should be noted that while Moscow was still the center of Soviet power, emphasis was placed on developing energy resources within the Russian Federation. Following the breakup, governments in newly independent republics to the south consequently began courting major foreign energy companies for help in developing resources that had been neglected by the Soviet authorities.

The first and initially most important of such challenges emerged from Kazakhstan, where exploitation of the giant Tengiz field would serve to redraw the map of global oil. With up to 26 billion barrels of oil originally in place, and with recoverable crude oil reserves estimated at 6 to 9 billion barrels, Tengiz is the sixth-largest oil field in the world. Discovered already in 1979, development began only in 1993, by the Tengizchevroil joint venture. The leading partner was Chevron, with a 50 percent stake, followed by ExxonMobil (25 percent), the government of Kazakhstan through KazMunaiGaz (20 percent), and the Russian-UK company LukArco (5 percent).[44]

In addition to the onshore Tengiz (and Korolev) fields, in 2000 a further discovery was made of the giant offshore Kashagan oil field, believed at the time to be one of the most important discoveries in the world in the preceding three decades. Operated by an international consortium, the

North Caspian Sea Production-Sharing Agreement, and run by Italian oil and gas company ENI, the Kashagan field is expected to hold 7 to 9 billion barrels of gross recoverable reserves, extendible to 13 billion barrels through partial gas reinjection.[45] Allegedly known in Shell circles as "cash all gone," the project has also been tagged as the most expensive energy project ever, having absorbed $116 billion.[46] Commercial production was finally begun in September 2013, nearly a decade late and five times over budget.[47]

Operation of the oil and gas fields in Kazakhstan has been marred by numerous conflicts in relations between the foreign operators and the governments of Russia and Kazakhstan. Environmental concerns relating to the high content of sulphur in Kazakh hydrocarbon reserves have formed part of such troubles. But the main reason why the Russian government has been involved again relates to control over transport.

Although Tengiz had been discovered long before the Soviet Union disintegrated, Moscow had been slow in realizing its potential. When Putin came to power, he discovered not only that Russian oil companies had lost the initiative in field development to the international oil majors, led by Chevron, but also that he was at a disadvantage against the long-standing and politically vastly more experienced president of Kazakhstan, Nursultan Nazarbaev. The fallback strategy was to focus on what Pavel Baev refers to as "securing 'benign' control over the transportation of the Kazakh oil to world markets."[48]

When exploitation of the Tengiz field began, Moscow was successful in ensuring that the export pipeline would be routed over Russian territory. The company that was created to build and manage the pipeline, the Caspian Pipeline Consortium (CPC), was started in 1992 as a development by the Russian, Kazakhstani, and Omani governments to build a pipeline to the Russian Black Sea port of Novorossiisk. Progress on the project remained stalled until 1996, when a restructure included eight production companies in the project. Among these companies were Chevron, Mobil, LUKoil, Royal Dutch Shell, and Rosneft. BP joined in 2003. Representing the only Russian pipeline that is not state-owned, shares in the consortium were divided fifty-fifty between the three states and the eight companies concerned. The first oil was loaded onto a tanker at the Novorossiisk Marine Terminal on October 13, 2001, and the first stage of the pipeline was officially inaugurated on November 27, 2001. Regular operations started in April 2003.[49]

While Kazakhstan and its foreign partners thus remained firmly within the Russian orbit, the case of Azerbaijan would present a very different story. As noted earlier, Baku has a long and proud history as a pioneer in oil extraction. The post–World War II era, however, saw emphasis being shifted to the north, and following independence in 1991, a period of serious neglect caused production to drop.[50] What changed the scene was the discovery of giant offshore oil and gas fields in the Caspian Sea.

The ensuing boom would serve to transform both Azerbaijan and the way in which the game over oil was played. The first stage was triggered by what Azeri president Heydar Aliyev referred to as the "deal of the century," a 1994 production-sharing agreement with a BP-led consortium to develop the giant Azeri-Chirag-Gunashli oil field.[51] Between 1997 and 2007, output from the field, estimated to hold 5.4 billion barrels, rose more than fourfold, from 180,000 to 800,000 barrels per day.[52]

In 1999, BP added to its success with discovery of the giant Shah Deniz field.[53] Sanctioned in 2003, it is estimated to hold 1.5 to 3 billion barrels of oil and 1.2 trillion cubic meters of gas, making it one of the largest gas condensate fields in the world. Commercial gas production from the first stage, which is expected to reach 8.6 billion cubic meters of gas per year, was begun in December 2006.[54] The second stage is expected to yield an additional 16 billion cubic meters of gas and up to 100,000 barrels of condensate per year, tripling overall production from the field. Shah Deniz is expected to come online by the end of 2017.[55]

What makes the case of Azerbaijan so important is that it highlights the need to distinguish between production facilities and assets in the ground, on the one hand, and means of ensuring that the energy flow reaches consumers, on the other. While the latter include rail and road transport, by far the most important role is played by pipelines. Without reliable access to pipeline transport, producers of both oil and—in particular—gas will quickly realize that assets in the ground have little value. The main focus of the games that have been played around Russian energy resources in the post-Soviet period has consequently been aimed at securing control over the existing pipeline grid, and over the construction of new pipelines.

The first real blow to Russia's inherited transport hegemony was the Baku-Tbilisi-Ceyhan (BTC) pipeline, which allowed Azerbaijan to export oil via Georgia to the southern Turkish port of Ceyhan.[56] Driven by Washington for political reasons, and by BP for commercial reasons, relating to its leading role in exploiting Azeri oil, the BTC is the second-longest oil pipeline in the world, after the previously mentioned Soviet-era Druzhba, which links Western Siberia with Europe. Construction on the BTC, designed for a capacity of 1 million barrels per day, began in 2002, and first oil was pumped in May 2005.[57] The main impact of this project was political, in the combined sense of allowing Baku leeway for political maneuvering between Russia and the European Union and of creating expectations for further pipeline projects to bypass Russia.

Of potentially greater importance than the BTC is its nonidentical twin, the Baku-Tbilisi-Erzurum (BTE) gas pipeline, which became operational at the end of 2006.[58] Also known as the South Caucasus Pipeline, it transports

gas from the Shah Deniz field via Georgia to Turkey. Its potential importance is derived from the fact that it constitutes a crucial link in a chain that
might supply substantial volumes of gas to Europe without crossing Russian territory. The reason why its importance is merely "potential" rests in
the fact that Azeri gas reserves are too limited for this link to assume any
strategic importance. Even when the second stage of the Shah Deniz is
completed, the long-term potential for the annual output of gas will peak at
about 30 billion cubic meters.[59]

Across the Caspian Sea, however, there is a combined long-term potential of gas from Kazakhstan, Uzbekistan, and above all Turkmenistan in
the range of 150–200 billion cubic meters, corresponding to about two-
thirds of Russia's long-term potential.[60] It was long believed that most if
not all of that supply was destined to pass via the Russian pipeline grid. The
first challenge to this belief was marked with the construction of a pipeline
from Turkmenistan to China. This was still acceptable to Moscow, for the
simple reason that it did not involve Europe. What might really change the
story is the construction of the Trans-Caspian Pipeline (TCP), a proposed
gas pipeline that would link Turkmenistan with Azerbaijan. This project has
been under discussion since the mid-1990s, but has been repeatedly delayed
by unresolved disputes over the exploitation of oil and gas resources in the
middle of the Caspian Sea.

The core of the problem rests in a legal dispute over whether the
Caspian is to be considered a sea or a lake. In the former case, it will be
governed by international law, granting bordering states exclusive rights
to resources in their offshore zones, which extend up to twenty kilometers from the coast. What remains is considered international waters. In
the latter case, the Caspian will be considered joint property and any
form of exploitation, including the construction of infrastructure, will require agreement by all littoral states. For close to three centuries, the
Caspian, the largest landlocked enclosed body of water on Earth, was an
exclusive interest first of Russia and Persia and then of the Soviet Union
and Iran.[61]

The demise of the Soviet Union in 1991 caused a dramatic change of
scene. As Carol Saivetz puts it, "Instead of two states—with agreements between them delimiting the rights of navigation, commerce and fishing—
there were now five."[62] Responding to the sudden transformation, both
Russia and Iran have insisted that the Caspian is a lake. This in effect de-
nies the three new states exclusive rights to resources in their offshore
zones, and calls for unanimous agreement on all projects.[63]

Having tried in vain to reach a negotiated solution, Moscow resorted to
a display of military might. It upgraded its Caspian flotilla with several new
ships, including a missile frigate, and equipped its local marine brigade
with new artillery and landing craft. A major military exercise was held in

August 2002. But reactions from both Kazakhstan and Iran were so negative that this would not be repeated.[64] Pending final resolution, several bilateral deals have been made to facilitate exploitation, but contention has remained regarding fields close to the center.[65]

As the TCP would need to cross the Caspian, and preferably so at the narrowest point, which is located between Turkmenistan and Azerbaijan, the project remains hostage to a resolution of who has rights to its central parts. Iran in particular has been holding out for a comprehensive legal solution. It has even been hinted, as part of the bargaining game, that in the case of a two-way agreement between Turkmenistan and Azerbaijan, which would ignore the interests of the other three states, Iran might in turn resort to military action.[66]

If it actually were to materialize, the TCP and the BTE would jointly constitute the first link in one of the most politically charged projects of the past decade, namely a 3,300-kilometer gas pipeline that would join the Caspian Basin with Central and Western Europe. Officially known as Nabucco, this project was conceived in 2002 by the Turkish energy company Botas and the Austrian energy company OMV. It envisions building a gas pipeline that would connect energy sources in the Caspian Basin, and possibly in the Middle East and Egypt, with Central and Western European gas markets. It would start at the Georgian-Turkish border and/or the Iranian-Turkish border, respectively; proceed via Turkey, Bulgaria, Romania, and Hungary; and end at Baumgarten in Austria. Investment costs, including financing costs for a complete new pipeline system, have been estimated at approximately €7.9 billion.[67]

Given the challenge that was presented by Nabucco to Gazprom's energy dominance, it is not surprising that the project has been surrounded by massive political infighting. For reasons that will be laid out in subsequent chapters, it remains highly unclear to what extent the intended transit countries will actually remain committed, and whether it will be possible to find sufficient volumes of gas to make the pipeline, with a capacity of 31 billion cubic meters annually, commercially viable.

Hyperdepression

By far the most striking of all the various controversies that surrounded post-Soviet economic reform was that it took so long for so many to recognize that things were going so badly wrong. Given everything that was known, or thought to be known, about the inefficiencies of central economic planning, it was not easy to accept that the introduction of a superior market economy could actually make things worse. Yet that was precisely what happened, and not only in Russia.

All of the countries that had practiced central economic planning were forced, without exception, to witness the transition to a market economy being associated with a "transformational recession." In some countries, the recession was short. In others, it would be drawn out. And in some cases, situations resembling failed states would result. In Russia, it would not be until 2007 that the level of GDP achieved in 1990 was once again attained. Given that China had a track record over the same period of an annual growth in GDP of about 10 percent, this represented a dramatic shift in the relative positions of Moscow and Beijing, a shift that is likely to dominate relations between the two former communist rivals over the foreseeable future.

The immediate impact on the Russian economy was to cause a veritable collapse of fixed capital investment, which fell during 1992 alone by 40 percent. While the initial fall in GDP was less steep, from 1991 to 1998 the Russian economy recorded a drop in output of well over 40 percent, depending on how one crunches the numbers. Given that the largest previous—peacetime—fall in GDP had been recorded during the Great Depression in the United States, when the US economy lost about 30 percent of GDP over four years, the Russian case does merit the label of a "hyperdepression." Compounding the damage, an explosive rise in prices by about 2,500 percent in 1992 was followed by several years of high and variable inflation, leading to a drastic shortening of the time horizon for investment decisionmaking and to a serious erosion of the very foundations of a prospective Russian market economy.[68]

But the failure to achieve fiscal order and monetary stabilization had serious effects beyond wages and pensions and the resulting widening of income inequality. By the mid-1990s, the notion of a "virtual economy," introduced by Clifford Gaddy and Barry Ickes, was gaining wide acceptance. It reflected the fact that the Russian "market" economy was becoming demonetized and barter was becoming ever more prevalent.[69] Being unable, or indeed unwilling, to raise sufficient taxes to cover gaping holes in the budget, the government resorted to playing pyramid schemes on the country's nascent financial markets. The result was severe damage to the banking system and, in the end, systemic failure.

In August 1998, the ruble was devalued and an effective default followed on about $40 billion in short-term treasury bills. The sheer magnitude of the crash, and the way in which Russian insiders were given preferential treatment, served to produce a range of conspiracy theories that would poison relations between Russia and the surrounding world for some time to come.[70]

In the spring of 1999, many observers thought that the game was over, that Russia would simply not be able to recover. Reflecting the general sentiment, *The Economist* quipped that Russia, having aspired for years to become a member of the Group of Seven (G7)—the richest industrialized nations—was now facing the prospect of membership in a less glamorous club of pariah nations like Sudan, Liberia, Congo, and Somalia: "poor, war-ridden places, some barely existing as states," that had borrowed money from the International Monetary Fund (IMF) and failed to repay their debts.[71]

Little did such observers know that out of the ashes of the financial meltdown would arise an aspiring energy superpower, ready to deploy its rapidly mounting petrowealth in a gambit to reclaim lost power and influence. Let us now turn to how Vladimir Putin embarked on his program of assembling an energy powerhouse.

Notes

1. The most authoritative source on Soviet oil is Gustafson, *Crisis amid Plenty.* See also Considine and Kerr, *The Russian Oil Economy;* and Grace, *Russian Oil Supply.*
2. Kotkin, *Armageddon Averted,* p. 15.
3. The often advanced view of the Soviet "satellite states" in Eastern Europe as an economic burden on the Soviet Union has been shown to be deficient, implying that Mikhail Gorbachev's policy of allowing these states to leave the Soviet orbit was conditioned by political motives, rather than by an economic inability to maintain the grip. Spechler and Spechler, "A Reassessment of the Burden of Eastern Europe on the USSR."
4. Kotkin, *Armageddon Averted,* p. 16.
5. See http://www.priweb.org/ed/pgws/history/pennsylvania/pennsylvania.html.
6. See further Levine, *The Oil and the Glory,* chaps. 1–2.
7. The story of early oil, and of early conflicts around oil, is told in Yergin, *The Prize,* pt. 1.
8. The story of the Nobels is told at length in Tolf, *The Russian Rockefellers.*
9. Gustafson, *Crisis amid Plenty,* pp. 22–23. The story of the long neglect of oil and gas in the Soviet Union is laid out in Campbell, *The Economics of Soviet Oil and Gas.*
10. Goldman, *Petrostate,* pp. 33–39.
11. Kotkin, *Armageddon Averted,* p. 15.
12. Gustafson, *Crisis amid Plenty,* p. 87.
13. Ibid., pp. 28–29.
14. Ibid., p. 64.
15. Ibid., pp. 29–31.
16. Ibid., pp. 32–33. For more detail on the gas campaign, see also ibid., chap. 5.
17. Ibid., pp. 39–40.
18. Ibid., pp. 55–56.
19. Ibid., p. 67.
20. Ibid., p. 47.
21. It may be worth noting here that in his book about the fall of the Soviet Union, Yegor Gaidar ascribes a large part of the blame for its collapse to the sharp fall in global oil prices. Gaidar, *Collapse of an Empire.*

22. Stent, "An Energy Superpower?" p. 79.

23. The following discussion draws largely on Goldman, *Petrostate,* pp. 61–63.

24. The background story on how these key players created their respective energy fiefdoms is told in Gustafson, *Wheel of Fortune,* chap. 3.

25. For a background account of how Rosneft was created, and how it was subjected to a process of slow strangulation by various outside interests, see Poussenkova, *Lord of the Rigs,* pp. 3–21.

26. On the process as a whole, see further Hedlund, *Russia's "Market" Economy,* pp. 256–260. For an account that questions whether the process really was all that scandalous, see Treisman, *"Loans for Shares" Revisited.*

27. Goldman, *Petrostate,* pp. 63–65.

28. "Moscow's Group of Seven," *Financial Times,* November 1, 1996, http://global.factiva.com/ha/default.aspx.

29. Bradshaw, "A New Energy Age in Pacific Russia," pp. 335–337. See also Bradshaw, "Soviet Far Eastern Trade."

30. For general background, see Bindemann, *Production-Sharing Agreements.*

31. Gustafson, *Wheel of Fortune,* pp. 178–180.

32. Bradshaw, "A New Energy Age in Pacific Russia," p. 337, citing Rutledge, *The Sakhalin II PSA.*

33. Bradshaw, "A New Energy Age in Pacific Russia," p. 350.

34. Goldman, *Petrostate,* p. 86.

35. For an overview of this project, see the English version of Sakhalin Energy's website, at http://www.sakhalinenergy.com/en.

36. Bradshaw, "A New Energy Age in Pacific Russia," pp. 338–341.

37. "Project History," http://www.sakhalin-1.com/Sakhalin/Russia-English /Upstream/about_history.aspx.

38. Ibid.

39. Bradshaw, "A New Energy Age in Pacific Russia," pp. 341–343.

40. "BP Signs Historic Russian Deal," *BBC News,* June 26, 2003, http://news.bbc.co.uk/2/hi/business/3021786.stm.

41. The conflict originated in 1997, when BP bought a 10 percent share in Sidanco for $484 million. Soon, however, it was elbowed aside by the owners of Tyumenneftegaz, who took control over one of Sidanco's prime oil fields. The ensuing legal dispute outraged the chief executive officer of BP, Lord Browne, and spooked other foreign investors. Still, the matter was settled in 2001, when the field was returned to Sidanco. Gradually—and to some, surprisingly—the former enemies were transformed into partners. "Pumping Up BP," *Bloomberg Businessweek,* February 23, 2003, http://www.businessweek.com/magazine/content/03_08/b382 1077.htm.

42. "Oil Trade Strengthens US-Russian Ties," *BBC News,* July 8, 2002, http://news.bbc.co.uk/2/hi/business/2116133.stm.

43. Baev, *Russian Energy Policy and Military Power,* p. 121.

44. See further Tengizchevroil's website, at http://tengizchevroil.kz/home_en /about_tco. Having reached an output of 285,000 barrels per day in 2002, an ambitious $7.2 billion expansion program that was begun in 2003 allowed output to rise to 540,000 barrels per day by 2008. The field also produces a substantial volume of gas, some of which is injected into the oil reservoir to create gas lift. Chevron, "Major Expansion at Tengiz Field in Kazakhstan Completed," September 2008, http://www.chevron.com/news/currentissues/tengiz.

45. ENI, "Kashagan," June 24, 2013, http://www.eni.com/en_IT/innovation -technology/eni-projects/kashagan/kashagan-project.shtml.

46. "Kazakhstan's Kashagan Tagged World's Most Expensive Energy Project," *Tengrinews,* November 29, 2012, http://en.tengrinews.kz/industry_infrastructure /Kazakhstans-Kashagan-tagged-worlds-most-expensive-energy-project-14913.

47. "Costly Kashagan Oil Field Begins Production to Relief of Kazakhstan," *Euronews,* September 11, 2013, http://www.euronews.com/2013/09/11/costly -kashagan-oil-field-begins-production-to-relief-of-kazakhstan.

48. Baev, *Russian Energy Policy and Military Power,* pp. 134–135.

49. For further detail, see the CPC's website, at http://www.cpc.ru. For a background on the Russia-Kazakhstan relationship, and on the troubles that have beset both Tengiz and the CPC, see also Torjesen, "Russia and Kazakhstan."

50. Between 1992 and 1997, Azeri crude oil production dropped from 222,000 to 180,000 barrels per day. It then rose, exceeding 1 million barrels per day by 2010. US Energy Information Administration, "Azerbaijan," September 10, 2013, http://205.254.135.7/countries/country-data.cfm?fips=AJ&trk=m#pet.

51. The political games surrounding negotiations on the agreement are described in Levine, *The Oil and the Glory,* chap. 11.

52. See BP, "Azeri-Chirag-Gunashli: The Largest Oil Field Under Development in the Azerbaijan Sector of the Caspian Basin," http://www.bp.com /sectiongenericarticle.do?categoryId=9006667&contentId=7015091#top; and BP, "Azerbaijan: On Track for Success," http://www.bp.com/liveassets/bp_inter net/globalbp/STAGING/global_assets/downloads/B/BPM_04two_P17-23 _azerbaijan .pdf.

53. Nasser Sagheb and Masoud Javadi, "Azerbaijan's 'Contract of the Century,'" *Azer,* Winter 1994, http://azer.com/aiweb/categories/magazine/24_folder /24_articles/24_aioc.html.

54. BP, "Production Begins at Shah Deniz Gas Condensate Field in the Caspian Sea," December 15, 2006, http://www.bp.com/genericarticle.do?categoryId=9006 615&contentId=7026800.

55. BP, "Shah Deniz Full Field Development," http://www.bp.com/lubricant home.do?categoryId=6070.

56. BP, "Baku-Tbilisi-Ceyhan Pipeline: Spanning Three Countries from the Caspian Sea to the Mediterranean Coast," http://www.bp.com/sectiongeneric article.do?categoryId=9006669&contentId=7015093.

57. Hydrocarbons Technology, "Baku-Tbilisi-Ceyhan (BTC) Caspian Pipeline," http://www.hydrocarbons-technology.com/projects/bp.

58. BP, "South Caucasus Pipeline: Supplying Gas to Meet the Needs of Regional Consumers," December 12, 2013, http://www.bp.com/sectiongenericarticle .do?categoryId=9006670&contentId=7015095.

59. Götz, "The Southern Gas Corridor and Europe's Gas Supply," p. 2.

60. Ibid.

61. The status of the Caspian Sea was originally settled by Persia and the Russian empire in the 1729 Treaty of Rasht. The last of many subsequent agreements was signed between the Soviet Union and Iran in 1940, describing the Caspian as an enclosed sea that belonged to the two countries. "The Caspian Sea: Extremely Complex Issues," *Voice of Russia,* November 9, 2011, http://english.ruvr.ru/2011/11/09 /60084572.html.

62. Saivetz, "Perspectives on the Caspian Sea Dilemma," p. 588.

63. Nies, *Oil and Gas Delivery to Europe,* pp. 49–50.

64. Baev, *Russian Energy Policy and Military Power,* pp. 58–59.

65. Alam, "Pipeline Politics in the Caspian Sea Basin," pp. 5–6.

66. Tatyana Mitrova, "The Magical Paper Pipeline," *Moscow Times,* August 5, 2009, http://www.themoscowtimes.com/opinion/article/the-magical-paper-pipeline /380203.html.

67. See further http://www.nabucco-pipeline.com.

68. Hedlund, *Russia's "Market" Economy.*

69. Gaddy and Ickes, "Russia's Virtual Economy." For a summary of the ensuing debate, see also Clifford G. Gaddy, "Russia's Virtual Economy," February 2008, http://www.brookings.edu/articles/2008/02_virtual_economy_gaddy.aspx.

70. See further Hedlund, "Russia and the IMF."

71. "Money Can't Buy Me Love," *The Economist,* February 4, 1999, p. 21, http://www.economist.com/node/184782.

4

Assembling
the Powerhouse

As President Putin's second term in office unfolded, evidence seemed to be mounting that the Kremlin was indeed bent on using the country's energy complex as a means by which to make Russia great again. There were those who claimed to see it coming, even before the sudden rise in hydrocarbon prices triggered the petrodollar bonanza. While most were still debating the seeming irrationality of the Kremlin's onslaught against Yukos Oil, some analysts could see a long-term political rationality.

Already in 2004, veteran commentator Peter Lavelle saw Putin being rationally "determined to re-order Russia's oil patch to serve national and international interests."[1] By early 2006, sociologist Vladimir Shlapentokh captured the Kremlin's ambition in presenting Russia as a "newborn superpower" and Putin as the "lord of oil and gas."[2] And by 2008, when Putin was preparing to take a temporary leave from the Kremlin, talk of a nascent Russian energy superpower was proliferating.

But this book does not subscribe to such blanket interpretations. Although the evidence is indeed suggestive of such interpretations, it is arguably more consistent with a policy of gradual adaptation to unfolding events than with the presence of an early master plan on how to use the sudden bonanza of hydrocarbon wealth. Above all, it is highly dubious that the use of hydrocarbon exports for foreign policy purposes really was a priority of the Putin regime. Domestic agendas relating to a reassertion of state control for its own sake also played a role, as did motives of sheer greed in orchestrating asset redistribution.

Irrespective of what reasons may have dominated, what remains is that consolidation of the country's energy resources and retention of state control over transport infrastructure did become increasingly important. Given, however, the events that had unfolded in the 1990s, assembling the energy powerhouse would be a tall order.

The standard story of how the oligarchy emerged under Yeltsin has three main components. The first details how a set of favored cronies of the regime was allowed to grab assets at bargain-basement prices. Being by far the most spectacular, it captured headlines and filled numerous scholarly volumes. To Marshall Goldman, this was the "piratization of Russia."[3] To Chrystia Freeland, it was the "sale of the century," a "Faustian bargain," or the "original sin" whereby Russia's young reformers created the oligarchs.[4] While others have been similarly critical, some, it should be noted, have been somewhat more sympathetic.[5]

The second component concerns the widespread practice of what came to be known as "optimization" of taxes—the finding of every loophole possible whereby the actual payment of taxes could be minimized. While there is general agreement that this was indeed widespread, the question of what long-term damage was done to Russian perceptions of the desirability of a market economy, more broadly, and to the acceptance of private property rights in resources, more specifically, will likely remain controversial.

The third part of the story was more conclusive, detailing how economic actors went about setting up of links with foreign partners and markets in a way that facilitated massive capital flight. There could be no denying the negative short-term impact of tax evasion on the government's fiscal position, and of capital flight on the supply of badly needed investable funds. The latter hemorrhage in particular was clearly devastating.[6]

The ambition to achieve a break with this form of crony capitalism run amok would proceed along two tracks. In addition to reimposing state control over domestic players, it would also entail rolling back the influence of major foreign oil companies. Again it should be noted that this was not a simple matter of state versus oil barons, or of state versus foreigners. While most of the domestic oil companies did resort to optimization of tax payments, oligarch Vladimir Bogdanov at Surgutneftegaz stood out in making sure that his company paid its taxes, at least as far as it was able.[7] And while most of the private oil companies would pursue their own narrow agendas for short-term profit, Vagit Alekperov at LUKoil was careful throughout in considering Russian foreign policy objectives.[8] Even with respect to the major foreign oil companies, we may find that some would be dealt with more harshly than others.

This said, there can be no denying that in terms of rhetoric as well as public policy the Putin era did represent a fundamental break with that of Yeltsin. There was a new sheriff in town, and there would be little time wasted driving home the message that oligarchs would henceforth be required to pay their dues and to stay out of politics. For those who were slow in reacting, the subsequent dismantling of Yukos Oil would set a powerful example.

This chapter details how these ambitions were pursued. It begins by discussing the cowing of the oligarchs and the rolling back of foreign oil. Broadening the perspective, it then shows how Gazprom embarked on a combined operation aimed at securing energy assets in the Caspian Basin and at building what may be referred to as a "ring fence" around the European energy market.

While the latter ambitions may be viewed as part of the Kremlin's foreign policy agenda, it is again important to keep in mind the caveat against perceptions of a master plan. Although cases would vary, commercial and political motivations would as a rule prove hard to separate. As Pavel Baev puts it, the drive to achieve a new form of greatness houses an important contradiction, juxtaposing "the goal of increasing the financial returns from energy export and the temptation to manipulate the privileges of an irreplaceable supplier for harvesting political dividends."[9]

Let us begin with the high-profile ambition to break the influence of the oligarchs, an influence that in many ways had defined the Yeltsin era as a whole.[10]

Breaking the Oligarchs

The real watershed in the transformation of corrupt but market-friendly oligarch-run businesses into an authoritarian Kremlin-controlled energy powerhouse may be dated to the previously mentioned ceremony in London, held in June 2003, where Lord Browne, then chief executive officer of BP, committed his company to the ill-fated TNK-BP joint venture. Only days later, while markets were still celebrating, the opening rounds were fired in a legal battle that would end in the de facto expropriation and dismantling of Yukos and the incarceration of the company's main owner, oligarch Mikhail Khodorkovsky.[11]

As chief executive officer of Yukos, Khodorkovsky had pushed hard not only for a revitalization of the Russian oil industry, aggressively pursuing an agenda of putting right the many technological shortcomings of the Soviet oil industry, but also for the introduction of transparency and accountability in Russian business circles.[12] The latter was likely not a reflection of a change in Khodorkovsky's personality, but rather of a realization that good corporate governance would result in a higher stock market valuation. And the rewards were lavish indeed. Yukos stock soared, with *Forbes* magazine, in its 2003 list of world billionaires, ranking Khodorkovsky as the twenty-sixth richest, with an estimated private fortune of $8 billion.[13]

To the Kremlin, the rising fortunes of the energy complex provided something of a mixed blessing. While the process did generate substantial revenues, it also had two highly provocative consequences. One was that it gave rise to political friction, as some oligarchs began sponsoring opposition political parties, and the other that it attracted a great deal of interest from foreign oil companies. The implied common denominator was that of a threatening shift of power over domestic as well as foreign policy into the hands of the owners and associates of privatized Russian oil companies. Their growing links with major foreign oil companies would make them harder to control, and their investment resources would give them influence over pipeline diplomacy.

The lightning rod for the Kremlin's mounting frustration would prove to be Khodorkovsky and Yukos Oil. The relationship between Putin and his least favored oligarch had been deteriorating steadily, due in no short measure to the openly provocative behavior of the latter. Although numerous theories have been advanced as to what caused the seemingly irrational "Yukos affair," Thane Gustafson is probably correct in suggesting that it was no single cause but rather the accumulation of numerous challenges that eventually sealed Khodorkovsky's fate.[14]

This said, what triggered the final showdown in the summer and fall of 2003 may well have been the combination of an intended merger between Yukos and Sibneft and a subsequent move by ExxonMobil to acquire a major stake in the new entity. The target was attractive indeed. The intended merger would have created the world's fourth-largest private oil producer, with 18.4 billion barrels in proven oil reserves and 5.9 trillion cubic meters in proven natural gas reserves. Had the deal gone through, YukosSibneft would have had a market capitalization of $35 billion. This would have vastly enhanced the ability of Khodorkovsky, as designated chief executive officer of the new company, to transform the Russian energy game. Just to show how close it really was, the merger was approved by the Russian antimonopoly ministry on August 14, 2003, leaving the shareholders to make the final decision.[15]

In September it was rumored on Wall Street that ChevronTexaco and ExxonMobil were preparing rival bids for 25 percent plus one share of the new oil giant, in a deal that would have been worth $11 billion.[16] According to subsequent rumors, ExxonMobil was prepared to offer $25 billion for a 40 percent share.[17] To the Kremlin, the writing on the wall must now have been clearly visible.[18]

The attack on Yukos had actually begun already, on July 2, when Platon Lebedev, chief executive officer of Group Menatep and a major stakeholder in Yukos at that time, was arrested and taken to the KGB's Lefortovo prison. Although at first he was not charged with offenses relating to Yukos, it soon enough transpired that this was indeed what the "affair" was about.

Following lengthy legal proceedings that included seizure of considerable documentation from Yukos offices, Khodorkovsky was himself arrested on October 26, 2003. Over the following months it became increasingly clear that the Kremlin was quite serious about its assault. With Khodorkovsky in prison, the almost completed merger between Yukos and Sibneft fell apart, and ExxonMobil was reduced to a passive onlooker.

Following Putin's March 2004 landslide reelection as president, Khodorkovsky remained incarcerated. Sitting in a shared cell in the Matrosskaya Tishina prison, with a private fortune that according to *Forbes* magazine had grown to $15 billion, he had good reason to experience mounting concern about his own future.[19] At the conclusion of what can only be referred to as a show trial, in May 2005 he was sentenced to nine years in a Siberian prison camp. Although that sentence was subsequently commuted to eight years, it still meant that the Kremlin's main enemy had been neutralized.[20]

On February 5, 2007, only months before Khodorkovsky would have been legally eligible for parole, new charges of embezzlement and money laundering were brought that in theory could have led to an added sentence of up to twenty-seven years. The Kremlin, busy preparing for the upcoming presidential election, quite obviously wanted a potential troublemaker to remain incarcerated. For incoming president Dmitry Medvedev, whose political image would be heavily marked by talk of the rule of law and a struggle against corruption, handling of the case would be viewed as something of a litmus test, one that he would fail miserably to pass.

Despite substantial pressure and criticism, both from abroad and from Russian opposition figures, on December 27, 2010, Khodorkovsky was found guilty. Three days later the judge handed down a sentence of an additional six years, for a total of thirteen and a half years, counting from his arrest in 2003. It was indicative of the regime's fear of angry reactions that the verdict was announced in the midst of the Christmas holiday season, when attention from the media and the general public was likely to be minimal.

As it turned out, reactions were both harsh and plentiful, domestically as well as internationally. From the side of the financial markets, one analyst was quoted by the *New York Times* as having said that "the Russian equity market would be worth several hundred billion dollars more if it weren't for the critical Western perception of Russia, and the Khodorkovsky case is the principal example of that perception."[21] From the side of the Kremlin, economic aide Arkady Dvorkovich expressed worry that "a considerable portion of at least the foreign community will have serious questions, and the assessment of risks working in the Russian Federation will rise."[22] From the side of the political opposition, opposition leader Vladimir Ryzhkov expressed fear of a new wave of emigration, with the Khodorkovsky ruling constituting "the last straw for thousands of talented citizens who have given up hope after 10 years of Vladimir Putin's leadership."[23]

By far the most spectacular reaction, however, was a public admission by an assistant to the presiding judge, Viktor Danilkin, that the trial had been a sham. In a broadcast interview, Natalya Vasileva, also press secretary at the Khamovnichesky court where the case was heard, claimed that the judge's original draft of the verdict had been rejected. He had instead been compelled to read a revised version, imposed from above and hand-delivered to the court while in session.[24]

The main beneficiary of the dismantling of Yukos was Rosneft, at the time the only piece of the old Soviet oil industry that had remained in state hands. As noted in Chapter 3, in the spring of 1998 the Kiriyenko government had tried to sell it too, but failed because of the approaching economic crisis. As the Kremlin set out to break up Yukos and to sell the pieces at rigged auctions, allegedly in order to recoup outstanding taxes, Rosneft came in handy.

The game plan was simple enough, consisting of three consecutive steps. The first was to present claims for back taxes that would eventually reach $28 billion.[25] The second was to freeze Yukos assets, thus making it impossible for the company to meet the tax demands. And the third was to proceed to sell its assets at a series of rigged auctions. Following much legal wrangling, including attempts by shareholders to bring suits in US courts, the process was brought to a formal end on August 1, 2006, when the Moscow Arbitration Court delivered a verdict of bankruptcy and liquidation of Yukos.[26]

Several reasons combined to make the Kremlin's assault and the eventual dismantling of Yukos Oil one of the most controversial events of the Putin era as a whole. First, both the legality and the accuracy of the original tax claim have been called into serious doubt. It may well have been true that Yukos management had engaged in creative accounting aimed at tax evasion, but in the Yeltsin era that was standard practice. Singling out Yukos for punishment must in consequence be viewed as a highly dubious action, as selective administration of justice, or even worse.

The size of the tax claim, moreover, was also clearly out of proportion. According to a management presentation from December 2004, the claim for back taxes would imply a total tax burden for the years 2000–2003 of 67 percent, 105 percent, 111 percent, and 83 percent of the company's revenue for the respective years in question. In comparison, the tax bill of Gazprom for 2003 was given at about $4 billion on revenues of $28.9 billion.[27] With the added facts of a court order freezing Yukos assets and the granting of merely days in which to settle the tax claim, it should be quite clear that this was an operation designed not to recoup taxes but to break Yukos. The degree of sheer vengefulness was such that, in Gustafson's words, "Yukos was not so much plundered as lynched."[28] Despite substantial efforts to win international litigation cases, the former stockholders have—to date—not been successful in making any substantial headway against the Russian state.[29]

A second reason why the Yukos affair has been so widely recognized as a politically motivated assault on the country's flagship oil company concerns the conditions under which its assets were auctioned off. The prized asset was Yuganskneftegaz, which at the time was producing about 1 million barrels of crude oil per day, representing about 60 percent of the Yukos total, and about 1.6 percent of the world total.[30] On December 19, 2004, Yuganskneftegaz was sold at an auction, again allegedly to recoup outstanding taxes.

The originally intended beneficiary was Gazprom, which had announced its intention to participate in the auction already in early December. At the time, there was little doubt that the deal would be done according to plan. Even the best-laid plans, however, will at times come to naught. In a surprise eleventh-hour move, the Yukos management team, under Steven Theede, turned to a court in Houston, Texas, with an application for Chapter 11 bankruptcy protection. Ruling to temporarily forbid the auction, the court issued a warning to Gazprom and the six foreign banks that had been lined up to provide financing not to take part. As the banks heeded the warning, the game plan had to be changed. Although Gazprom might have been able to find other sources of financing, it was clearly spooked by the risks entailed in subsequent litigation by Yukos stockholders. An unfavorable ruling would have exposed Gazprom's considerable foreign assets to the risk of seizure. Consequently, Gazprom decided to pull out.[31]

The single bidder at the auction was instead an obscure company named Baikal Finance Group, which had been created only two weeks before the event. Legally registered at an address in Tver that was home to a vodka bar, it had a share capital of no more than 10,000 rubles (about $3,000). The price it paid for Yuganskneftegaz was $9.3 billion, representing just over half of the company's estimated market value. According to an assessment commissioned by the Russian government itself a few months prior to the fire sale, Yuganskneftegaz had been valued at between $15 billion and $17 billion.[32] Only days later, Baikal Finance Group was in turn taken over by Rosneft, which would prove also to have been the source of financing for the deal. In a sharp comment, Andrei Illarionov, at the time still Putin's senior economic adviser, blasted the auction as the "scam of the year."[33] Following the absorption of Yuganskneftegaz, Rosneft emerged as Russia's second largest oil company.[34]

The conclusion of the Yukos affair sent a powerful message to other members of the former oligarchy, who would prove more than willing to bow to the Kremlin's demands. In September 2005, oligarch Roman

Abramovich accepted to surrender Sibneft to Gazprom for $13.1 billion. Representing the biggest-ever takeover in Russia, the deal brought Gazprom a fair bit of the way toward becoming an energy supergiant. In order to secure the deal, it arranged to borrow $14 billion from Western banks.[35] Although Abramovich may not have been too happy about being muscled out of the oil business, during the loans-for-shares proceedings he and Boris Berezovsky had succeeded in snapping up Sibneft at a mere $100 million. The net gain thus would come to $13 billion.

The background story of how Sibneft was created and taken over is typical of the culture of backroom dealings that was prevalent at the time. According to Paul Klebnikov, it was Abramovich, at the time a brash young oil trader, who approached Berezovsky with a plan for carving out two of the best Rosneft assets—the Omsk refinery and the Noyabrneftegaz oil production facility—and packaging them into a new oil company. And it was Berezovsky's political connections that made the deal possible.

In the summer of 1995, Sibneft was incorporated, behind the back of the Ministry of Fuel and Energy. Through the loans-for-shares scam, Berezovsky, having first muscled out those with vested interests in these assets, managed to acquire 51 percent of the shares in the new company at a mere $100.3 million. Two years later, Sibneft would have a market capitalization of $5 billion.[36] The exact circumstances under which Abramovich subsequently acquired Berezovsky's stake in Sibneft remain unclear.

In 2009, Berezovsky entered a £2 billion lawsuit in a London court, claiming that his former business partner had used "threats and intimidation" to coerce him into selling his stake at below value. Abramovich tried to have the case dismissed, but in March 2010 the High Court of Justice ruled that the case should go ahead, and in February 2011 three appellate-court judges ruled not to overturn that decision.[37] The trial began in October 2011 and was concluded in January 2012. When the verdict was finally handed down, in August 2012, the court ruled in favor of Abramovich. Judge Elizabeth Gloster told the courtroom that she "found Mr. Berezovsky an unimpressive, and inherently unreliable, witness, who regarded truth as a transitory, flexible concept."[38]

For another, albeit far less spectacular, illustration of the backroom dealings that built the Russian oil industry, we may turn to Russneft (not to be confused with Rosneft), a small oil company that was founded and owned by billionaire Mikhail Gutseriev. Following a year of steadily increasing pressure, in July 2007 Gutseriev announced that he was giving up control over his company. His initial attempt to resist selling, and to make public the pressures that were brought to bear on him, was interesting to watch but in the end proved futile.[39] The main reason why the case is worth noting, despite the fact that Russneft accounted for no more than 3 percent of Russian crude oil production, rests in the nature of the attack.

Gutseriev was trained as a petroleum engineer. He started out in business in Chechnya in the 1980s, and in 1995 became a Duma deputy. Leaving the Duma in 2000, he returned to business to become president of Slavneft. In 2002 he founded Russneft and went on to win a number of awards for his performance.[40] In 2006–2007 the company was subjected to a series of tax and other investigations by Russian authorities. Some of Gutseriev's assets were frozen, and he was told not to leave the country but managed to escape to London via Baku. Russian authorities issued an international arrest warrant, and tried but failed to have him extradited from Britain. Meanwhile, he was negotiating to sell the company to Oleg Deripaska's company Basic Element.

Although Gutseriev claimed that this was a campaign against him personally, former Duma Speaker Gennady Seleznev argued that it was a battle not against Gutseriev but for his assets: "I wouldn't rule out it happening today to Deripaska and tomorrow to Rosneft." Philip Hanson cites the latter as evidence of how the game for control over Russian energy assets has been played, emphasizing Seleznev's allegation that even Rosneft might be in danger of having its assets seized.[41]

Basic Element did buy Russneft in 2007, for $3 billion, financed in part by a $2.7 billion loan from Sberbank, but failed to obtain clearance for the deal from the federal antitrust body. Under the subsequent impact of the global financial crisis, Deripaska fell on hard times, and in January 2010 he was forced to sell Russneft back to a group of companies controlled by Gutseriev. The price was $600 million and a pledge to assume responsibility for an additional $6 billion in debt.[42]

Returning to the story of Gazprom's acquisition of Sibneft, which was to be renamed Gazpromneft, it should be noted that this was an important acquisition indeed. Gazprom, having the largest known gas reserves in the world, and accounting for close to a fifth of global gas production at that time, now also emerged as a major player in oil. As there were other players on the field competing for the slot as Russia's number one oil producer, this was clearly bound to create friction.

In 2004, well before the Yukos auctions, agreement had been reached on a merger between Rosneft and Gazprom that would have created a true energy giant. In the spring of 2005, however, the deal was suddenly scrapped. Although this was very much in line with Putin's personal vision of creating a national energy champion, the Gazprom clan had clearly underestimated the opposition. Sergei Bogdanchikov, the chief executive officer of Rosneft, clearly did not relish the idea of playing second fiddle to Gazprom's Aleksei Miller.[43] Bogdanchikov now faced the unattractive option of being made head of a new subsidiary, the aforementioned Gazpromneft, which would have been headquartered in St. Petersburg. What likely tipped the scales was that Bogdanchikov received support from

Igor Sechin, who was head of the Rosneft board and a key Kremlin insider.[44]

In preparation for the showdown, Rosneft had been playing a deliberate game involving court actions, debt creation, and transfer pricing schemes, all of which were aimed at ensuring that Rosneft would not be taken over by Gazprom. A Russian legal expert has even held up this "anti-takeover" defense as worthy of being included in textbooks.[45] Following the subsequent dismantling of Yukos, and Rosneft's takeover of Yuganskneftegaz, the game was transformed. Rosneft and Gazprom were now of equal size and importance, with the former in clear ascendance.

Although the two energy giants have often been at odds with each other, both Rosneft and Gazprom remain firmly under Kremlin control. Together they provide a formidable basis for domestic as well as foreign energy policy. Their cohabitation, however, has not been entirely without problems. The simple fact that Rosneft has acquired substantial interests in gas, and that Gazprom has done the same in oil, suggests that further turf battles are to be expected. This will have consequences both for their respective protectors within the upper levels of the bureaucracy and for Russian energy policy more broadly.

Rolling Back Foreign Oil

On a parallel track, the Kremlin complemented its assault against the domestic oligarchs with a drive to roll back the influence of the major foreign oil companies over Russian energy policy. The first act in the drama was played out at and around Sakhalin Island, where Shell and Exxon-Mobil had been investing heavily in a long-term presence based on highly favorable production-sharing agreements. These were now set to backfire.

The first victim of the Kremlin's rollback was Royal Dutch Shell. Given that the production-sharing agreement allowed the foreign partners to recoup costs before the sharing of revenues could begin, it was not surprising that Moscow watched with mounting frustration as cost overruns at Sakhalin II accumulated at a staggering rate. Russia's anticipated share in the returns was thus being pushed further and further into the future. To this could be added a vigorous international campaign by various nongovernmental environmental organizations claiming that serious ecological damage was being done. By December 2006, Shell, faced with threats of a $50 million lawsuit and the risk of having its concession revoked, felt compelled to strike a deal.[46]

Following a meeting in the Kremlin between Prime Minister Putin and the chief executive officers of Gazprom, Shell, Mitsui, and Mitsubishi, it was announced that the foreign partners had agreed to sell half of their respective shares to Gazprom. More precisely, the deal implied that Shell would reduce its stake from 55 to 27.5 percent, and that Gazprom would come out with 50 percent plus one share. The price that Gazprom thus paid for assuming control over Sakhalin Energy was a mere $7.45 billion.[47] This was the equivalent, according to a Shell spokesman, of "paying to enter on the ground floor, as if they were a shareholder at the beginning."[48]

Subsequently, the Russian government added insult to injury by leaking a document purporting that the three foreign companies had also agreed to absorb $3.6 billion in mounting cost overruns, outside the terms of the production-sharing agreement. As this would bring forward the date of full cost recovery, it would also bring forward the date when revenue sharing could begin. Once Gazprom had assumed full control, which took place in April 2007, the regulatory pressures disappeared, and the project has since "won accolades for its environmental record."[49]

For the sake of accuracy, if not fairness, it should be recalled that the Sakhalin II production-sharing agreement in particular has been viewed as inherently biased against Russia. It allowed the Shell-controlled Sakhalin Energy Investment Corporation the right to recoup all its costs plus a 17.5 percent rate of return—before Russia would get a 10 percent share of the proceeds from what was being extracted out of the ground.[50]

To what extent the Sakhalin Island environmental groups that were pursuing Shell, and that finally got the Russian Ministry of Natural Resources to take action, had serious grounds for complaint is a more complex issue. Before the final showdown, Shell had undertaken extensive and costly efforts to deal with issues ranging from indigenous minorities and gray whales to the routing of pipelines and establishing safeguards against oil spills, all aimed at securing a clean bill of health.[51]

This said, it remains hard indeed to believe that the main motivation for the attack was anything but political, in the sense of securing a larger share of the revenue for the Russian side. Since Shell was still making a profit, it accepted to play by the new rules, leaving for its senior management to express its pleasure and gratitude at having come out of the fray with at least something left to show.

The next victim was the previously mentioned TNK-BP joint venture. At the time of the original deal, BP had nurtured grand ambitions to develop the giant Kovytka gas field in Eastern Siberia. Discovered already in 1987, the field had proven reserves of nearly 2 trillion cubic meters and more than 83 million tons of gas condensate.[52] After four years of fruitless negotiations, BP was approaching realization that its own plan for export of gas to China conflicted fatally with Gazprom's ambition to do the same. The breaking point proved to be a clause in the license concerning production targets. Being denied permission to build its own pipeline to China, and faced with a blank refusal by Gazprom to pump gas westward, the company's only option was to sell its gas on the local market. As this fell far short of the stipulated volumes, TNK-BP was faced with the same threat that had confronted Shell—the risk of losing its license. Consequently, in June 2007, TNK-BP agreed to sell its 63 percent stake. The buyer, again, was Gazprom.[53]

Under the terms of the agreement, TNK-BP accepted to sell Gazprom its 63 percent stake in Rusia Petroleum, the company that held the license for the Kovytka gas field. And it agreed to sell its 50 percent interest in the East Siberian Gas Company, which was charged with a regional gasification project. Gazprom would pay a total of no more than $700–900 million for the lot. As had been the case with Shell after losing Sakhalin II, BP was reduced to smiling and to accepting a consolation price in the form of a call option to buy 25 percent plus one share in Kovytka at a later date. Then president and chief executive officer of TNK-BP, Robert Dudley, noted that this was "an important development in the future growth of TNK-BP."[54]

Next in line was ExxonMobil, whose operation of the Sakhalin I oil and gas field had been linked from the very outset with plans for exports to China. In October 2006, ExxonMobil accordingly signed a preliminary agreement with the China National Petroleum Corporation (CNPC). But Gazprom, having a legal monopoly on all export of gas, would not allow a private gas pipeline to China.[55] It instead demanded that the full output from Sakhalin I be sent via the Sakhalin-Khabarovsk-Vladivostok (SKV) pipeline, the launch of which was planned to coincide with the 2012 Asia-Pacific Economic Cooperation (APEC) summit in Vladivostok. Plans for a second liquefied natural gas plant were also mentioned.[56]

Faced with this opposition, in May 2009 the ExxonMobil-led consortium agreed to sell 20 percent of Sakhalin I gas to Gazprom.[57] On July 31, at a ceremony to inaugurate the SKV pipeline, Prime Minister Putin underscored that domestic energy needs must take priority over exports.[58] The likely final outcome again seemed to be that of a foreign oil company caving in to pressure, and of Gazprom expanding its might even further.

Leaving Sakhalin Island and Eastern Siberia, we find Gazprom embroiled in similar controversy also at the other end of the country. Offshore in the Russian sector of the Barents Sea lies the Shtokman field, one of the world's largest natural gas fields. Discovered in 1988, its reserves are estimated at 3.9 trillion cubic meters of gas and 56 million tons of gas condensate. Of this, 3.8 trillion cubic meters of natural gas and more than 53.3 million tons of gas condensate are located within Gazprom's licensed area. With the first phase aiming to produce 23.7 billion cubic meters of natural gas, final output is expected to reach 70 billion cubic meters, comparable to the annual gas output of Norway.[59]

Due to the extreme Arctic conditions prevailing in the area, and a sea depth that varies from 320 to 340 meters, it was realized early on that Gazprom would not be able to go it alone. In September 2005, five foreign companies—Statoil, Norsk Hydro, Total, Chevron, and ConocoPhillips—were consequently selected as finalists in a search for partners to develop the field. Then the Kremlin's political agenda was transformed, and in October 2006 a decision was made to reject all potential foreign partners. Remaining aware, however, of the need for foreign technology, in February 2008 Gazprom agreed with Total and (merged) StatoilHydro to set up the Shtokman Development Company. Charged with organizing the design, financing, construction, and operation of the first phase of the Shtokman infrastructure, upon completion the foreign companies' shares were to be transferred to Gazprom.[60]

It was deeply symptomatic of the changing times that where the early Sakhalin pioneers—Shell and ExxonMobil—had succeeded in getting the Kremlin to accept production-sharing agreements that were clearly biased against Russia, when what was then thought to be the final deal on Shtokman was made, the foreigners ended up offering their precious technology for a mere fee, rather than an ownership stake or even a share in output. In August 2012, moreover, Statoil would announce that it had written off around 2 billion crowns ($336.2 million) of investment and handed back its shares in the project. The reason was that the partners had failed to meet an established June 30 deadline for an agreement on how to proceed.[61] Putin's Russia had morphed into a very different kind of partner than that presided over by Boris Yeltsin. The times of bargain-basement dealing had come and gone.

Rounding off the story of trouble faced by big oil in Russia, in the summer of 2008 TNK-BP was shaken by a bitter internal power struggle that caused its chief executive officer, Robert Dudley, to flee the country.[62] On December 1, following a long series of visa hassles and accusations of espionage that caused the entire expatriate management team to leave Russia, he was forced to resign. At the core of the battle was a conflict between BP and its Russian partner, the Alfa Group, which succeeded, in May 2009, in having its own president, Mikhail Fridman, installed as the new chief executive officer of TNK-BP.[63]

Given the overwhelming importance of TNK-BP to overall BP operations, representing a quarter of the company's output and a fifth of its total reserves, this was no small matter.[64] A casual observer might perhaps have thought that in BP management circles there should have been some cause for reflection. There was the specific case of lessons never really learned from BP's losses in struggles with the Alfa Group before the TNK-BP adventure, and there was the more general case of what appears to be the bottom line of foreign involvement in Russian energy: foreigners were welcome to contribute their superior technology, and to make handsome profits for a time, but were not to expect to be allowed any form of controlling interest.

A powerful indication that no such lessons had been contemplated, or at least not learned, arrived at the outset of 2011. On January 14, markets were stunned by the announcement of a major deal between BP and Rosneft, aimed at exploring the Kara Sea on Russia's Arctic continental shelf.[65] The announcement had several interesting dimensions. Most important, perhaps, was that the technical side of the deal entailed a share swap whereby BP offered 5 percent of its shares, valued at $7.8 billion, in return for 9.5 percent of Rosneft shares. BP in consequence would become the biggest nonstate shareholder in Rosneft, which is 75 percent controlled by the Russian government, and Rosneft would become the second-largest shareholder in BP.[66]

From a public relations perspective, this may have been viewed as a way for BP to impress on markets that despite the disaster with the explosion of the Deepwater Horizon drilling platform in the Gulf of Mexico, it was still a serious player. The commercial angle also seemed to represent a shrewd way for BP to acquire a secured seat at the table for future exploration of Russia's Arctic hydrocarbon wealth. The real key, however, was that following its troubles first with Sidanco and then with the TNK-BP venture, BP management obviously saw a need to secure protection straight from the very top. This was delivered, it seemed, by Prime Minister Putin on a silver platter.[67]

Although the commercial side of the deal may have appeared sound, there was also a political dimension that would come back to haunt BP. Given the way in which Rosneft had picked up the wreckage after the dismantling of Yukos, it was to be expected that BP would be subjected to heavy criticism for the de facto legitimization of the Kremlin's behavior, and for what some held to represent a purchase of stolen goods. A powerful indictment along these lines was fielded by Bruce Misamore, the former chief financial officer at Yukos.[68]

Added venom was provided by US congressman Edward Markey, a top Democrat on the House Natural Resources Committee, who claimed that "BP once stood for British Petroleum. With this deal it now stands for Bolshoi Petroleum."[69] With others claiming that it should be more rightly referred to as "Bolshevik Petroleum," and that BP's action would complicate even further the aftermath of Deepwater Horizon, it was clear to one columnist that the deal had "much more to do with tectonic shifts in geopolitics than with oil."[70] Having first undertaken what many British viewed as a shakedown of BP, to the tune of $20 billion plus for damages in the Gulf of Mexico, US lawmakers were now accused of being resentful of a deal that was jointly blessed by the Russian and British governments.

The deal with Rosneft provoked legal action from the Russian billionaire co-owners of TNK-BP, who obviously feared that they would become sidelined.[71] Given that the deal appeared to be protected by Putin himself, the very fact that the Alfa Group chose open confrontation may have come as a surprise to BP. Having been twice burned already, by these very same partners, the company may have thought that this time they had ensured adequate protection. Subsequent events, however, would prove that doing business in Russia can never carry any guarantee, of any kind. Following a four-month legal battle to save the deal, marked by a series of adverse rulings, by mid-May 2011, BP had to face the fact that its proposed alliance with Rosneft had collapsed. The prize of Arctic hydrocarbon exploitation was again back on the market.[72]

Most important of all, the Rosneft deal illustrated that the Kremlin had been right in discounting the risk that its heavy-handed way of treating foreign partners would lead to negative reactions. Symbolically, it was left for Robert Dudley to put together the deal with Rosneft. Having been appointed to succeed Tony Hayward as chief executive officer at BP following the Deepwater Horizon disaster, among his first chores was to return to Moscow, two years after he had fled, in order to pursue further negotiations on the company's fate.[73]

This, however, was far from the end of the story. The saga of BP involvement in Russia was set to continue, with surprising new twists and turns along the road. In October 2012, Rosneft suddenly announced that it was to take over TNK-BP. The Russian group AAR was paid $28 billion in cash to get out, and BP was offered a package of cash and nearly a 20 percent stake in Rosneft.[74] Whether this will prove to be a final and lasting deal remains to be seen.

Let us proceed now to look at Russian ambitions to secure the energy resources in the Caspian Basin and to lock in the European Union market for its gas exports. Both would be marred by mounting conflicts.

Securing the Caspian Basin

While the Kremlin's ambition to impose effective control over domestic energy resources was important enough, the real key to success in assembling an energy powerhouse rested not in Russia proper but in the region surrounding the Caspian Sea. As noted earlier, the breakup of the Soviet Union was associated with the emergence of a set of aspiring new energy powers in Central Asia and in the South Caucasus. As these newly independent players began to look for outside help in developing their energy resources, the stage was set for a new round of the great game played out between the British and Russian empires over the course of the nineteenth century.

The historical parallel was frequently drawn.[75] This time, however, the players had multiplied to include not only Russia and Britain but also China, the United States, and the European Union. And the competition had been more narrowly focused on achieving control over the region's energy resources. At stake, more specifically, was control over the transport of energy out of the region. For as long as Russia would be able to maintain its inherited Soviet-era hold on the pipeline grid, both governments and energy companies in the region would have to face the fundamental fact that reserves of oil and gas in the ground have little value.

Throughout the 1990s, it also did seem as though Russia would be able to retain its grip. When Kazakhstan began developing the giant Tengiz field, Moscow could make sure that the export pipeline was routed over Russian territory. It was when it began to look as though a resurgent Russia was about to walk off with the spoils that the notion of an emerging Russian "energy superpower" made its appearance. In the words of Fiona Hill, "Russia is back on the global strategic and economic map. It has transformed itself from a defunct military superpower into a new energy superpower."[76]

The first serious challenge to such beliefs emanated from developments in Azerbaijan. The construction of the Baku-Tbilisi-Ceyhan and the Baku-Tbilisi-Erzurum oil and gas pipelines opened up the threat of a further major bypass option being built—the European Union's Nabucco gas pipeline. If the latter were to be realized, it would deprive Moscow of its effective monopoly control over energy transport from the Caspian Basin to customers in the European Union. Consequently, there was an implied need to secure long-term control over the sources of gas in the region. The real key to success here rested in Turkmenistan, and in its enigmatic president, Saparmurat Niyazov. Also known as Turkmenbashi, the "Father of the Turkmen," Niyazov had long been considered a loyal vassal to Moscow, seemingly content with allowing Russia to derive massive gains from captive Turkmen energy exports.

In the Soviet era, Turkmenistan had been an important provider of gas to other Soviet republics, supplying about 90 billion cubic meters annually. In return, it had received a hard currency quota based on its presumed share in exports to Europe. Following the breakup of the Soviet Union, Ashgabat began demanding payment for gas deliveries in hard currency and at "world prices." The outcome was to be a long series of incidents involving nonpayment and delivery interruption. Given that Ukraine was the biggest customer, taking about 25 billion cubic meters annually, it would be at the focus of many such disputes.[77]

In November 1995, an attempt was made to solve the underlying problems by forming a separate entity, named Turkmenrosgaz, which was charged with handling all sales of Turkmen gas. A joint venture between Turkmenneftegaz (51 percent), Gazprom (45 percent), and a private trading company named Itera (4 percent), it had a brief but important existence. In November 1997, all deliveries of Turkmen gas outside Central Asia were stopped, and Ashgabat unilaterally dissolved Turkmenrosgaz, citing nonpayment by Itera of debts for sales to Ukraine. Events that were played out in the wake of this confrontation would provide important early indications of what was to follow later. Four main issues were involved: the contract price for gas; the persistent inability of Ukraine to pay its bills; the role of intermediary trading companies such as that of Itera; and the Kremlin's apprehension that Ashgabat would seek export routes for its gas that would bypass Russia.

The immediate consequence of the cessation of exports in 1997 was that Turkmen production of gas dropped precipitously, from 84.3 billion cubic meters in 1991 to merely 13.3 billion cubic meters in 1998. The associated loss in export revenue in turn led Ashgabat to seek other outlets. It began exporting gas to Iran. A first pipeline, with a capacity of 8 billion cubic meters, was launched in 1997.[78] But also, and far more importantly, Ashgabat signed an agreement with the Turkish energy company Botas to deliver 30 billion cubic meters annually via the Trans-Caspian Pipeline.

Deliveries of gas to Ukraine were resumed in January 1999. But in April the flow again was stopped by Ashgabat, citing continued failure by Kiev to pay its bills and a debt that had swelled to $100 million. Clearly inspired by the Kremlin's fears of the TCP becoming a reality, in December Gazprom embarked on a project to mend fences with Turkmenistan.

In 2000, an agreement was reached on long-term deliveries of Turkmen gas to Russia. Meanwhile, trouble had developed also in relations between Turkmenistan and Azerbaijan. As the international partners pulled out, it appeared that the TCP was dead. Momentum was again building for Russia. In April 2003, President Putin and President Niyazov finally signed an agreement that had been on the table since December 1999. Touted at the time as a landmark deal, it called for Turkmenistan to supply 2 trillion cubic meters of natural gas to Russia through 2028.

At the signing ceremony in the Kremlin, Aleksei Miller, the chief executive officer of Gazprom, hailed the agreement as "a revolutionary breakthrough in the cooperation between the two great gas powers." Turkmen president Saparmurat Niyazov stated that "we are ready to supply to Russia up to 100 [billion cubic meters] of gas starting from 2010."[79]

The original intention was to begin modestly, with 5–6 billion cubic meters in 2004 and up to 10 billion cubic meters in 2006. During this initial period, Russia would be paying $44 per thousand cubic meters, half of which in cash and the rest in goods and services. Russian purchases would increase to 60–70 billion cubic meters in 2007 and to 70–80 billion cubic meters in 2009. What the price would be at these later stages was left unclear.[80] This, however, was to prove no more than a temporary respite.

The core of the problem continued to revolve around pricing. In early December 2004, Ashgabat demanded that Russia and Ukraine accept a substantial price increase. This led to a renewed cessation of the gas flow by the end of the year. Although separate negotiation allowed deliveries to Ukraine to be resumed after a few days, deliveries to Russia remained suspended through April 2005, reflecting just how complex the relation was between Gazprom and the Kremlin on one side and Turkmenistan on the other.

Early signs that the rules of the game were about to undergo serious change were noted in the last year of the life of Turkmenbashi. In April 2006, Niyazov flew to Beijing to conclude a deal on a 7,000-kilometer pipeline that would allow China to purchase 30 billion cubic meters of gas per year for thirty years, starting in 2009.[81] Although Russia would remain the major route for Turkmen export, the China deal did mark that the playing field was being opened up. The Kremlin could no longer count on retaining its monopoly position. The main cause for concern again was that the pipeline to China would be followed by a pipeline route to the West, in the form of the TCP and Nabucco.

Added fuel for such fear was provided by growing cooperation also between Turkmenistan and Iran. By far the most sensible option would be to link fields in Turkmenistan with existing infrastructure in Iran, allowing both transit to the West and swaps between north and south within Iran. Due mainly to resistance by the United States, this has not been given serious consideration in the larger energy game. Yet Ashgabat and Tehran were developing their own links. Spurred on by conflicts with Gazprom, in 2008 they decided to expand prior cooperation with a second pipeline. Inaugurated in 2010, it raised eventual capacity to 20 billion cubic meters annually.[82]

The pivotal question in this context has been to what extent Turkmenistan may actually be able to meet the commitments involved in playing a "multivectored" game, based on rivalry between Russia, China, and the West. Given that some estimates of total Turkmen gas reserves, at the time of increased Turkmen foreign activity, ran as high as 22 trillion cubic meters, there was plenty of room for speculation.[83]

During a visit by German foreign minister Frank-Walter Steinmeyer to Ashgabat in November 2006, Niyazov had added to the excitement by claiming that the newly discovered Yolotan-Osman field held no less than 7 trillion cubic meters of gas.[84] As this would represent more than double the reserves in Russia's high-profile Shtokman field, it was no wonder that the statement attracted substantial attention. Did it imply that Ashgabat was about to emerge from its long-standing isolation?

On December 21, it was suddenly announced that Niyazov had died. The events that surrounded this announcement were symptomatic of the closed and clandestine nature of the regime. There were rumors that the announcement had been deliberately delayed, that there had been purges of rival contenders for power, and that the border with Uzbekistan had been sealed for fear of outside intervention. The accession to power of Turkmen deputy prime minister Gurbanguly Berdymukhammedov, who was appointed acting president, was in clear violation of the Turkmen constitution, which stipulated that the chairman of parliament should step in as acting president and that the acting president in turn could not be nominated for the presidency.[85] Following Berdymukhammedov's election as president of Turkmenistan on February 11, 2007, a process of cautious reform was initiated and the previous policy of strict neutrality gave way to a gradually increasing foreign policy activism. But Russia still appeared to have the upper hand.

The peak of the Kremlin's ambition to secure the Caspian Basin was reached in the spring of 2007. Following lengthy negotiations, on May 12 President Putin finally managed to secure a deal with Kazakhstan, Turkmenistan, and Uzbekistan to build a gas pipeline, the Prikaspiiskoe (Pre-Caspian) line, which looked set to substantially alter the map of the game. Designed to hug the northern shore of the Caspian, it was to ensure that the bulk of Central Asian gas would flow north into the Russian grid.[86] The deal was generally viewed at the time as a final Russian victory in the great game.

A Stranglehold on Europe

What is evident from the account thus far is that by far the most important "weapon" in the Kremlin's arsenal has been its inherited control over the Soviet-era energy transport infrastructure. While state-owned Transneft has a near-monopoly on all oil pipelines, Gazprom controls the entire grid of gas pipelines. On the domestic scene, this has allowed the Kremlin to lock in a stranglehold over nominally private and independent producers, foreign as well as domestic. The logical next step would be for this stranglehold to be extended to cover exports of gas to Europe.

The ambition to build the aforementioned "ring fence" around the European energy market would have two main dimensions, in the form of major new pipeline projects to the north and to the south. A supplementary dimension, completing the ring in the fence, would be to aim for a stake also in gas supply to Europe across the Mediterranean.

At the time that Putin returned to the Kremlin, the latter was still of peripheral importance. Import of natural gas to Europe from the south remained dwarfed by imports from the east and the north. A breakdown of the sources of supply to the EU-27 countries for 2010 shows that indigenous production, though in decline, still accounted for 35 percent of the total. Of the remainder, 22 percent came from Russia and 19 percent from Norway. Algeria, Libya, Nigeria, and Egypt jointly accounted for only 15 percent.[87] (Appendix 6 provides detail on development of the European gas market, from 1994 onward.)

A rapid expansion of export capacity for gas across the Mediterranean may cause this to change. Three pipelines are already in place, and three more are under construction. As a result, Algerian capacity in particular is expected to increase greatly, from 76 billion cubic meters in 2008 to 102 billion cubic meters in 2015. The Trans-Saharan (NIGAL) pipeline is also proposed, to connect Nigeria with Algeria and onward to Europe.[88]

Gazprom has clearly wished to be part of this development. In 2009, it signed a $2.5 billion deal with the Nigerian National Petroleum Corporation to form the Nigaz joint venture,[89] and it is looking at participation in a pipeline from Algeria, known as Galsi, that would connect with Italy via Sardinia or with France via Corsica. Together with Algerian Sonatrach, it could develop an African hub at Beni Saf.[90]

Leaving aside the question of imports across the Mediterranean, which from Gazprom's point of view remained peripheral, we shall remain focused on the Kremlin's ambitions to lock in the European gas market by building new pipelines of its own. This will be largely in accordance with the first two counts in Karen Smith Stegen's previously cited "energy weapon" model,[91] and it calls for a brief digression into the composition of the inherited Soviet-era transport infrastructure.

The problem that the Kremlin has had to face is that the vast set of pipelines that transport oil and gas from Western Siberia to markets within the European Union cross the territories of Ukraine, Belarus, and Moldova. (Appendixes 7–9 provide detail on existing and planned pipelines for oil and gas.)

The real workhorse in this network is the previously mentioned Druzhba oil pipeline, in service since 1964. At about 4,000 kilometers, it is still the longest pipeline in the world. It starts in Tatarstan, in the heart of Russia, collecting oil from Western Siberia, the Urals, and the Caspian Basin, and stretches all the way into Central Europe. At Mozyr in southern Belarus, it splits into a northern branch that proceeds across Belarus into Poland and Germany, and a southern branch that crosses Ukraine. At Uzhgorod, on the western border of Ukraine, it splits again, into separate lines for Slovakia, Hungary, and the Czech Republic. It also has a connecting spur, the Odessa-Brody pipeline, that allows export of oil via the Black Sea.

When Druzhba—the "Friendship" pipeline—was originally built, it was at the heart of controversy between the United States and its European NATO allies, regarding the wisdom of making Europe dependent on supply of energy from the Soviet Union. In the post-Soviet era, it has been at the heart of a different form of controversy—Russian ambitions to cut Ukraine and Belarus out of the transit trade by building bypass options. We shall have reason to return to these matters in Chapter 8. Here we shall remain focused on gas, the transport of which presents a far more complex picture.

The main route for export of Russian gas to Europe is the Soviet-era Bratstvo (Brotherhood) pipeline, which transits Ukraine. Launched in 1967, it consists of a set of trunk pipelines that run from the main Russian gas fields at Orenburg, Urengoi, and Yamburg to Uzhgorod on the western border of Ukraine, and further on to countries in Europe. It has a total capacity of 130 billion cubic meters annually. There is also a Soviet-era pipeline, with a capacity of 20 billion cubic meters annually, from Central Asia transiting Russia and Ukraine to the Balkans.

Two lesser gas pipelines cross Belarus. One is the Soviet-era Siyanie Severa (Northern Lights), which was built in steps from 1967 until 1985. As in the case of the Brotherhood pipeline, it is actually a system of pipelines, with a total length of about 7,400 kilometers. It has a capacity of 25 billion cubic meters annually. The second is the more recent Yamal-Evropa (Yamal-Europe) pipeline, which runs parallel to the Northern Lights. In operation since 1999, it has a capacity of 33 billion cubic meters annually. The total export capacity for gas via Ukraine and Belarus thus comes to 208 billion cubic meters annually. In addition, there is also an existing Soviet-era pipeline to Finland, known as the Finland Connector, with a capacity of 20 billion cubic meters annually, and a more recent pipeline to Turkey, the Goluboi Potok (Blue Stream), with a capacity of 16 billion cubic meters annually.[92] If the latter are included, the total export capacity to Europe rises to 244 billion cubic meters annually.

As the Kremlin set out to erect its "ring fence" around the European energy market, its main objective was to ensure that no challenge would emerge to Russian control over the transport infrastructure. Beginning with the southern dimension, this entailed preventing bypass options such as the European Union's Nabucco project from becoming a reality.

Gazprom already had one route, the aforementioned Blue Stream pipeline, which carries gas from southern Russia across the Black Sea to Turkey. Built by a Netherlands-based joint venture between Gazprom and Italian oil and gas company ENI, called Blue Stream Pipeline B.V., it was originally intended as a long-term strategic cooperation project between the two countries. The project was technically challenging, entailing the construction of two offshore pipelines laid at a maximum depth of 2,150 meters. Gas flow started in 2003 and is intended to continue until 2025, peaking at 16 billion cubic meters per year.[93] The offshore part of the 1,250-kilometer pipeline is owned by the joint venture, and the respective land sections are owned by Gazprom and by the Turkish energy company Botas.

Moscow's ambition of preventing Nabucco from being built was not the only factor at play here. Considering Moscow's parallel desire to also reduce its dependence on Ukraine, Belarus, and Moldova as transit states for gas export to Europe, it was logical that an extension of the cooperation with Turkey would be up for discussion. First suggested in August 2002, in August 2005 Vladimir Putin and Recep Tayyip Erdogan officially proposed the construction of a Blue Stream II, and announced a decision to extend Blue Stream I to southeastern Europe.[94]

Discussion of this extended project was marred, however, by the fact that cooperation on Blue Stream I had been beset with trouble from the very outset. The core of the problem was a pricing dispute, which in turn was related to questions regarding Turkish demand for natural gas. Only months after the gas had actually begun to flow, a Russian official appeared at an international energy conference in Istanbul with a speech alleging that Ankara was double-crossing Moscow by backing out of the Blue Stream agreement in order to obtain natural gas at a cheaper price from Azerbaijan's previously mentioned giant Shah Deniz field.[95] The conflict caused the official inauguration to be postponed until November 2005. With added reluctance to trust in Turkey as a partner against Nabucco, Russia would soon decide to seek another path.

In June 2007, Gazprom joined with its Italian partner ENI to work out plans for a pipeline to be known as South Stream that would link the Caspian Basin with southern and central Europe. Bypassing Turkey, it would run under the Black Sea from southern Russia to Bulgaria, where it would branch off into a southern route to Greece and Italy and a northern route to Hungary.[96] Originally designed for a capacity of 31 billion cubic meters annually, it would match the rival Nabucco pipeline. The stakes, however, would soon go even higher.

At a meeting at the Black Sea coast resort town of Sochi on May 15, 2009, Russia agreed with Italy, and with transit states Bulgaria, Greece, and Serbia, to enlarge the South Stream project, to be operational by 2015, to a capacity to 61 billion cubic meters annually. There were good reasons at the time to suspect that this initiative was mainly a political effort to slow the growing momentum of the EU. According to one commentator, the expanded capacity figure seemed "purely arbitrary and possibly improvised." Gazprom had already upped the ante in February, to a capacity of

47 billion cubic meters annually, and was now committing to a further substantial hike. The financing also seemed unclear. Before the Sochi meeting, the total project cost was estimated at $19–24 billion. With the envisioned further capacity enhancement, that number would go even higher.[97] And this was proposed in the midst of the global financial crisis.

No matter what one chooses to believe about motivations, the event was clearly indicative of just how tough competition had become between the two pipeline projects. Since it was highly unlikely that both Nabucco and South Stream could ever become jointly commercially viable, the great game over the Caspian Basin was in the process of being transformed into a more specific great game over who would control gas supply to Europe. Who will emerge as the winner remains to be seen.

Turning now to the northern dimension of Russian gas supply policy, we may find an equally controversial manifestation of the very same type of game.[98] At the time of the breakup of the Soviet Union, about 90 percent of Russian exports of gas to Europe proceeded via Ukraine,[99] a transit that would be marked by severe and continuing conflicts.

Determined to reduce the scope for such conflicts, in 1997 Gazprom joined with the Finnish company Neste (later Fortum) to form a joint company called North Transgas Oy, which entered into partnership with the German company Ruhrgas (later E.ON). The purpose was to build an underwater pipeline through the Baltic that would connect Vyborg in Russia with Greifswald in Germany. A joint feasibility study was commissioned in 2001, and in 2002 the Gazprom management committee approved a schedule of project implementation. In 2005, Fortum sold its 50 percent stake to Gazprom, which was then the sole owner of North Transgas Oy.[100] On September 8, 2005, Gazprom, BASF, and E.ON signed a basic agreement on the construction of a pipeline, and on November 30, 2005, the new entity, named the North European Gas Pipeline Company (later Nord Stream), was incorporated in Zug, Switzerland. Construction of the Russian onshore section of the pipeline was begun on December 9, 2005.[101]

The Nord Stream pipeline was designed to be 1,220 kilometers long and to consist of two parallel lines. The first, with a transmission capacity of about 27.5 billion cubic meters annually, was to be completed in 2011, and the second in 2012, doubling annual capacity to around 55 billion cubic meters. This would be enough to supply more than 25 million households in Europe. Total investment in the offshore pipeline was projected at €7.4 billion.[102]

Several factors combined to surround this project with great controversy from its very start. One of the more important was that both Poland and the Baltic States viewed it as a stratagem that would allow Gazprom to shut off their energy supply without disturbing the flow to Germany. Vociferous protests would in consequence be heard, to the point even of conjuring up images of a new axis between Moscow and Berlin. In 2006, Polish foreign minister Radoslaw Sikorski upped the ante by explicitly comparing Nord Stream to the notorious Molotov-Ribbentrop Pact, which preceded the Nazi German assault on Poland.[103] Adding to suspicions about clandestine ambitions, the Russian side also was hard-pressed to explain why it preferred a more complex and environmentally dubious underwater solution to a much less costly route over land.

The Nord Stream project as a whole provides by far the best illustration of what has been mentioned here about internal divisions between EU member states. Given the geography of the Baltic Sea region, the pipeline consortium was in effect held hostage to approval by at least some of the coastal states. Although national territorial waters do not extend more than 12 nautical miles from the coastline, exclusive economic zones extend 200 nautical miles out, and in the case of the Baltic Sea they actually meet at the middle.

Since the three Baltic States could not be counted upon to grant permission for pipeline construction within their respective economic zones, a pivotal role was assigned to Sweden, which has a very long coastline. At an early stage, it was even hoped that the pipeline could be connected to a Swedish national distribution grid, thus increasing the size of the market for Nord Stream gas. Finland was also to be involved, as were Denmark and Germany, albeit with far less controversy.

In domestic public debates about whether the Swedish government should give a green light for the consortium to proceed with construction within the country's economic zone, arguments against were at first focused on military security issues. A particular role was played here by fears of involvement by the Russian navy in protecting the installation, and by suspicions that the pipeline would be used as a platform for installing listening devices for detection of the activities of Swedish submarines.

Since arguments of this kind could clearly not be openly expressed by any of the concerned governments, critics soon found other ways of attempting to prevent the project from being realized. Obstacles that were officially raised would consequently focus instead on environmental concerns, ranging from disturbance of marine habitats to risks associated with munitions dumped after the conclusion of World War II.[104]

What made the whole issue so intriguing to watch was that during the six months when the process of seeking permission was at its most critical phase, the rotating presidency of the EU was held by Sweden. Being squeezed between Germany, which in effect was a partner with Russia in the project, and Poland and the Baltic States, which were keen on blocking it, the Swedish government was in a delicate position. In public, it went to great lengths assuring that it viewed the whole matter as a question of approval based on environmental concerns only. Behind the scenes, however, plans were being discreetly drawn up on how approval could be delayed indefinitely, by raising ever more complicated ecological concerns and by eventually simply issuing a refusal and allowing the matter to be buried in an international court.[105]

In the end, however, it would be the Nord Stream consortium that prevailed. Following a lengthy process of amply financed and highly professional lobbying, the balance swung in favor of approval, which was granted in December 2009. Approval by the governments of Finland, Denmark, and Germany followed shortly thereafter.[106]

Apart from working to produce a positive spin in the media, the Nord Stream consortium had also succeeded in recruiting a number of senior business and political figures as "ambassadors," or as outright consultants to promote the project. By far the most prominent on this list was Swedish prime minister Fredrik Reinfeldt's former chief of staff, Ulrika Schenstrom, who most likely had been privy to internal government deliberations on how to handle the Nord Stream application. In Finland, where public opinion was less hostile, the consortium succeeded in recruiting former prime minister Paavo Lipponen to act as an independent consultant.

While it remains uncertain whether South Stream will actually be completed, the construction of Nord Stream has been completed. The first of the two lines was officially inaugurated in November 2011, at a ceremony in Lubmin on the German coast of the Baltic Sea, where the pipeline makes landfall. The second line went into commercial operation in October 2012.[107] Whether Gazprom and its German partner will in turn be able to count on prices that cover the rapidly mounting costs is a different issue, one, moreover, that will not have any impact on the pipeline itself. However, in reflection of its determination to defy EU calls for "unbundling" and a reduced dependence on Russian energy, in May 2012 the Nord Stream consortium announced that it had launched a feasibility study on the potential for constructing two additional pipelines that would double its capacity to provide gas from Russia to the EU market.[108]

Recalling again the model framework for the "energy weapon" suggested by Karen Smith Stegen, with the benefit of hindsight it is tempting to see a three-stage strategy whereby the Kremlin first went about securing control over extraction, then proceeded to secure control over transportation, and in a final stage aims also to control distribution, entailing takeovers of national distribution networks. Despite the argument here against the presence of an early master plan of some sort, the outcome, looking beyond possible intentions, will nevertheless remain important in supporting perceptions by outside observers that there has been an intentional strategy at play.

Projects like South Stream and Nord Stream have served to enhance fears that the Kremlin, once it has secured control over the lion's share of energy supply to the European Union, will be in a position to use this lever-age in order to break any potential resistance to allowing Gazprom to pur-chase national distribution networks. This makes up an important part of the case against the Kremlin for wielding an energy weapon.

Outright threats along such lines have also been made. A case in point was marked in April 2006, when British regulators moved to block an anticipated bid by Gazprom for Centrica, Britain's largest gas distributor. At a subsequent meeting with ambassadors of the EU-25 states in Moscow, Gazprom chief executive officer Aleksei Miller bluntly advised that the EU should not block Gazprom's "international ambitions." Otherwise, the com-pany would redirect supplies to other markets.[109]

Numerous statements to the same effect have been subsequently issued, in response to moves by the EU to counter Gazprom's ambitions to lock in the European energy market. The hardening rhetoric has not just been detri-mental to the prospects for developing a mutually beneficial policy of energy security, which would be aimed at sustainable resource development and an economically rational energy transport infrastructure. From a narrow Russian point of view, it may also turn out to have been rather ill-advised.

Assertive Russian behavior in foreign energy relations has been fraught with dangers, with the perceived bullying triggering reactions that go beyond negative reporting in the media. Several neighboring countries have responded with concrete measures aimed at reducing dependence on the Russian pipeline grid and on Russian energy deliveries. Before looking in more detail at the counterforces that have emerged, let us digress to take a closer look at Gazprom. Due to its sheer size and the nature of its opera-tions, it was destined to make up the very heart of the Russian energy com-plex, though its performance would leave much to be desired.

Notes

1. Lavelle, "OPEC Dethroned."

2. Cited from *Johnson's Russia List,* February 9, 2006, item 18, http://www.cdi.org/russia/johnson/2006-39-18.cfm.

3. Goldman, *The Piratization of Russia.*

4. Freeland, *Sale of the Century,* p. 22.

5. For example, Gustafson, *Wheel of Fortune,* chap. 3.

6. Tikhomirov, "Capital Flight from Post-Soviet Russia."

7. Gustafson, *Wheel of Fortune,* p. 122.

8. Ibid., pp. 120–121.

9. Baev, *Russian Energy Policy and Military Power,* p. 157.

10. For extensive accounts of the emergence and role of the Russian oligarchs, see Fortescue, *Russia's Oil Barons and Metals Magnates;* and Hoffman, *The Oligarchs.*

11. The international coverage of the Yukos affair has been massive. For a few influential contributions, see Gustafson, *Wheel of Fortune,* chap. 7; Hanson, "Observations on the Cost of the Yukos Affair"; Hanson, "The Russian Economic Puzzle"; Poussenkova, *Lord of the Rigs;* and Tompson, "Putting Yukos in Perspective."

12. The role of Yukos Oil in creating the Russian "oil miracle" that marked the early Putin era is detailed in Gustafson, *Wheel of Fortune,* pp. 201–221.

13. "The 10 Most Powerful Billionaires," *Forbes,* March 17, 2003, http://www.forbes.com/global/2003/0317/050.html.

14. Gustafson, *Wheel of Fortune,* pp. 312–318.

15. "YUKOS/Sibneft: Corporate Governance Risk Increased," *Troika Dialog,* April 2, 2004, http://ir.gazprom-neft.com/fileadmin/user_upload/documents/troika-2004-04-02-eng.pdf. For detail on the prospective new entity, see also Gazprom's investor presentation at http://www.gazprom-neft.ru/investor/presentations/other/Yukos-Sibneft-eng.pdf.

16. "ExxonMobil Corporation, ChevronTexaco Corp. Eyeing 25% Stake in Yukos; Stake Valued at Approximately $11 Billion—WSJ," *Wall Street Journal,* September 15, 2003, http://global.factiva.com/ha/default.aspx.

17. "ExxonMobil Corporation in Talks to Take Stake in Yukos," *Financial Times,* October 2, 2003, http://global.factiva.com/ha/default.aspx. On the nature of speculation in the market concerning possible mergers, see also "Arrest and Detention of Khodorkovsky Cools the Anticipation of Merger," *Paneurasian,* September 18, 2003, http://www.paneurasian.com/yukosmerger.html.

18. For a detailed account of the backroom dealings between Yukos and its potential US partners, see Gustafson, *Wheel of Fortune,* pp. 297–300.

19. "Scandals," *Forbes,* February 24, 2004, http://www.forbes.com/2004/02/24/cz_bill04_scandalslide.html?thisSpeed=20000.

20. As in the case of the Yukos affair, international coverage of the fate of Khodorkovsky, the former chief executive officer of Yukos, has been massive. For a brief overview of his rise to power, and of the ensuing attack by the Kremlin on both him and his creation, see Goldman, *Petrostate,* pp. 105–123. Valuable continuing coverage from inside Khodorkovsky's defense counsel has been provided on a website maintained by his main legal adviser, Robert Amsterdam, at http://www.robertamsterdam.com.

21. Chrystia Freeland, "The Raw Face of Capitalism, Kremlin Style," *New York Times,* January 6, 2011, http://www.nytimes.com/2011/01/07/world/europe/07iht-letter07.html.

22. Anatoly Medetsky, "Dvorkovich Fears Verdict Risk," *Moscow Times,* January 20, 2011, http://www.themoscowtimes.com/business/article/dvorkovich-fears-verdict-risk/429255.html.

23. Ibid.

24. Gregory L. White, "Russian Tycoon's Trial Is Called a Sham," *Wall Street Journal,* February 15, 2011, http://online.wsj.com/article/SB10001424052748703584804576143842582744356.html?mod=WSJ_topics_obama.

25. Pleines, "Developing Russia's Oil and Gas Industry," p. 77.

26. Torbakov, "Yukos Bankruptcy." For a detailed timeline of events played out during the Yukos affair as a whole, see http://www.khodorkovskycenter.com/media-center/timeline-yukos-affair.

27. Powerbase/Public Interest Investigations, "Yukos," http://www.powerbase.info/index.php/YUKOS.

28. Gustafson, *Wheel of Fortune,* p. 314.

29. Of all the various legal actions that have been taken by the former shareholders, the most high-profile is a suit brought in the European Court of Human Rights. The case was accepted as admissible in January 2009, and hearings took place in March 2010. Representing the first decision ever by the Court to hear a case against a publicly quoted company, the claim for damages also was the largest ever submitted to any court. The damage claim of $98 billion is an estimate of what Yukos would have been worth had its most valuable properties not been stripped away in 2007, when the company in effect ceased to exist. In April 2011, the Court found that Russian authorities had violated the rights of Yukos when the company was broken up, but rejected the allegation that this had been politically motivated. The question of monetary compensation was deferred. At the time of writing it is still pending. See Andrew E. Kramer, "European Court Ready to Hear Yukos Case," *New York Times,* March 4, 2010, http://www.nytimes.com/2010/03/04/business /global/04iht-yukos.html?_r=1; and Gregory L. White, "European Rights Court Delivers Split Yukos Ruling," *Wall Street Journal,* September 21, 2011, http://online .wsj.com/article/SB10001424053111904194604576582142899283926.html. See also "Khodorkovsky at the European Court of Human Rights," http://www.khodor kovsky.com/legal/international-forums.

30. Erin E. Arvedlund, "Russia to Sell Big Yukos Unit at Low-End Price," *New York Times,* October 13, 2004, http://query.nytimes.com/gst/fullpage.html?res=9D 03E3DF1E3BF930A25753C1A9629C8B63.

31. For a background on how Yuganskneftegaz instead ended up in the hands of Rosneft, see Poussenkova, *Lord of the Rigs,* pp. 60–66.

32. Dresdner Kleinwort Wasserstein had suggested that the unit was worth between $15.7 and $18.3 billion, but also added that, with all potential risk taken into account, the value could drop to $10.4 billion; "Russia 'Plans Partial Yukos Sale,'" *BBC News,* October 12, 2004, http://news.bbc.co.uk/2/hi/business/3736074 .stm. Proceeding to the auction, the Russian government, which itself was the source of risk, conveniently used the lower valuation.

33. "Putin Aide Slams Yukos Sell-Off," *BBC News,* December 28, 2004, http://news.bbc.co.uk/2/hi/europe/4129875.stm.

34. The two remaining subsidiaries of Yukos—Samaraneftegaz and Tomskneft— were sold to Rosneft at a further auction in May 2007, at the price of $13.2 billion. Rutland, "Putin's Economic Record," p. 1058.

35. Steve Marshall, "Gazprom Swallows Up Sibneft," *Upstream,* September 28, 2005, http://www.upstreamonline.com/live/article99244.ece.

36. Klebnikov, *Godfather of the Kremlin,* pp. 194–208.

37. Jennifer Lipman, "Chelsea's Abramovich Loses Berezovsky Lawsuit Appeal," *Jewish Chronicle Online,* February 23, 2011, http://www.thejc.com/news /uk-news/45619/chelseas-abramovich-loses-berezovsky-lawsuit-appeal.

38. Tom Peck, "Berezovsky Humbled by Verdict that Leaves Reputation in Tatters," *The Independent,* August 31, 2012, http://www.independent.co.uk /news/uk/home-news/berezovsky-humbled-by-verdict-that-leaves-reputation-in -tatters-8099260.html.

39. "Behind Russia's 'Russneft Affair,'" *Forbes,* August 3, 2007, http://www .forbes.com/2007/08/02/russneft-russia-oil-biz-cz_0803oxfordanalytica.html.

40. Russneft, "President of the Company Mikhail Safarbekovich Gutseriev," December 14, 2013, http://eng.russneft.ru/president_1.

41. Hanson, "The Resistible Rise of State Control in the Russian Oil Industry," pp. 17–18.

42. "UPDATE 1-Russia's Deripaska Sells Russneft to Founder-Paper," *Reuters*, January 5, 2010, http://uk.reuters.com/article/idUKLDE6040DA20100105.

43. For an attempt at telling the inside story, see "Russia: A Merger Fails, A Power Struggle Is Revealed," *Stratfor*, May 19, 2005, http://www.stratfor.com /russia_merger_fails_power_struggle_revealed.

44. Gustafson, *Wheel of Fortune*, pp. 338–341.

45. Poussenkova, *Lord of the Rigs*, p. 68.

46. Abrahm Lustgarten, "Shell Shakedown," *CNN Money*, February 1, 2007, http://money.cnn.com/magazines/fortune/fortune_archive/2007/02/05/8399125 /index.htm.

47. Bradshaw, "A New Energy Age in Pacific Russia," p. 352.

48. Abrahm Lustgarten, "Shell Shakedown," *CNN Money*, February 1, 2007, http://money.cnn.com/magazines/fortune/fortune_archive/2007/02/05/8399125 /index.htm.

49. Bradshaw, "A New Energy Age in Pacific Russia," p. 352.

50. Lustgarten, "Shell Shakedown."

51. Bradshaw, "A New Energy Age in Pacific Russia," pp. 349–351. On the takeover as a whole, see also Heinrich, "Under the Kremlin's Thumb," pp. 1551–1553.

52. Dusseault, "Russia's East and the Search for a New El Dorado," p. 80.

53. Heinrich, "Under the Kremlin's Thumb," pp. 1550–1551.

54. BP, "BP and TNK-BP Plan Strategic Alliance with Gazprom As TNK-BP Sells Its Stake in Kovykta Gas Field," June 21, 2007, http://www.bp.com/en /global/corporate/press/press-releases/bp-and-tnk-bp-plan-strategic-alliance-with -gazprom-as-tnk-bp-sells-its-stake-in-kovykta-gas-field.html.

55. Gazprom's formal monopoly on export was introduced in a 2006 law governing gas exports. Balmaceda, "Russia's Central and Eastern European Energy Transit Corridor," p. 143.

56. Itoh, *Russia Looks East*, p. 34.

57. "Gazprom Grabs 20% of Sakhalin-1 Gas," *Upstream*, May 5, 2009, http://www.upstreamonline.com/live/article177547.ece.

58. "ExxonMobil Will Be Pushed to Provide Gas for Pipeline," *Moscow Times*, August 3, 2009, http://www.themoscowtimes.com/business/article/exxonmobil-will -be-pushed-to-provide-gas-for-pipeline/380054.html.

59. Gazprom, "Shtokman," http://www.gazprom.com/production/projects /deposits/shp.

60. A framework agreement on the main terms of the cooperation was signed between Gazprom and Total on July 13, 2007, and between Gazprom and Statoil-Hydro on October 25, 2007. According to the terms of the agreement, Gazprom would hold a 51 percent stake in Shtokman Development AG, leaving stakes of 25 percent for Total and 24 percent for StatoilHydro. See further "REG-TOTAL S.A. Gazprom, Total, and StatoilHydro Create Shtokman Development Company for Phase One on the Shtokman Gas Field," *Reuters*, February 21, 2008, http://www.reuters.com/article/pressRelease/idUS178328+21-Feb-2008 +BW20080221.

61. "UPDATE 1-Statoil Writes Off $336 mln Shtokman Gas Investment," *Reuters*, August 7, 2012, http://www.reuters.com/article/2012/08/07/statoil-shtokman-idUSL6E8J76LB20120807.

62. Stanley Reed, "Dudley Flees Russia in TNK-BP Shareholder Fight," *Bloomberg Businessweek*, July 24, 2008, http://www.businessweek.com/global biz/content/jul2008/gb20080724_783018.htm.

63. "BP and AAR Agree on New Management Structure for TNK-BP," *Scandinavian Oil and Gas Magazine,* October 24, 2011, http://www.scandoil.com /moxie-bm2/news/bp-and-aar-agree-on-new-management-structure-for-t.shtml.

64. "Deadline Looming for Rosneft and BP," *Moscow Times,* May 16, 2011, http://www.themoscowtimes.com/business/article/deadline-looming-for-rosneft -and-bp/436822.html.

65. Howard Amos, "BP, Rosneft in Landmark Swap," *Moscow Times,* January 17, 2011, http://www.themoscowtimes.com/business/article/bp-rosneft-in-landmark -swap/428957.html.

66. BP, "Rosneft and BP Form Global and Arctic Strategic Alliance," January 14, 2011, http://www.bp.com/en/global/corporate/press/press-releases/rosneft-and -bp-form-global-and-arctic-strategic-alliance.html.

67. Again, there may have been reason here to consider the past, notably so given that President Putin had been present also to give his blessing to the original TNK-BP deal that was concluded in London.

68. "BP's Laundering Job," *Moscow Times,* January 21, 2011, http://www.the moscowtimes.com/opinion/article/bps-laundering-job/429362.html.

69. Steve Maley, "Rep. Ed Markey (D) on the BP/Russia Deal," *RedState,* January 17, 2011, http://www.redstate.com/vladimir/2011/01/17/rep-ed-markey-d -on-the-bprussia-deal.

70. Sam Barden, "Sam's Exchange: BP-Rosneft—A Game of Political Chess," *RIA Novosti,* January 19, 2011, http://en.rian.ru/columnists/20110119/162205858 .html.

71. Anatoly Medetsky, "Billionaires Take BP Deal to Court," *Moscow Times,* January 28, 2011, http://www.themoscowtimes.com/business/article/billionaires -take-bp-deal-to-court/429896.html.

72. "BP Defeat Puts Arctic Back on Market," *Moscow Times,* May 19, 2011, http://www.themoscowtimes.com/business/article/bp-defeat-puts-arctic-back-on -market/437074.html.

73. Andrew E. Kramer, "Next Leader for BP Meets Russian Officials in Moscow," *New York Times,* August 4, 2010, http://www.nytimes.com/2010/08/05 /business/05dudley.html?_r=0.

74. Roland Oliphant, "$61 Billion Deal Makes Rosneft the Largest Publicly Traded Oil Firm," *Moscow Times,* October 23, 2012, http://www.themoscow times.com/business/article/61-billion-deal-makes-rosneft-the-largest-publicly -traded-oil-firm/470147.html.

75. Ahrari, *The New Great Game in Muslim Central Asia;* and Kleveman, *The New Great Game.* For an early media reference to the notion of a new great game, see "The New Great Game in Asia," *New York Times,* January 2, 1996, http://www .nytimes.com/1996/01/02/opinion/the-new-great-game-in-asia.html.

76. Hill, *Energy Empire,* p. i. See also Hill, "Russia: The 21st Century's Energy Superpower?"; Baev, "Russia Aspires to the Status of 'Energy Superpower'"; Saivetz, "Russia: An Energy Superpower?"; and Goldman, *Petrostate.*

77. This background account is drawn from Stern, *The Future of Russian Gas,* pp. 72–79. See also Pirani, "Turkmenistan: An Exporter in Transition."

78. "Turkmenistan Opens New Iran Gas Pipeline," *BBC News,* January 6, 2010, http://news.bbc.co.uk/2/hi/8443787.stm.

79. Igor Torbakov, "Russian-Turkmen Pacts Mark Strategic Shift for Moscow in Central Asia," *Eurasianet,* April 14, 2003, http://www.eurasianet.org/departments /insight/articles/eav041503.shtml.

80. Ibid.

81. Stephen Blank, "Turkmenbashi in Beijing: A Pipeline Dream," *Eurasianet,* April 9, 2006, http://www.eurasianet.org/departments/business/articles/041006a .shtml.

82. "Turkmenistan Opens New Iran Gas Pipeline."

83. "Turkmenistan: Playing the Energy Export Field," *Eurasianet,* March 16, 2008, http://www.eurasianet.org/departments/insight/articles/eav031708f.shtml.

84. "Turkmenistan: Potential 'Super-Giant' Emerges on Energy Scene," *Eurasianet,* November 12, 2006, http://www.eurasianet.org/departments/insight /articles/eav111306b_pr.shtml.

85. See further Blank, "Turkmenistan and Central Asia After Niyazov."

86. The core of the deal was to expand a spur of a the Central Asia–Center (CAC) gas pipeline, a Soviet-era pipeline network linking Turkmenistan and Russia, to a total annual capacity of 44 billion cubic meters. Kazakhstan was involved because the new pipe would cross its territory, and Uzbekistan was involved because it was to be linked to the pipe via a connector. The existing route, known as the CAC-3, was capable of handling only minor volumes. Following the suggested expansion, by 2012 it was to have a capacity of 20 billion cubic meters. With all these works completed, including plans for refurbishing two additional lines, Russia would be able to almost double its imports of Central Asian gas to roughly 90 billion cubic meters, up from about 50 billion cubic meters. See "Russia Registers Victory in Caspian Basin Energy Game," *Eurasianet,* May 13, 2007, http://en .wikipedia.org/wiki/Central_Asia-Center_gas_pipeline_system; "Russia Celebrates Its Central Asian Energy Coup," *Eurasianet,* May 15, 2007, http://www.eurasianet .org/departments/insight/articles/eav051407a.shtml; and Sergei Blagov, "Russia Celebrates Its Central Asian Energy Coup," *Eurasianet,* May 15, 2007, http://www .eurasianet.org/departments/insight/articles/eav051607.shtml.

87. Eurogas, *Eurogas Statistical Report 2011,* p. 8.

88. Nies, *Oil and Gas Delivery to Europe,* pp. 90–93.

89. "Gazprom Seals $2.5bn Nigeria Deal," *BBC News,* June 25, 2009, http://news.bbc.co.uk/2/hi/8118721.stm.

90. Nies, *Oil and Gas Delivery to Europe,* p. 92.

91. Smith Stegen, "Deconstructing the 'Energy Weapon.'"

92. Nies, *Oil and Gas Delivery to Europe,* p. 70.

93. Offshore Technology, "Blue Stream Natural Gas Pipeline," http://www .offshore-technology.com/projects/blue_stream. See also Gazprom, "Blue Stream," http://gazprom.com/production/projects/pipelines/blue-stream.

94. Offshore Technology, "Blue Stream Natural Gas Pipeline."

95. Mevlut Katik, "Blue Stream Pipeline's Future in Doubt amid Russian-Turkish Pricing Dispute," *Eurasianet,* June 1, 2003, http://www.eurasianet.org /departments/business/articles/eav060203a.shtml.

96. Gazprom, "South Stream," http://www.gazprom.com/production/projects /pipelines/south-stream.

97. Socor, "Sochi Agreements and Aftermath Deflate South Stream Hype."

98. For a broad overview, see Godzimirski, "The Northern Dimension of Russian Gas Strategy."

99. Nies, *Oil and Gas Delivery to Europe,* p. 19.

100. Hydrocarbons Technology, "Nord Stream Gas Pipeline (NSGP), Russia-Germany," http://www.hydrocarbons-technology.com/projects/negp.

101. Gazprom, "Nord Stream," http://www.gazprom.com/production/projects /pipelines/nord-stream.

102. Nord Stream, "The Pipeline," http://www.nord-stream.com/pipeline.

103. Ahto Lobjakas, "Reports Suggest Danish PM Front-Runner for NATO Seat," *Radio Free Europe/Radio Liberty,* March 10, 2009, http://www.rferl.org /content/Reports_Suggest_Danish_PM_FrontRunner_For_NATO_Seat/1507459 .html. See also Ariel Cohen, "The North European Gas Pipeline Threatens Europe's Energy Security," October 26, 2006, http://www.heritage.org/research/Europe /bg1980.cfm.

104. See further Larsson, *Nord Stream, Sweden, and Baltic Sea Security.*

105. Support for this interpretation, which was widely rumored at the time, is provided by an interdepartmental strategy document that was leaked to Sweden's national public television station. See "Hemligt dokument säger nej till gasledning," *SVT Nyheter,* December 7, 2006, http://svt.se/2.53332/1.717462/hemligt_dokument _sager_nej_till_gasledning.

106. Nord Stream, "Sweden and Finland Grant Permits to Nord Stream," November 5, 2005, http://www.nord-stream.com/press-info/press-releases/sweden -and-finland-grant-permits-to-nord-stream-255.

107. "Second Line of Nord Stream Goes Into Commercial Operation," *ITAR-TASS,* October 8, 2012, http://en.itar-tass.com/archive/683257.

108. "Nord Stream Studies Two More Pipelines," *United Press International,* May 14, 2011, http://www.upi.com/Business_News/Energy-Resources/2012/05/14 /Nord-Stream-studies-two-more-pipelines/UPI-97361336991400.

109. Torbakov, "Europe Rejects Gazprom's Ultimatum."

5

Gazprom and
the Peculiarities of Gas

The story of Russian energy has essentially two different sides, one relating to oil and the other to natural gas. This may seem trivial to note. Thus far the book has implicitly treated the Russian energy complex as a whole. This chapter, however, takes a step further. In any discussion of the influence of hydrocarbons on Russian development, it is essential that a line be drawn between the respective cases of oil and gas. There are good reasons for this, reasons that go to the heart of differences in the formulation of strategies for economic and political gain and that consequently shed light on the prospects for performance.

In his magnum opus about Russian oil, Thane Gustafson sets out by noting that in terms of energy content, Russia produces about as much gas as oil, about 500 million tons of oil equivalent each year. Importantly, however, while Russia exports three-quarters of its oil output, it consumes nearly two-thirds of its gas at home, and the latter at regulated low prices. Exports of oil consequently generate about four times the revenue earned from exports of gas: "Thus, without much exaggeration, one could say there is a division of roles: oil pays the bills abroad, while gas subsidizes the economy at home."[1]

What Gustafson refers to as a division of roles will be shown in this chapter to go far beyond matters of trade and fiscal policy. The two sides of the Russian energy story have been separated also by differences in approach to foreign policy, to privatization, and to the scope for foreign involvement. Perhaps most important, they have been marked by a distinct lack of cooperation in formulating strategies for common gain. In looking more closely at the peculiarities of Russian gas, I argue that the root cause of these differences rests in the specific nature of gas transport requirements.

While oil may be transported in a variety of ways, including pipeline, rail, and indeed road, gas predominantly requires pipelines. Although technology has been made available that allows gas to be liquefied and transported on special-purpose LNG tankers, this requires heavy investment and to date has been seriously developed only by countries like Indonesia, Malaysia, Algeria, and especially Qatar. (Appendix 4 provides detail on the development of liquefied natural gas from 2000 onward.) Developments on the Sakhalin continental shelf have shown that Russia will eventually gain a presence in this market as well, but this is still in its early stages. Consequently, the country remains dependent on fixed pipeline grids.

The key feature of this dependence is that a pipeline provides a firm link between seller and buyer, sometimes known as an "umbilical cord of steel," that makes it difficult to speak of a market price. Once a pipeline has been built, the parties are locked in and the stage is set for pricing disputes to follow. This explains why the pricing of Russian gas exports has become so heavily politicized. But the practice of signing long-term contracts for piped gas also explains why it is movement in the price of oil that has been the most immediate cause of fluctuations in export earnings. In the Russian case, the prices for piped gas have tended to be linked to movements in the price of oil, with a lag of six to nine months.

In a broader perspective, we may note that control over pipeline assets had a fundamental impact also on the different ways in which the respective oil and gas industries developed in the wake of the collapse of the Soviet Union. As the oil industry was broken up and privatized, it attracted a great deal of involvement by foreign energy companies, ranging from the major global companies to specialized service companies. The gas industry in contrast remained monolithic and beyond the reach of foreign interests. Dressed in new corporate garb, as RAO Gazprom, it would maintain an essential continuity with the old Soviet Ministry of Gas.

Of importance here to the very special role that would be played by Gazprom in the Kremlin's ambition to assemble a Russian energy powerhouse is the natural gas giant's control over pipelines. This arguably has been the key factor in maintaining the company's dominant role as national producer, in blocking expansion by major foreign energy companies, and indeed in blocking ambitions by oil companies to exploit the associated gas that is often found together with deposits of oil. A few stylized facts will serve to bring home the overall importance of Gazprom.

The first relates to its sheer size. Accounting for 18 percent of global reserves and 14 percent of global production as of 2012, Gazprom has an obvious place in any discussion of the global importance of natural gas. On the domestic scene, moreover, its role is paramount. Accounting for 72 percent of Russia's total domestic reserves and 74 percent of total domestic production, Gazprom caters to an overwhelming share of domestic final energy use.[2]

Over and above its role as supplier of gas for industry, and for power generation, where gas is a key fuel, the company has also made deliberate efforts to increase the use of natural gas in the household sector. Known as gasification, this was a key element already of Soviet urbanization and modernization strategy. Entailing the construction of new transmission and distribution networks to make pipeline gas available in new geographical areas, this has remained a priority. During the financially good years of 2005 to 2009, Gazprom invested 90 billion rubles in the gasification of new regions. Consequently, the proportion of households that received pipeline gas rose from 54.2 to 63.2 percent.[3]

Considering that the company has an inherited de facto monopoly on the country's gas pipeline grid, and a newly introduced legal monopoly on exports of natural gas, its role is highlighted even further. In short, even if Gazprom had been a purely commercial operation, run for the financial benefit of its shareholders, which has clearly not been the case, it would still have been a very special kind of operation. Gazprom in consequence simply cannot be viewed in isolation, either from domestic politics or from foreign energy security concerns.

What makes the whole set of games that have been played around Russian energy resources so opaque, and so intriguing, is that it has been so hard to draw a line between the commercial interests of Gazprom and the political interests of the Kremlin. The peak of the company's influence symptomatically coincided in time with the proliferation of worries in foreign circles about Russia's ambitions to become an energy superpower, with some even questioning which of the two—Gazprom or the Kremlin—represented the true center of power in the Russian Federation. Until the onset of the global financial crisis, the company enjoyed such a degree of political protection, and of preferential treatment in fiscal matters, that it could be viewed as an integral part of the Kremlin administration. But that was not to last.

By the time that Vladimir Putin returned to the Kremlin, to reclaim his formal role as president of the Russian Federation, the fortunes of Gazprom were in decline. Previous political protection was eroding. Independent producers were encroaching on the company's turf. Fiscal preferences were being trimmed, and the attitude from EU regulators was hardening. Still, important legacies remain that go beyond the specific role of Gazprom in Russian energy policy, and in the Kremlin's alleged ambition to build an energy superpower. Most important, the case sheds important further light on the role of multiple and at times conflicting agendas.

As discussed in Chapter 1, Markku Kivinen suggests that what has been good for Gazprom may not by necessity have been good also for Russia. Here we may add Margarita Balmaceda's well-documented claim that conventional accounts of a contrast between purely commercial interests and alleged Russian "energy imperialism" fail to account for "agency and policy differentiation among the recipients of Russian energy, and indeed for differentiation between actors in Russia itself."[4] In short, behind a seemingly straightforward conflict between commercial interests in maximizing profits and political interests in using energy to project power over neighboring countries are hosts of conflicting private and bureaucratic interests that have impacted negatively on investment strategies and project selection.

This chapter provides background for discussion of the reasons behind these developments. It outlines how Gazprom was created, how it was abused under Yeltsin, how it received a new but hardly reformed management under Putin, how its relations to foreign customers came to be marked by the involvement of shady intermediaries, and how the company was affected by the global financial crisis. But first, a few words about the emergence of a modern Russian gas industry.

The Emergence of Russian Gas

The history of Russian gas, compared to that of oil, is of much more recent origin. According to Jonathan Stern, an authority on this matter, the "birth of the modern Russian natural gas industry is generally held to be the building of the first long distance (845 km) natural gas pipeline (between Saratov and Moscow) commissioned in 1946."[5]

The agency that was tasked with this construction, Glavgaztopprom, had been introduced in 1943, as a directorate within the Council of People's Commissars. Under Nikita Khrushchev, the nascent gas industry was broken up and placed under the authority of regional economic councils, the *sovnarkhozy*. As part of the "reset" that followed Khrushchev's ouster, the Soviet Ministry of the Gas Industry was introduced in 1965.[6]

Although early discoveries of major gas deposits had been made already in the 1950s and 1960s, the Soviet leadership had been slow in realizing the extent of these prospects. It was only with the launch of a typically Soviet "gas campaign" in 1980 that the industry really took off, and that the Soviet economy consequently also became truly addicted to energy.

Several factors combined to generate highly favorable conditions during the early phase of exploration. Most important, resources could be focused on a limited number of supergiant fields. Each had a small number of production wells, and all had their main deposits at fairly shallow depths. In stark contrast, moreover, to the case of Kazakh gas, which has a high content of sulphur, West Siberian gas has a low content of "aggressive components." At least initially, it also had sufficient natural pressure to do without compressor stations at the first sections of transport pipelines. All of this helped sustain initially impressive rates of output.[7]

As in the case of oil, however, and even more so, the low-hanging fruit has now been plucked. The need to engage in intensified exploration may be reflected in the fact that more than 90 percent of Gazprom's production has been sustained by only six fields.[8] With the exception of Orenburg in southern Russia, the core of the resource base has remained firmly located in Western Siberia. It consists mainly of three supergiant fields that were discovered in the middle to late 1960s, and that peaked early on—Medvezhe in 1983, Urengoi in 1987, and Yamburg in 1994. (Orenburg was discovered in 1970 and peaked in 1985.) Although the increasing depletion of the first three supergiants was temporarily offset by the discovery, in 2001, of the supergiant Zapolarnyi field, this offset, in turn, peaked in 2005.[9] Looking toward the future, new fields will have to be developed in remote frontier regions that pose vastly greater challenges.

The needs for more complex technology have already been demonstrated on the Sakhalin continental shelf, where highly contentious participation by major foreign oil companies was deemed essential in order to master the challenges involved in offshore drilling under Arctic conditions. The supergiant Shtokman field offers great promise, but again under Arctic and offshore conditions that are beyond the current technological capabilities of Gazprom. Fields on the Yamal peninsula have competed with Shtokman for attention and resource allocation, but here as well, highly promising future rewards will have to be bought at the expense of major investment in technology as well as infrastructure.[10]

A particularly important dimension of the quest to extract West Siberian gas has been related to the epic construction of major transport pipelines. While this task was facilitated by the geographical concentration of the main fields, pipelines still had to be built over great distances, traversing areas of very rough terrain. Most of Western Siberia is made up of huge swamps that freeze in winter and by spring become impassable.

Gazprom undertook and successfully completed the construction of a massive grid of pipelines, the backbone of which consists of a set of wide-diameter (56-inch) high-pressure trunk lines. According to the company's website, the Unified Gas Supply System (UGSS), the world's largest gas transmission system and a Gazprom monopoly, consists of an impressive 159,500 kilometers of trunk lines and branches. The UGSS has 219 pipeline compressor stations, with a capacity of 42 million kilowatts, and a total of twenty-five underground storage facilities. The average transmission distance within the country is 2,901 kilometers, extending to 3,322 kilometers for export.[11]

It should be recognized that there is unquestionable achievement involved here. Yet there is also a Soviet legacy of shoddy production and of neglected maintenance that is coming back to haunt the present-day Gazprom management. Most of the system was built in the 1970s. It was accomplished under severe time pressure and with Soviet production standards that included poor-quality corrosion protection and compressor stations that would prove to have low levels of efficiency and reliability. By 2008, the share of the pipeline system that was more than twenty years old had increased to 67 percent, up from 47 percent in 2003. Almost one-quarter of the system was more than thirty-three years old and approaching the end of its design life.[12] The implied lack of needed investment underscores the importance of taking a closer look at the financial health of the company, which presents a rather sordid picture.

In further contrast to the case of oil, which was marked by the emergence of a number of competing private oil-producing companies, with the pipeline assets placed in a separate state monopoly called Transneft, the integrity of the former Soviet Ministry of Gas would remain intact. Over and above its critically important control over the UGSS, Gazprom also succeeded in retaining a command structure that is eerily similar to that of the Soviet era.

The combined absence of competition and transparency has offered great opportunities for well-positioned insiders to place their own narrow interests above those of the company, and by implication above the interests of the country as a whole. Importantly, and unfortunately, this was equally true under the respective presidencies of Boris Yeltsin and Vladimir Putin; and Dmitry Medvedev, for all his talk of modernization and the rule of law, would bring little if any positive change.

In order to understand how it was possible for a nominally private company to achieve the kind of power and influence that Gazprom long wielded over domestic as well as foreign policy, we must return to the turbulent times of the Soviet dissolution.

Our Home Is Gazprom

Toward the end of the Soviet era, the previously separate oil and gas industries were merged under one umbrella. The merger was in line with the general trend of experimentation that was associated with Mikhail Gorbachev's perestroika. The idea was that ministerial structures should retreat to a more strategic and regulatory function, allowing lower-level production associations more leeway for operational control and decisionmaking. More specifically, the reform entailed an amalgamation of the Ministry of the Gas Industry, the Ministry of the Oil Industry, and the Ministry of Petroleum Refining into a new Ministry of the Oil and Gas Industry of the Soviet Union.[13]

Given the general turbulence of the time, insiders found themselves looking at vast opportunities for personal enrichment. As already noted, in November 1991, Vagit Alekperov, who was then acting minister of oil, succeeded in carving out part of the oil industry and repackaging it as a private oil company, which he named LUKoil and placed under his own control. Important to consider here is the influence and political dexterity of two of the ultimate insiders of the time: the former head of the Ministry of Gas, Viktor Chernomyrdin, and his long-standing comrade-in-arms at the ministry, Rem Vyakhirev.[14]

Preempting what would happen to the Ministry of Oil, in August 1989 Chernomyrdin stepped up to the plate. Having served as head of the Ministry of the Gas Industry since 1985, he had only just been appointed first deputy minister in the newly amalgamated ministry. From this vantage position, he reached out and secured permission from the Soviet leadership for what amounted to a real coup. Using a newly introduced possibility to create "state concerns," he set his old ministry aside from the new, transforming it into the country's first hybrid state-corporate enterprise, under the name of Gazprom. Although 100 percent ownership of the new entity remained with the state, Chernomyrdin switched his title to chairman of the board and chief executive officer.[15]

The notion of a "state concern" was an important buzzword of the day, capturing an ambition to decentralize the economy. The great paradox of Chernomyrdin's move was that a successful ambition to retain the gas ministry as a monolith under his own control could be passed off as being in line with ambitions to decentralize. His added ambition, however, to ensure that the whole of the Soviet Ministry of Gas would remain intact, was soon to be frustrated—by the simple fact that the Soviet Union disintegrated. Gazprom would in consequence be a purely Russian "state concern."[16] Much effort would subsequently be devoted to efforts aimed at reassembling the grip of the Soviet-era ministry over gas assets across the former Soviet space and beyond.

The collapse of the Soviet Union was fateful not just in the sense that it unleashed a set of roving predators bent on reaping short-term private gain. It also brought in its wake a new Russian government that was bent on marketizing reform, in effect paving the way for the predatory ambitions of the elite. To Gazprom, this was to prove a mixed blessing.

The government's main champion in the promotion of market relations was the State Property Committee, which, among other things, advocated a breakup of Gazprom into competing joint stock companies. Its offensive peaked in November 1993, when a presidential decree called for a breakup not only of Gazprom but also of the three vertically integrated oil companies that had been established in 1992—Yukos, Surgutneftegaz, and LUKoil. In addition, it also called for a three-year ban on production and refining companies holding shares in trunk-line companies.[17] The very same demands would be subsequently repeated in the aforementioned ambitions by the European Union to achieve a breakup of Gazprom and an "unbundling" of pipeline assets.[18] All would be to little avail. Gazprom was protected.

The perhaps unexpected savior in the early stage was Yegor Gaidar, who would remain insistent that breaking up Gazprom was not in Russia's best interest.[19] More sustained protection would then be provided by Vladimir Putin. At an October 2003 meeting with German chancellor Gerhard Schröder, held in the Russian city of Yekaterinburg, President Putin made it very clear who was calling the tune: "The gas pipeline system is the creation of the Soviet Union. We intend to retain state control over the gas transportation system and over Gazprom. We will not divide Gazprom. And the European Commission should not have any illusions. In the gas sector, they will have to deal with the [Russian] state."[20]

The main line of argument from Gazprom's side was that technological and other reasons called for the integrity of the company to be maintained. In this quest, it was successful. Two presidential decrees issued in June 1992 established, respectively, that the Unified Gas Supply System should remain exclusive federal property and that it was vital for the national economy to maintain a rapid development of the gas industry. Hidden in the latter decree was a provision that gave Gazprom rights, without tender or competition, both to oil and gas fields it was already working and to promising fields not yet opened. By 1995, Gazprom would have secured licenses for a total of eighty-one fields, comprising 68.5 percent of the country's total proven reserves.[21] For the lucky few who were well connected, the value of protection from the Kremlin seemed hard indeed to overstate.

In May 1992, President Boris Yeltsin had yielded to demands that the young reform economists in his government must be joined by someone senior, with more experience. Following his subsequent appointment of Chernomyrdin as deputy prime minister, he allowed the stewardship of Gazprom to be passed to Rem Vyakhirev, who was appointed both chairman and chief executive officer. The Chernomyrdin-Vyakhirev tandem would not be shaken, however. On the contrary. The crowning achievement of their partnership was marked in November 1992, when Yeltsin issued a presidential decree transforming the "state concern" Gazprom into an independent and private joint stock company. Importantly, the decree also declared that Gazprom would assume full ownership of the UGSS, including responsibilities ranging from research and development to production and infrastructure, as well as domestic "gasification" and exports.[22]

In December 1992, Chernomyrdin succeeded Yegor Gaidar as prime minister, a post he would retain until March 1998. With this move, Gazprom had been rendered immune to any form of outside attempts at calling for transparency and accountability. The implications would be far-reaching indeed.

When sales of shares in the new joint stock company began in February 1993, the process proceeded according to stipulations laid out in the founding decree. The Russian Federation should hold a minimum of 40 percent of the shares. A further minimum of 15 percent was to be sold to insiders (workers and management) at preferential prices, and a minimum of 20 percent offered to the population in exchange for privatization vouchers.

As was the case in most other privatization deals at the time, the understanding of "preferential prices" would be very kind to insiders. In late 1992, Gazprom was officially valued at $298 million. This may be compared to a market value that was estimated in Western sources as ranging from $250 billion to $740 billion.[23] Privatization proceeded based on the lower figure—meaning, at a mere thousandth of the estimated market value. The windfall gain that was thus passed on to the company's shareholders was truly remarkable.

Equally remarkable was the way in which Gazprom's management team went about ensuring that public sales of shares would not lead to a loss of control over the company. The first step was to disregard the insistence of the State Property Committee that sales to the general public in exchange for privatization vouchers should take place at open auctions. By relying on closed auctions only, the company could decide who would be allowed to participate and thus also determine the initial distribution of shares. Via such essentially rigged auctions, 33.9 percent of the shares were sold to physical persons residing in regions that were home to Gazprom's main operations. By the spring of 1995 the company would have more than 1 million shareholders. In a further step to ensure that this wide dispersion of shares would not lead to emerging threats against insider control, a set of restrictive rules were established regarding trade in the company's shares on secondary markets, forcing prospective sellers to give management first right of purchase.[24]

With one-third of company shares having thus been safely distributed among the general public, the rest would be clear sailing. Gazprom bought 10 percent of its own shares. A further 15 percent were sold to its employees, and of the 40 percent stake that was retained by the state, 35 percent was assigned to Vyakhirev by proxy. With the latter step in particular, the package as a whole had been neatly sewn together. Insider control over the operation was secured from the very outset.

All that remained now was to ensure that no threat could emanate from foreign investors. This was accomplished via a presidential decree in 1997 that capped foreign ownership of Gazprom shares at 20 percent, and limited this to American depositary shares traded in London and New York.[25]

The first American depositary shares in Gazprom had been issued in 1996, and they would be a constant source of irritation. Quickly dubbed by the financial community as a "ring fence," the system meant that American depositary shares were traded at prices that were substantially higher than for domestically traded shares. But also, since American depositary shares accounted for no more than 3 percent of the nonlocal traded free float, interested foreign investors were tempted to buy shares via Russian brokerages that bought on their own accounts. It has been suggested that as much as 10 percent of Gazprom shares may have been owned by foreign entities, through "gray schemes" that were tolerated by the Russian government and Gazprom.[26] The system consequently had the dual effect of preventing transparency regarding the ownership structure and of acting as a drag on the company's degree of capitalization.[27]

The so-called ring fence would remain in place until the end of 2005. The main reason why this effective market separation could remain in force for so long was linked to the perceived need of retaining control. The Kremlin did realize that the setup resulted in numerous anomalies, but also feared what might happen were it to be abolished without first securing state control. The latter might of course also be interpreted as an ambition to maintain secure control by key political insiders.

What eventually made the lifting of the ring fence possible was a consolidation of state ownership in the energy sector. The core feature was a purchase by the state, in June 2005, of 10.7 percent of Gazprom stock, bringing state ownership of shares in the company to 51 percent. The context of the deal was complex, involving a sale of the stock by a Gazprom subsidiary to the state-owned company Rosneftegaz, which was created to hold the state's 100 percent stake in the oil company Rosneft. Rosneftegaz paid $7.2 billion. The money was raised from banks, and subsequently repaid by floating shares in Rosneft.[28] As previously mentioned, the broader ambition had been to create a merged Gazprom-Rosneft behemoth under Kremlin control. Although nothing would come of this, the operation did result in a unified market and in soaring Gazprom share prices.

Before leaving the question of Gazprom ownership, it is noteworthy to consider the one foreign company that did actively pursue options to acquire Gazprom stock. This was German company Ruhrgaz (later E.ON), which eventually also would end up as partner with Gazprom in the Nord Stream project to build a gas pipeline from Russia to Germany. In December 1998, Ruhrgaz was allowed to purchase 2.5 percent of Gazprom stock at $660 million, and in May 1999 it acquired a further 1 percent at $200 million. It also ended up controlling an additional 1.5 percent via Gerogaz, a joint venture with Gazprom.[29] This, however, was to remain a very special case, reflecting the close links between Gazprom and Ruhrgaz/E.ON.

And, it was not to last. In December 2010, E.ON sold its Gazprom shares for €3.4 billion.[30]

Ruled over by the Chernomyrdin-Vyakhirev tandem, Gazprom was transformed into a seemingly inexhaustible source of both financial and political gain for its masters. In the run-up to the 1995 elections to the Russian Duma, Prime Minister Chernomyrdin set up his own political party, named Nash dom Rossiya (Our Home Is Russia). Symptomatically, Russian street humor would simply refer to it as Nash dom Gazprom (Our Home Is Gazprom). Although the bid was not successful, leaving the party with no more than 10 percent of the vote, it did reflect the political importance of Gazprom as a source of funding.

Exactly what went on behind the scenes during the turbulent 1990s has not been possible to establish, but the circumstantial evidence has been striking indeed. By far the most controversial part of the story concerns persistent allegations that Chernomyrdin made a personal fortune via the process of privatization. Although he denied having owned any stock in the company while serving in the government, it was interesting to note that in 1998 *Forbes* magazine included him on its list of the world's 200 richest billionaires.[31] Marshall Goldman also emphasizes how several of the spin-offs and subsidiaries of Gazprom came to resemble a pure Chernomyrdin-Vyakhirev family business, with children and relatives appearing as owners and managers.[32]

An important high-level source of critique against alleged wrongdoings at Gazprom was Boris Nemtsov, who served first as a highly successful mayor of Nizhnyi Novgorod and then as first deputy prime minister under Chernomyrdin. According to him, Gazprom's management team engaged in ploys of asset-stripping and diversion of holdings that involved a maze of some 300 subsidiary companies, including banks.[33] This alleged looting of state property could take place despite the fact that the state itself owned 40 percent of Gazprom shares.

Another outspoken critic of such practices was Boris Fedorov, who had served as minister of finance and as head of the Russian tax service. Having moved to the United Financial Group, a Moscow brokerage firm, he managed to mobilize sufficient shares to claim a seat on the Gazprom board of directors. His allegation was that executives succeeded for almost a decade in stripping Gazprom of $2 billion a year. In a similar vein, William Browder, who managed by far the largest foreign hedge fund in Russia, lists seven dubious transactions that resulted in the loss of about 10 percent of Gazprom's total natural gas reserves, worth about $5.5 billion.[34]

One of the most daring, albeit eventually unsuccessful scams aimed at personal enrichment was devised already in 1993, when a group of core insiders were issued options to purchase 30 percent of the government's share of Gazprom stock—at cheap preinflation face value. Following heavy criticism from Nemtsov, the scam was finally halted by Yeltsin in December 1997.[35] Recalling the market separation that was produced by the "ring fence," it is also notable that in early 2001 a group of insiders were allowed to profit from a conversion of 1.4 percent of domestically traded shares into American depositary shares that traded at double value. Attempts by minority shareholders to learn the identity of the lucky few would not be successful.[36]

While there has been no shortage of criticism against what was happening at Gazprom, there have also been more sympathetic voices. One is Jonathan Stern, who argues that the case of Gazprom is not really all that different from what has been happening in similar energy utilities around the world. Stern not only draws an explicit parallel between alleged misdeeds at Gazprom and the various forms of creative corporate behavior that caused the US energy giant Enron to collapse, but also, and more importantly, emphasizes that many of the accusations that have been leveled against Gazprom "consist of newspaper reportage or simple assertions with little attempt at verification."[37]

The parallel between Gazprom and Enron may come across as a bit of overstretch, above all so given the very different political roles played by the respective energy giants. But the point about anecdotal and circumstantial evidence is certainly valid. For the purpose at hand, however, to exactly what extent various predators really did succeed in fleecing Gazprom, and whether a case really could have been built against them, is beside the point. What we are left with is a sordid track record of poor output performance, and the fact that the company's protectors did not take criticism lightly. The latter in particular was brought home following Chernomyrdin's dismissal in March 1998.

The alleged reason for Boris Yeltsin to dismiss the government as a whole was that he had begun to fear that his prime minister harbored unacceptable ambitions to succeed his ailing patron as president. Be this as it may, to Chernomyrdin there was some compensation involved. He was first appointed government representative on the Gazprom board of directors, and in mid-1999 he was voted chairman of the board.[38] To Vyakhirev, however, the removal of his former boss from the government implied increased exposure. When Yeltsin in turn also left office, it was apparent that the rules of the game were about to change.

The way in which Gazprom had been run had produced a mounting groundswell of anger, both over asset-stripping and over the general culture of waste and extravagance that formed part of Gazprom's corporate culture. The company's lavish Moscow headquarters, built at a cost of $150 million, was a case in point.[39] Although Fedorov was certainly not alone in feeling a sense of outrage, he was a leading voice in calls for an independent auditor to be called in, and for Vyakhirev to be relieved of his duty before his contract expired.

The latter in particular may well have been the reason behind subsequent attempts to extract vengeance. As detailed by Goldman, Fedorov was subjected to attacks that ranged from a series of venomous articles in the press to threats of incarceration, visits by organized crime figures, and eventually even the poisoning of his dog, all of which caused him to seriously fear for his life.[40] Suddenly, however, it all came to an abrupt end. As the saying goes, there was a new sheriff in town.

Under New Management

When power over the Kremlin was transferred to Vladimir Putin, who was duly elected president in March 2000, control over Gazprom was logically placed high on the agenda of the new regime. Action, moreover, was both swift and effective. In June 2000, Chernomyrdin was removed from his post as chairman of the board, and Dmitry Medvedev was inserted in his place. In May of the following year, Vyakhirev was in turn removed as chief executive officer and replaced by Aleksei Miller. Both of the new appointments were "friends of Putin," having worked alongside him in the St. Petersburg mayor's office. As a reflection of the dignity of these appointments, in March 2008 Medvedev would in turn be (s)elected president of the Russian Federation.

With a simple stroke of his KGB pen, Putin had thus succeeded where Fedorov and others had failed—in breaking the long-standing cronyism of Gazprom's senior management. At first, it did look as though the company was now on the high road to recovery. Three reasons combined to provide this impression. First and foremost was the rise in global oil prices. As this gradually translated also into a rise in gas prices, it boosted the company's bottom line.

Second was the decision to undertake a phased increase in domestic prices for gas. During the 1990s, Gazprom had suffered heavy losses from being required to supply gas to domestic users at prices that did not cover costs, and from being barred from responding to nonpayment of bills by cutting off further deliveries. According to the company's own calculations, total losses from domestic sales from 1999 to 2003 amounted to $25 billion. Breakeven would not be achieved until 2005.[41]

The third reason to believe that Gazprom was indeed on the mend was also the most spectacular. Protected by Putin, the new management embarked on a highly successful campaign of clawing back what had been spun off from the company under Yeltsin.[42] Many of these deals had involved the independent gas-trading company Itera. One of the first steps taken by Aleksei Miller was to repurchase Purgaz, a gas-producing company that had supplied 70 percent of Itera's own output.[43] Soon thereafter, Gazprom also retook control from Itera over Severneftegazprom, the license holder of the South Russkoe gas field, which would be chosen as the source of gas for the Nord Stream pipeline.[44] Other major deals included the return to Gazprom of control over the petrochemicals giant Sibur, a feat that included a symbolic arrest of the company's chairman, Yakov Goldovsky, in Miller's office lobby (Goldovsky subsequently fled the country).[45] And we must not forget the coercive repurchase of shares in Stroytransgaz, a giant engineering contractor that had been at the focus of asset redistribution schemes involving friends and relatives of Chernomyrdin and Vyakhirev.[46]

For all their successes in such schemes of asset repossession, the new management team would prove to be far less capable as managers of a gas company. Those who may have thought that breaking the power of the Yeltsin-Chernomyrdin-Vyakhirev triangle over Gazprom operations would lead to the introduction of transparency, sound business operations, and greater efficiency in gas production would wake up to a very different reality. Looking back at developments during the first two terms of the Putin presidency, we may conclude that nothing much changed—aside from the guards and the sheer size of the rents. The main purpose of the operation had clearly not been to improve Gazprom's performance, but merely to achieve asset redistribution.

By far the most detailed indictment of how the fleecing of Gazprom continued, and even intensified, after Yeltsin had left the Kremlin has been produced by Boris Nemtsov, in association with Vladimir Milov. Both may claim deep inside knowledge, the former from his time as first deputy prime minister in 1997–1998 and the latter from having served as deputy minister of energy in 2002. According to their estimate, based on a detailed listing of various shady deals, the total value of assets shifted out of Gazprom control on Putin's watch amounted to no less than $60 billion, to which could be added $20 billion in cash losses sustained via transfer pricing schemes and overvalued acquisitions.[47]

By the time that Putin handed over the presidency to Dmitry Medvedev, for temporary keeping, Gazprom would consequently be in seriously bad shape. The new management team that was inserted by Putin and led by Medvedev had failed to safeguard the interests of the company and by implication, given its dominant position in the Russian economy, also of the Russian people at large. The most damning accusation maintains that during the good years of growing demand and high energy prices, Gazprom had seriously neglected investment in its core business—that of gas extraction. During the first two terms of the Putin presidency, companies in the mainly privatized oil sector secured a more than 50 percent increase in output. Over the same period, Gazprom succeeded in increasing its output by no more than 7.4 percent, from 512 billion cubic meters in 2001 to 549.7 billion cubic meters in 2008.[48] Given the important role that was so obviously assigned to the company, as the hard core of the Russian energy powerhouse, its dismal output performance is of quite some importance. The causes, moreover, have a lot to do with conflicting agendas and with the mode of governance that flows from the Kremlin.

Looking toward the future, it might seem that despite its poor output performance, Gazprom remains in good shape, with eighty years of proven gas reserves at current extraction levels, as commonly maintained. A closer look, however, calls for qualification. First, it should be recognized that Russian estimates of reserves in the ground include deposits that are not yet being worked. According to Stern, once giant new discoveries such as Shtokman and Yamal have been excluded, the remaining life span of reserves at current levels of extraction is reduced to thirty-eight years according to Russian estimates, and to a mere twenty-four years according to stricter international estimates.[49]

To this may be added that traditional fields—such as Urengoi and Yamburg—that have been worked since the 1980s are being depleted, and that bringing the new fields into production will require heavy investment in infrastructure, as well as the acquisition of more advanced technology. It is against this background that one cannot take lightly the range of accusations of predatory management that have been aimed at Gazprom. In fact, Nemtsov and Milov claim that the value lost due to various asset-stripping machinations is, in their estimation, "approximately equal to the cost of bringing the Shtokman, Bovanenkovo and a number of other major new gas fields into production."[50]

The numbers they cite in support of this claim are striking indeed. Over the period 2001–2007, with energy prices at record levels, Gazprom invested just over $27 billion in developing gas extraction, which really should have been its main priority. Meanwhile, a total of $44.6 billion was spent on acquisitions, two-thirds of which were outside the gas business.[51] Included here were assets in the oil industry (Sibneft and Tomskneft) and in the power-generation industry (RAO Unified Energy System and Mosenergo), but also assets wholly outside the energy field, ranging from media (Gazprom-Media) and banking (Gazprombank) to various recreation facilities across the country.[52]

That Gazprom's management had other objectives in mind than those of efficient gas extraction is clearly reflected in the fact that between 2003 and 2007 the company's operating costs (excluding taxes) rose from $4.90 to $14.80 per barrel of oil equivalent. Included here were an increase in employment, from 391,000 to 445,000 personnel, and a disproportionate increase in total cost of wages, from $3.7 billion to $9.7 billion. Despite enjoying substantial fiscal favors from the government, Gazprom consequently was falling ever deeper into debt. When Putin was first elected president, in 2000, the company owed $13.5 billion. By the end of 2007, on the eve of the global financial crisis, it ominously owed $61.6 billion, corresponding to two-thirds of its income.[53]

Of the many reasons that combined to produce this sorry outcome, the pride of place must go to the slew of schemes that served to dilute value and strip assets. Prominent on the latter count is the string of shady intermediaries involved in transacting gas supplies from the Caspian Basin via Ukraine and on to Europe. Let us turn now to look in more detail at these.

The Role of Intermediaries

Until 1994, all Russian gas trade with countries within the Commonwealth of Independent States (CIS) was handled exclusively by Gazprom. Reflecting the importance of such trade, all deals made were based on long-term intergovernmental agreements that were signed by presidents or prime ministers. These agreements provided a comprehensive framework covering matters that ranged from sales, transit, prices, and tariffs to underground storage and the formation of joint ventures.[54] The breakup of the Soviet Union disrupted this arrangement, causing a fragmentation of suppliers, persistent pricing problems, and supply disruptions.

Over the period 1991–1995, Gazprom gas exports to other CIS states declined from 90 to 73.2 billion cubic meters, and by 2001 the number had dropped to a low of 39.6 billion cubic meters. By the end of the Yeltsin era, given that a large share of remaining deliveries to Ukraine, Belarus, and Moldova were made in return for transit services, Gazprom had withdrawn almost fully from actual trade with other CIS states.[55] Given the broad range of problems, political as well as financial, that so suddenly came to beset its previous monopoly position as supplier of gas, allowing intermediaries to step in may have been both wise and logical. It was, however, not a decision that was taken for reasons of business alone.

It all began with the previously mentioned Itera, founded in 1992 to trade consumer goods with Turkmenistan. Headquartered in Jacksonville, Florida, in 1994 it moved into natural gas and began dealings with Gazprom. Given the important role of gas in Turkmen exports, the initial move was quite logical. No doubt it was also supported by the fact that the company had strong connections with the president of Turkmenistan. Over the coming years, however, Itera would evolve into a small business empire of its own, expanding from the role of intermediary in trade to becoming a major independent gas producer.

One of the most controversial stages in its brief career was begun in 1997, when the company was authorized by Gazprom to take over some of the latter's output in the Yamalo-Nenets autonomous region in Siberia. This background was linked to the problems of nonpayments that marked the time. The governor of the region first agreed with Gazprom that it could pay its local taxes in kind—meaning in gas deliveries. He then sold the gas in question to Itera, which in turn resold it at a substantial profit. According to media estimates, the purchase price was in the range of $2 to $5 per thousand cubic meters, and the final sale price was between $40 and $80 per thousand cubic meters. In 2001, deals of this kind would be banned by the Federal Audit Chamber of the Duma.[56]

By the end of the Yeltsin era, Itera would have 130 subsidiaries with operations in twenty-four countries.[57] In 2000, it produced nearly 18 billion cubic meters of gas, purchased 30 billion cubic meters on commission from the Yamalo-Nenets region, and purchased an additional 35 billion cubic meters from Central Asia. In that year, it sold over 85 billion cubic meters of gas, 40 billion cubic meters of which within Russia. By 2001, it had actually bypassed Gazprom as a supplier of gas to other CIS states, delivering 50 billion cubic meters as opposed to Gazprom's 39.6.[58]

That such a seemingly insignificant start-up company could rise to such prominence, in a field so economically important and so heavily politicized, is interesting. The exact ownership of this nominally US company has not been possible to ascertain, but Marshall Goldman suggests that relatives of Gazprom managers have been among the key stockholders.[59] The main point is that from 1994 until well into the 2000s, Gazprom showed a remarkable preference for allowing its business to be conducted via front companies with short life spans and hefty earnings records. It is hard indeed to avoid suspicion that the latter have served mainly as vehicles for asset-stripping and transfer pricing schemes.

Following the replacement of the old Gazprom management team with friends of Putin, Itera was squeezed out. The simple means chosen was to withdraw access to Gazprom pipelines. Faced with near bankruptcy, the company had to accept to resell its prime assets back to Gazprom. As noted, the latter would make up the mainstay of chief executive officer Aleksei Miller's high-profile program of "asset reacquisition."

The first sign that Itera was about to reach the end of its existence arrived toward the end of 2002, when it was announced that beginning in January 2003, Gazprom would itself take over the shipment of Turkmen gas to Ukraine. Soon enough, however, it transpired that nothing much had really changed. In March, it was announced that Itera had simply been replaced by EuralTransGas (ETG), a previously unknown trading company that was registered in Hungary and said to be owned by a few Hungarian and Romanian individuals. The sudden appearance of this new entity sparked a wave of allegations of corruption and links to organized crime.[60]

ETG had been awarded a three-year contract for shipping Central Asian gas. During 2003, it carried a total of 35 billion cubic meters of Turkmen gas, as a result of which it succeeded in recording a commercial turnover of approximately $2 billion, with a net $220 million profit from sales to Ukraine.[61] For reasons that would trigger even more speculation, the saga of ETG would be short indeed. Perhaps the allegations of shady characters operating in the background proved to be too much.

Already in July 2004 it was announced that Gazprom subsidiary Gazeksport had joined with Austria's Raiffeisen Bank in forming yet another intermediary gas-trading company. The new entity was named RosUkrEnergo and given a broad mandate. In addition to being responsible for acquisition, transit, and delivery of gas from Turkmenistan, it was also tasked with maintaining and upgrading the Ukrainian pipeline system. It was designed to carry 44 billion cubic meters of gas in 2005, and 60 billion cubic meters annually starting in 2007. The contract with EuralTransGas was terminated ahead of time, at the end of 2004.[62]

The role and fate of RosUkrEnergo would turn out to be even more intriguing than those of its immediate predecessors. As part of the settlement of the January 2006 gas crisis between Russia and Ukraine, it transpired that RosUkrEnergo had been elevated from a mere transporter to assuming responsibility as the operator of all Ukrainian gas imports, not only from Central Asia but from Russia as well. In Ukraine, this was followed by the creation of yet another intermediary, UkrGazEnergo, which was given rights to distribute gas directly to industrial users. The implication was that the new company could proceed to pocket substantial profits from the financially strongest domestic consumers. Contractual obligations to supply district heating companies and residential users, who were often unable to pay their bills, were meanwhile left with the national distribution utility, Naftogaz, which in consequence would be brought close to bankruptcy.[63]

Over the coming years, the controversial role of intermediaries would be of far greater importance than the recurring pricing conflicts. Following a crisis in early 2008, it was agreed that intermediaries should be dropped—UkrGazEnergo in March and RosUkrEnergo "some months later." As part of the resolution of the 2009 gas crisis, which caused a serious deterioration in relations between Russia and the European Union, it was again agreed that RosUkrEnergo should be dropped, but this agreement was not implemented. On the contrary, the company would remain at the heart of political intrigue. In November 2011, the recently jailed former prime minister of Ukraine, Yulia Tymoshenko, filed a lawsuit at a court in New York against RosUkrEnergo and its co-owner Dmytro Firtash, alleging fraud, violation of human rights, and extortion.[64]

It is hard to dismiss suspicions that the frequent gas disputes between Russia and Ukraine have involved a broader circle than simply Russian players. Perhaps an even greater role has been played by Ukrainian domestic conflicts, particularly those between Tymoshenko and her erstwhile companion President Viktor Yushchenko. As Margarita Balmaceda puts it, even lacking insider information, "it is possible to conclude that 'someone' did not want the agreements to be fulfilled."[65]

Falling from Grace

While the times remained good, all of this could continue without anyone noticing or at least paying much attention. By the summer of 2008, just before the global financial crisis erupted, Gazprom was still the third most valuable company in the world. It had an estimated worth of some $350 billion, and was in hot pursuit of General Electric for the number one slot. But it was unable to weather the crisis, which shrank its estimated worth to $120 billion and its ranking to fortieth place.[66]

The main reasons behind this dramatic tumble were linked to the sharp economic recession in Europe, which brought falling energy demand and falling energy prices, and to the parallel surge in imports of cheaper liquefied natural gas triggered by the surge in US shale gas production. During the first quarter of 2009, Gazprom's exports of gas fell by 56 percent, compared to the same period in 2008.[67] Forced to respond with production cutbacks, the company reduced its output of gas in May 2009 by 14 percent compared to the previous month, and by 34 percent compared to May 2008.[68]

With the drop in demand, the price of gas was also falling sharply. According to a report published in the Russian newspaper *Vedomosti* on March 23, 2009, Gazprom had sold gas to Europe in 2008 at an average price of $409 per thousand cubic meters. With a projected average price for 2009 that now stood at $258 per thousand cubic meters, down from a projected $280 just weeks earlier, it was estimated that revenues would drop from $73 billion to $44 billion.[69] There was panic in the air.

Viewed against this radically different background, the two deals that had earlier been considered major triumphs for Russian energy policy suddenly began to appear instead as major liabilities. The landmark twenty-five-year deal to purchase Turkmen gas that had been signed in 2003 meant that Gazprom was locked into contracts for gas it no longer needed, thus forcing it to instead cut output from lower-cost Russian sources.

Compounding the damage, the March 2008 agreement to pay "European" prices for gas from Turkmenistan, Kazakhstan, and Uzbekistan meant that Gazprom would now also have to pay higher prices to its suppliers than it could charge to its customers. According to an agreement reached during a visit by Putin to Tashkent in September 2008, Gazprom would pay, on average, $340 per thousand cubic meters in 2009. That very same gas would sell in Ukraine at an average of about $230 per thousand cubic meters, with prices charged to consumers in Europe dropping to an average of perhaps $280.[70] The massive losses that the company was now beginning to incur, estimated by one source at $3.5 billion for 2009, could be seen as a fee to be paid for its monopoly position in the Caspian Basin.[71]

The times when the Kremlin could rely on Gazprom as a combination cash cow and foreign policy tool appeared to have ended. Acting on this impression, Russia's southern neighbors began to ratchet up their own ambitions. In the wake of the August 2008 war in Georgia, Azerbaijan stepped forward to enhance its role as energy hub for the Caspian Basin. At a November 13–14 energy summit in Baku, with Russian representatives conspicuously absent, Azerbaijan signed two intergovernmental agreements— one to supply Georgia with gas for five years, and one to allow export of 25 million tons of oil annually from Kazakhstan via Azerbaijan.[72]

While this must have been bad news indeed, both for Gazprom and for the Kremlin, there would be still worse to come. As will be detailed in Chapter 6, the brief "gas war" that erupted between Russia and Ukraine in January 2009 would provoke the European Union into a more activist policy involving threats of serious intervention against Gazprom interests. And in the midst of the financial crisis, China would move to capitalize on Russian weakness, making important inroads into both oil and gas in Eastern Siberia and in the Far East.

But the main reason to speak of a true fall from grace rested within, in the beginning erosion of protection from the top. By 2009, Putin was becoming increasingly insistent that Gazprom provide equal access for the independent producers to its gas pipelines. In 2010, he threatened that if Gazprom did not take a more proactive stance in developing its capacity to supply gas to industrial customers, third parties would be encouraged to step in. And in 2012, he would lash out against corruption at Gazprom, calling for guilty parties to be flushed out and thrown in prison.[73]

In the background, Rosneft chairman Igor Sechin was maneuvering skillfully, not only to promote Rosneft interests over those of Gazprom, but also to support non-Gazprom producers. In the words of an industry commentator, "We believe that Novatek's rise is the result of the government and Sechin in particular telling Gazprom 'You must make room for independent gas.'"[74] The pervasive role of conflicting clandestine agendas was thus yet again brought to the fore. And Gazprom was now on the losing side. By the end of 2012, the Kremlin would come to view its erstwhile favorite as a clear liability. In the words of an observer, "The Kremlin needed to change horses."[75]

Perhaps the most important reason behind this shift in political patronage was that Gazprom had remained so stubbornly fixated on its longstanding practice of supplying gas via pipeline, under long-term contracts and with prices linked to the price of oil. What served to render this policy so suddenly obsolete was the US discovery of technology that made it possible to extract large volumes of unconventional gas, mainly shale gas. The shale boom arrived seemingly out of nowhere. In the words of longstanding US energy expert Daniel Yergin, "This revolution arrived with no fanfare, no grand opening ceremony, no ribbon cutting. It just crept up."[76] (Appendix 5 provides detail on the development of shale gas in the United States and on global shale gas reserves.)

While the US energy industry began adapting early, in 2007, general political awareness of the potential involved was triggered only in June 2009. In a surprise announcement, the US Committee on Potential Gas raised its biennial estimate of unproven US gas resources by 45 percent, from 32.7 to 47.4 trillion cubic meters. Ongoing developments were well in line with this much-cited announcement. A parallel study by Wood Mackenzie indicated that unconventional gas production in the contiguous forty-eight US states had increased from 33 percent of total production in 2000 to 59 percent in 2009, and was expected to rise to 73 percent by 2020.[77] Although the category of unconventional gas includes several different sources, with at times unclear lines of distinction, it was shale gas that was the real driver.[78]

US production of shale gas increased from 21 billion cubic meters in 2005, to 63 billion cubic meters in 2008, and to 192 billion cubic meters in 2011. Measured as a share of total US production of natural gas, shale rose from below 5 percent in 2005 to 23 percent in 2010. By 2035, it is expected to reach 380 billion cubic meters, making up 49 percent of the total.[79] The impact on total US production of natural gas has been substantial. Output rose from 511.1 billion cubic meters in 2005 to 570.8 billion cubic meters in 2008, to 651.3 billion cubic meters in 2011. By 2010 the United States had bypassed Russia to become the world's largest producer of gas, and by the end of 2011 it accounted for 20 percent of world production, compared to Russia's 18.5 percent.[80]

The transformation proceeded in three stages. First, between 2005 and 2009, the United States looked set to become one of the largest import markets for liquefied natural gas. Qatar in particular made substantial investments in the plants needed to liquefy gas for transport on special-purpose LNG tankers. As Qatar had the third-largest reserves of natural gas in the world, after Russia and Iran, this seemed a sensible thing to do. Between 2005 and 2010, Qatar's output of LNG increased by more than 150 percent. In the latter year, it accounted for 26 percent of total LNG exports, followed by Indonesia (11 percent), Malaysia (10 percent), and Australia (9 percent). The main importers have traditionally been Japan and South Korea. In 2010, they together accounted for 47 percent of global trade in LNG.[81] But the main driver for expansion was the US market.

In its 2005 annual energy outlook, the US Energy Information Administration predicted that in order to meet growth in demand, and to offset the expected drop in indigenous production, by 2010 the United States would need to import 70 billion cubic meters of gas annually. Given actual production of LNG in 2010, this would have amounted to a global market share of 23 percent, second only to Japan. Based on such expectations, US regasification capacity increased sevenfold between 2002 and 2010.[82] And Qatar was not alone in building capacity to meet the demand. In 2009–2010, an extra 9 billion cubic meters of global liquefaction capacity came online.[83]

The second stage, beginning in 2009, was marked by the emergence of the United States as a self-sustaining producer of gas. With rising global capacity for LNG exports, and with newly constructed US import terminals being idled, large volumes of LNG gas were rerouted instead to Europe, where a gas glut resulted. Qatar alone increased deliveries to Europe during 2009 by 114 percent, to reach 15.9 billion cubic meters.[84] The impact of the oversupply put downward pressure on prices and placed growing emphasis on spot market pricing. To Gazprom, this meant not only falling prices but also falling market shares.

The third stage, still unfolding, began as upward revisions indicated that the United States has sufficient reserves of recoverable unconventional gas to last for many years to come. According to Yergin in 2010, at current levels of extraction the United States has "about 120 years of proved and potential supply—a number that is bound to go up as more and more shale gas is found."[85] In its 2013 biennial assessment, the US Committee on Potential Gas made a further upward revision of the technically recoverable US natural gas resource base by 25.7 percent, from 53.7 trillion cubic meters at the end of 2010 to 67.5 trillion cubic meters at the end of 2012.[86] The implication is that a former major market for imports of gas has suddenly emerged, instead, as a potential exporter, not only of gas but perhaps also of oil.[87]

In January 2012, Qatar's oil minister, Abdullah bin Hamad Al Attiyah, announced plans to reverse the flow, so that its giant Golden Pass regasification terminal on the US Gulf Coast could instead begin exporting US shale gas. Cheniere Energy, one of the first companies to build a US regasification plant, at Sabine Pass, had already secured regulatory approval to begin exports in 2015.[88] Consequently, Russia, having been overtaken by the United States as the world's largest producer of natural gas in 2010, was now also looking at the prospect of facing competition from US liquefied natural gas in its own export markets.

A potential future fourth stage relates to the fact that significant shale gas reserves may be found also in a number of European countries. Estimated total recoverable reserves amount to 33–38 trillion cubic meters, compared to total conventional reserves in Europe of no more than 2.4 trillion cubic meters. Europe's unconventional gas resources may suffice to cover European gas demand for at least sixty years.[89]

The bottom line is that the combined effects of the shale gale have put a new twist on Russian ambitions to lock in the European energy market. If Poland in particular succeeds in exploiting its reserves, it may be transformed from a major customer into a net exporter within the European Union. Gazprom chairman Aleksei Miller has tried to put a brave face on things, arguing that shale gas cannot serve as a substitute for Russia's ample supply of conventional gas.[90] Yet there can be little doubt that the future will look very different from what was generally believed as late as 2005. We shall have reason to return to the implications for Russia of these various issues in Chapter 8.

The consequences that conflicting agendas and predatory governance will have for Gazprom's performance—measured in terms of vulnerability, ill-considered investment strategy, poor prospects for technological development, and gross neglect of maintenance of a rapidly aging and deteriorating infrastructure—do not seem to be of much concern to the Russian regime. By early 2011, having weathered the global financial crisis, both Gazprom and the Kremlin would again begin to exude the confidence of an emerging energy superpower, seemingly unfazed by the ongoing shale gas revolution. But before looking at how they went about picking up the pieces, we must look at how other countries reacted to Russia's mounting assertiveness in foreign energy relations.

Notes

1. Gustafson, *Wheel of Fortune*, p. 3.
2. Data for 2012 are from Gazprom's website, at http://www.gazprom.com /about. Russia is the world's largest exporter and the second-largest producer of natural gas, after the United States, with about a quarter of the world's total proven reserves; US Energy Information Administration, "Russia," http://www.eia.gov /countries/cab.cfm?fips=RS.
3. Pirani, *Elusive Potential*, p. 83.
4. Balmaceda, "Russia's Central and Eastern European Energy Transit Corridor," p. 137.
5. Stern, *The Future of Russian Gas*, p. 1.
6. Kryukov and Moe, *Gazprom*, p. 15.
7. Ibid., pp. 9–10.
8. Stern, *The Future of Russian Gas*, p. 58.

9. For details on reserves, peak production, and rates of depletion at Gazprom's major fields, see Stern, *The Future of Russian Gas,* pp. 7–9, especially tabs. 1.4 and 1.5.

10. See further Stern, *The Future of Russian Gas,* pp. 10–19.

11. Gazprom, "Gazprom in Questions and Answers," http://eng.gazprom questions.ru/?id=6. For maps and capacity estimates of the Russian gas pipeline network, see East European Gas Analysis, "Major Gas Pipelines of the Former Soviet Union and Capacity of Export Pipelines," http://www.eegas.com/fsu.htm#Tab.

12. Henderson, *Non-Gazprom Gas Producers in Russia,* p. 221.

13. Kryukov and Moe, *Gazprom,* p. 19.

14. For a brief background on these two important players, see Goldman, *The Piratization of Russia,* pp. 105–106.

15. Goldman, *The Piratization of Russia,* p. 106.

16. Kryukov and Moe, *Gazprom,* pp. 19–20.

17. Ibid., p. 25.

18. For a brief account of similar ambitions by the Organization for Economic Cooperation and Development and others, see Stern, *The Future of Russian Gas,* pp. 187–188.

19. Gustafson, *Wheel of Fortune,* p. 71.

20. Cited in Fredholm, *Gazprom in Crisis,* p. 1.

21. Kryukov and Moe, *Gazprom,* pp. 29–33.

22. Ibid., pp. 32–34.

23. "A Russian Gas Giant May Get Some Foreign Fuel," *Bloomberg Businessweek,* November 27, 1994, http://www.businessweek.com/stories/1994-11 -27/a-russian-gas-giant-may-get-some-foreign-fuel.

24. Kryukov and Moe, *Gazprom,* pp. 36–38.

25. Originally developed in 1927, the system of American depositary receipts is designed to allow investors to trade in non-US corporations on US financial markets. Denominated in US dollars, these receipts are issued by four major commercial banks as of 2013. Individual shares in foreign corporations that are represented by American depositary receipts are referred to as American depositary shares. The specific mode of trade varies according to agreement with the particular foreign company. See http://en.wikipedia.org/wiki/American_Depositary_Receipt.

26. "Abolishing Gazprom's 'Ring Fence' and Russia's Big Bang," *RIA Novosti,* October 17, 2005, http://en.rian.ru/analysis/20051017/41800342.html.

27. Stern, *The Future of Russian Gas,* pp. 170–171.

28. Sergei Blagov, "Russian Govt Agrees to Buy 10.7 % of Gazprom for $7.15 bn," *ICIS,* June 15, 2005, http://www.icis.com/Articles/2005/06/15/685674/russian -govt-agrees-to-buy-10.7-of-gazprom-for-7.15bn.html.

29. Goldman, *The Piratization of Russia,* p. 107.

30. Peter Dinkloh, "E.ON Sells Stake in Gazprom for £2.8bn," *The Independent,* December 2, 2010, http://www.independent.co.uk/news/business/news /eon-sells-stake-in-gazprom-for-16328bn-2148726.html.

31. Goldman, *The Piratization of Russia,* p. 102.

32. Ibid., pp. 107–110.

33. Ibid., p. 108.

34. Ibid.

35. Ibid., p. 107.

36. Ibid., p. 113.

37. Stern, *The Future of Russian Gas,* pp. 188–192, 198–200.

38. Goldman, *The Piratization of Russia,* p. 113.

39. Ibid., p. 114.

40. The story is of particular interest in that subsequent investigations revealed how leading newspapers had been paid to participate in the campaign. A prominent example was that of *Vedomosti,* one of Russia's most respected business newspapers, which allegedly had accepted $6,000 each for four articles attacking Fedorov. Following Vyakhirev's departure from Gazprom, the attacks were halted and some of the papers even published retractions. Goldman, *The Piratization of Russia,* pp. 114–115.

41. Stern, *The Future of Russian Gas,* pp. 43–44.

42. See Henderson, *Non-Gazprom Gas Producers in Russia,* pp. 59–60.

43. Valeria Korchagina, "Gazprom Brings Purgaz Back Under Its Umbrella," *St. Petersburg Times,* December 18, 2001, http://www.sptimes.ru/index.php ?action_id=2&story_id=6155.

44. Stern, *The Future of Russian Gas,* p. 190.

45. "The Nemtsov White Paper, Part II (Section 2)," *La Russophobe,* September 25, 2008, http://larussophobe.wordpress.com/2008/09/25/the-nemtsov -white-paper-part-ii-section-2.

46. Goldman, *The Piratization of Russia,* p. 116.

47. Nemtsov and Milov, "Putin and Gazprom," p. 17.

48. Gazprom, "Gazprom in Questions and Answers," http://eng.gazprom questions.ru/?id=7.

49. Stern, *The Future of Russian Gas,* p. 201. The former is the traditional Soviet method, which estimates reserves that are physically recoverable and in a sense measures the country's total mineral wealth. The latter estimate—undertaken by the Society of Petroleum Engineers—defines a reserve by whether it is economically feasible to produce and consequently whether it is responsive to world oil prices. Russian companies report both of these estimates, one to the government and the other to the international community. See further Gustafson, *Wheel of Fortune,* pp. 389–390.

50. Nemtsov and Milov, "Putin and Gazprom," p. 17.

51. Ibid., pp. 7–8.

52. Established as a joint stock company already in 1990, Gazprombank would become Russia's largest non-state-owned bank. Gazprom-Media was established in 2000 to consolidate the substantial media assets acquired during the 1990s, including prestigious *Izvestiya* and the NTV television channel. In 2005, Gazprom-Media was taken over by Gazprombank.

53. Nemtsov and Milov, "Putin and Gazprom," pp. 9–10.

54. Stern, *The Future of Russian Gas,* pp. 67–68.

55. Ibid., pp. 68–70, especially tabs. 2.1 and 2.2.

56. Goldman, *The Piratization of Russia,* p. 111. It should be noted that Stern disputes the veracity of these media accounts, and cites investigations both by the Federal Audit Chamber and by PriceWaterhouseCoopers that failed to uncover any irregularities in relations between Gazprom and Itera. That the latter made substantial profits is, however, beyond question, as is the fact that no other independent company came even close to its privileged status. Stern, *The Future of Russian Gas,* pp. 22–23.

57. Goldman, *The Piratization of Russia,* p. 112.

58. Stern, *The Future of Russian Gas,* pp. 22, 69.

59. Goldman, *The Piratization of Russia,* pp. 110–111.

60. The shady story of such allegations is laid out in great detail in Kupchinsky, "Gazprom's European Web."

61. Stern, *The Future of Russian Gas,* pp. 93–94.

62. Socor, "New Gas Trader to Boost Turkmenistan-Ukraine Transit."

63. Balmaceda, "Intermediaries and the Ukrainian Domestic Dimension," pp. 9–10.

64. "Tymoshenko-RosUkrEnergo Case to Be Considered in U.S. Under New Rules," *RAPSI News,* February 27, 2012, http://www.rapsinews.com/judicial_news /20120227/260534205.html.

65. Balmaceda, "Intermediaries and the Ukrainian Domestic Dimension," p. 10.

66. "Gazprom's New Weakness Offers Opportunity, *Moscow Times,* May 27, 2009, http://www.themoscowtimes.com/opinion/article/gazproms-new-weakness -offers-opportunity/377459.html.

67. Ibid.

68. "Gas Production Down, Oil Unchanged,"*Moscow Times,* June 3, 2009, http://www.themoscowtimes.com/business/article/gas-production-down-oil -unchanged/377676.html.

69. "Gazprom Squeezed by Central Asian Contracts," *Eurasianet,* March 23, 2009, http://www.eurasianet.org/departments/insightb/articles/eav032409d.shtml.

70. Andrew E. Kramer, "Falling Gas Prices Deny Russia a Lever of Power," *New York Times,* May 15, 2009, http://www.nytimes.com/2009/05/16/world/europe /16gazprom.html?pagewanted=1&_r=1.

71. "Gazprom Squeezed by Central Asian Contracts."

72. "Energy Summit in Baku Advances Regional Energy Cooperation," *Eurasianet,* November 23, 2008, http://www.eurasianet.org/departments/insightb /articles/eav112408.shtml.

73. Howard Amos and Irina Filatova, "Putin Targets Corruption at Gazprom," *Moscow Times,* October 3, 2012, http://www.themoscowtimes.com/business/article /putin-targets-corruption-at-gazprom/469178.html.

74. Henderson, *Non-Gazprom Gas Producers in Russia,* pp. 37–38.

75. John Lough, "Rosneft Replaces Gazprom as Super-Champion," *Moscow Times,* October 26, 2012, http://www.themoscowtimes.com/opinion/article/rosneft -replaces-gazprom-as-super-champion/470458.html.

76. Yergin, "Global Markets Feel the Force," p. 14.

77. Cited in Kuhn and Umbach, *Strategic Perspectives of Unconventional Gas,* p. 13.

78. The terminology may be a bit confusing. Conventional natural gas is extracted from porous reservoirs where the gas can migrate easily to the well bore and then on to the surface in a relatively free flow. It can appear in isolated deposits or together with oil, when it is known as associated gas. Unconventional gas, in contrast, is extracted from rock formations where the permeability is so low that the gas cannot migrate easily. Three of the main sources are coal-bed methane, which often occurs in coal mines and can be produced with oil industry techniques; tight gas, or tight sands, where the gas is stuck in very hard rock or in nonporous sandstone or limestone; and shale gas, which is derived from fine-grained shale deposits and requires advanced fracturing techniques. See "Unconventional Natural Gas Resources," *NaturalGas,* December 14, 2013, http://www.naturalgas.org/overview /unconvent_ng_resource.asp.

79. US Energy Information Administration, "What Is Shale Gas and Why Is It Important?" December 5, 2012, http://www.eia.gov/energy_in_brief/about_shale _gas.cfm.

80. BP, *BP Statistical Review of World Energy, 2012,* p. 22.

81. International Gas Union, *World LNG Report 2010,* p. 6.

82. Ibid., p. 21.

83. Kuhn and Umbach, *Strategic Perspectives of Unconventional Gas,* p. 17.

84. Orttung and Overland, "Russia and the Formation of a Gas Cartel," p. 60.

85. Yergin, "Global Markets Feel the Force," p. 15.

86. Potential Gas Committee, "Potential Gas Committee Reports Significant Increase in Magnitude of US Natural Gas Resource Base," April 9, 2013, http://potentialgas.org/press-release.

87. A substantial check on the rampant optimism was provided in January 2012, when the US Department of Energy cut its estimate for natural gas reserves in the important Marcellus shale formation by two-thirds, citing improved data on drilling and production. The estimate on total reserves of shale gas in the United States was cut to 482 trillion cubic feet, down from the 2011 estimate of 827 trillion cubic feet, representing a decrease of more than 40 percent. Christine Buurma, "U.S. Cuts Estimate for Marcellus Shale Gas Reserves by 66%," *Bloomberg News,* January 23, 2012, http://www.bloomberg.com/news/2012-01-23/u-s-reduces-marcellus-shale-gas-reserve-estimate-by-66-on-revised-data.html.

88. Peter Kelly-Detweiler, "LNG Export Economics: A Look at Frontrunner Cheniere," *Forbes,* December 5, 2012, http://www.forbes.com/sites/peterdetwiler/2012/12/05/lng-export-economics-a-look-at-frontrunner-cheniere.

89. Kuhn and Umbach, *Strategic Perspectives of Unconventional Gas,* p. 8.

90. Orttung and Overland, "Russia and the Formation of a Gas Cartel," p. 55.

6

Counterreactions

By the time that Vladimir Putin took a temporary leave from the Kremlin in March 2008, it seemed as though Russia's ambition to become an energy superpower was well on track. The real side of the Russian economy had emerged out of the depression of the Yeltsin era, and the prospects for continued growth were looking good. Russia's financial situation had been transformed from one of basket case on the verge of a sovereign default to a position of impressive strength. Domestic energy producers had been brought back under firm Kremlin control, and foreign oil interests had been cut down to size. Energy resources in the Caspian Basin appeared to have been locked in, and with the two-pronged strategy of Nord Stream and South Stream, the European Union was finally looking at the prospect of mounting dependence on the goodwill of the Kremlin.

Consequently, this was also the time that outside observers began to worry, quite seriously, that Russia was about to secure a position of influence over Europe that was stronger even than that during the Cold War. In June 2009, for example, Marshall Goldman voiced concern that Europe was sleepwalking into an increasingly dangerous level of dependence on Gazprom, which was seen to have close links to the Russian government: "Russia is using energy as a political weapon and I would argue that it is stronger than during the Cold War when it had nuclear weapons."[1]

As will be shown in Chapter 7, the global financial crisis would cause a major transformation of the game board and the emergence of new forms of strategic behavior. There were, however, broader reasons than simply fiscal ones that combined to produce a change of scene. The Kremlin's increasingly assertive behavior caused new lines of confrontation to emerge. This was the case not only to the south, where both Turkmenistan and Azerbaijan began to play increasingly independent games around the exploitation and marketing of their respective energy resources, but also with respect to the EU to the west and to China to the east, both of which constitute vital markets for Russian energy exports. The main driver of these emerging conflicts is linked to pipelines—to the pricing of gas transported via existing pipelines, and to rival agendas concerning the building of new pipelines.

Trouble to the South

The first indications that the Kremlin's ambition to secure the Caspian Basin was headed for trouble came in the wake of the previously mentioned death, in December 2006, of Turkmen president Saparmurat Niyazov. Faced with mounting assertiveness by the new Turkmen regime, led by President Gurbanguly Berdymukhammedov, Moscow decided to take a proactive stance. By agreeing to substantial increases in the purchase price of gas, it clearly hoped to preempt any potential further reorientation of energy flows. On March 11, 2008, Gazprom in consequence accepted to pay what was then known as "European prices" for Central Asian gas, beginning in 2009.[2]

In order to appreciate the importance of this step, it should be noted that early in the decade Gazprom had been paying prices in the range of $25–$35 per thousand cubic meters. At the time of the deal, the price paid to Turkmenistan had risen to $180 per thousand cubic meters, and it was now expected that in 2009 it would rise to perhaps $300.[3]

The Kremlin, lulled into complacency by the rapidly rising prices on all commodity markets, and by its accumulation of stunning petrowealth, apparently felt confident that it would have little trouble shifting the added burden onto the shoulders of EU consumers. In early March 2008, Gazprom chief executive officer Aleksei Miller went on record anticipating that the average price for gas in Europe in 2008 could reach as much as $400 per thousand cubic meters.[4]

The following week saw three further developments with important implications for ongoing speculation on the size of Turkmen gas reserves. On March 12, 2008, an agreement was reached to transfer to Ashgabat Soviet-era geological and geophysical data that had been held in Moscow. On March 17 the British firm Gaffney, Cline, and Associates was commissioned to undertake a survey of potential new gas fields, and on March 19 a top Turkmen energy official revealed that the country expected to increase its output by 50 billion cubic meters in the "near future."[5]

With these moves, the stage was set for Turkmenistan to enter into the fray of the great game as a major player in its own right. On March 24,

Berdymukhammedov made a visit to Turkey, deliberately raising expectations for a deal on Turkmen gas for the Trans-Caspian Pipeline and Nabucco, and during a visit to Ashgabat, on April 9–10, an EU troika received a promise of export of 10 billion cubic meters to the EU. Although it was left unclear how such export would be routed, this did serve to ratchet up expectations. On May 19–20, Berdymukhammedov made an official visit to Baku. Representing the first such event since 1996, it successfully laid to rest a long-standing conflict over Azeri debt for Turkmen gas deliveries, accumulated over the years since 1991.[6] The main implication seemed to be that the way ahead for building the critical and profoundly controversial TCP had been cleared.

In late May 2008, the Kremlin made an unsuccessful effort to shore up what now seemed to be a mercilessly turning tide. During a tour of the region, Gazprom's Aleksei Miller found both Berdymukhammedov and Uzbek president Islam Karimov to be unavailable. In stark contrast to this effective humiliation of the Kremlin, US envoy Richard Boucher made a parallel tour of the region, lobbying for the TCP and Nabucco, and Berdymukhammedov, at the NATO summit in Bucharest on May 30, had a symbolically important one-on-one meeting with US president George W. Bush.

Throughout June 2008, numerous Western delegations also visited Tashkent, the capital of Uzbekistan, seeking to repair the damage caused by negative reactions to the Andijan massacre in May 2005. Among other things, assurance was offered that further credits from the US Agency for International Development would not be linked to demands for further democratization.

On July 1, 2008, Miller did meet Berdymukhammedov in Ashgabat but failed to secure a firm commitment to the Russian position. Only days later, newly elected Russian president Dmitry Medvedev made a tour of Azerbaijan, Turkmenistan, and Kazakhstan. The main item on the agenda was an offer to buy all Azeri gas at "market" prices.[7] As Baku was already selling gas to Europe at market prices, there was little apparent sense in this offer, and it was not made at the most opportune of times.

Ever since the collapse of the Soviet Union, relations between Russia and Azerbaijan had been troubled by Russian involvement in the conflict over Nagorno-Karabakh, an ethnic Armenian region located within the Soviet republic of Azerbaijan. Following its declaration of independence, made at the end of 1991, an armed conflict erupted that is still to be resolved. In this conflict, Moscow has assumed the role of patron for Armenia, to the point even of signing, in 1997, a treaty on mutual military assistance, should either side be attacked.[8]

Despite such underlying tension, Azerbaijan had been an importer of Russian gas until the end of 2006, when Gazprom suddenly announced substantial price hikes. The apparent reason was an effort by the Kremlin to put increased pressure on Georgia by bringing about a halt in its gas imports from Azerbaijan. The rather unsubtle means chosen was to more than double the price charged to Azerbaijan and Georgia, from \$110 to \$235 per thousand cubic meters of gas, while keeping the price charged to Armenia unchanged.[9]

Declaring that it would not submit to "commercial blackmail," Baku responded by halting all further purchases of Russian gas, and by stopping shipments of oil via the Baku-Novorossiisk pipeline. According to a contract signed in 2004, Azerbaijan would purchase 4 billion cubic meters of gas per year until 2009, at a price of \$52 per thousand cubic meters. Despite this agreement, the asking price had been climbing steadily and the latest hike was apparently one too many.[10] Subsequent relations would be frosty, with Baku ignoring all offers of cooperation from Gazprom.

Regarding relations between Turkmenistan and Russia, during a visit to the Beijing Olympics in August 2008, Berdymukhammedov opened the new political season by promising to increase exports to China by an additional 10 billion cubic meters, to reach 40 billion cubic meters.[11] The Russian agreement to pay higher purchase prices for gas had apparently not been effective in curbing Turkmen ambitions to play a more independent game. Given the high stakes that were involved in these various political plays, there was a great deal of excitement in the air when the result of the aforementioned audit of Turkmen gas reserves by Gaffney, Cline, and Associates was made public. Presented on October 13, 2008, the announcement did live up to the best of expectations: "Based on our current understanding, Gaffney/Cline believes that the Yolotan field has a low estimate of 4 trillion cubic meters, a best estimate of 6 trillion cubic meters and a high estimate of 14 trillion cubic meters."[12]

With a best estimate of reserves in the Yolotan-Osman field that was five times larger than those of the Dauletabad field, previously Turkmenistan's main gas field, the new find would be approximately the fourth- or fifth-largest gas field in the world. To put the numbers into perspective, by the end of 2010 Russia had 44.8 trillion cubic meters of proven gas reserves, followed by Iran with 29.6 and Qatar with 25.3.[13] Now feeling itself part of the club of major players, Ashgabat announced an intention to increase its gas export to 125 billion cubic meters by 2015.[14] The stage was now clearly set for conflict, and the trigger would be related to the so-called east-west gas spur that had been intended to link Turkmenistan to the previously mentioned Prikaspiiskoe (Pre-Caspian) pipeline.

During a visit to Moscow in late March 2008, Berdymukhammedov learned that Gazprom was no longer interested in financing the construction, as originally intended. In response, Ashgabat let it be known that it was considering an international tender for the contract. On April 3, a posting on the website of the Turkmen state news agency announced that "the era of monopolies in this segment of the world economy is a thing of the past."[15] Hidden behind talk of needs to explore options for diversification was a thinly veiled threat that Turkmen gas might after all be diverted to feed the TCP and Nabucco.

Less than a week later, on April 9, an explosion damaged a gas pipeline near the Turkmenistan-Uzbekistan border, causing a disruption of Turkmen exports. The incident was reminiscent of the previously mentioned explosions that damaged Russian export pipelines to Georgia in 2006. Exactly what caused the blast again was unclear. Ashgabat accused Gazprom of turning off the gas flow without proper warning, thus causing a rapid buildup of pressure. Moscow pointed at metal corrosion and negligent maintenance by the Turkmen side. Irrespective of reason, the incident produced serious political fallout. At an energy security conference held in Ashgabat on April 23–24, 2008, Berdymukhammedov took the opportunity to proclaim energy independence: "Today we are looking for conditions to diversify energy routes and the inclusion of new countries and regions."[16] It was also clearly stated that Russia should not expect any form of price discounts.

Gazprom's response was to refuse resumption of imports, and to put pressure on Ashgabat. Citing falling demand and sliding prices on European gas markets, on June 1 Gazprom deputy chairman Valery Golubev made light of the need to honor contractual agreements, arguing that either the price or the volumes would have to be changed: "We've proposed to limit the volume because Turkmen gas is purchased at European prices. [But] Europe is not buying gas at European prices today. We have nowhere to sell your gas." Analysts estimated that Ashgabat was consequently suffering losses of up to $1 billion per month.[17] It would seem hard to imagine a more powerful incentive for Turkmenistan to shift its export focus toward the TCP and Nabucco.

The flow of gas would not be resumed until January 2010, following a deal between Gazprom and Turkmengaz, the signing of which was overseen by Russian president Medvedev and Turkmen president Berdymukhammedov. The agreed volumes, moreover, clearly reflected how things were changing. According to the 2003 "landmark deal," Russia had agreed to purchase 80–90 billion cubic meters of Turkmen gas per year. In the years preceding the rupture, flows had not exceeded 50 billion cubic meters, and according to the new deal they would stop at 30 billion cubic meters. Future prices, moreover, would be based on a fluctuating European price formula, aimed at putting an end to pricing disputes.[18]

In conclusion, while Russia had succeeded in causing serious damage to its own position as monopolist on the transport of gas from Turkmenistan, the deal between Medvedev and Berdymukhammedov also reflected that the prospects for Nabucco's success remained in limbo. Although Ashgabat in consequence did appear to be the projected winner, the true size of its total gas reserves remained enigmatic. According to allegations made in a Russian newspaper in October 2009, based on inside sources from the Turkmen oil and gas industry, estimates had been overstated by as much as three times. If true, this would vastly reduce the ability of Ashgabat to continue playing in the energy industry's big league. Gaffney, Cline, and Associates, however, declared that it was sticking to its numbers, thus ensuring that the guessing game would continue.[19] We shall have reason to return to the matter in Chapter 8.

Let us proceed now to look at Russia's relations to the European Union, which have proven to be in every bit as exciting as those to countries in the Caspian Basin—and clearly related to the latter.

Trouble with the European Union

Until the end of 2005, the Kremlin had been successful in maintaining the image of Russia as a reliable supplier of energy to the European Union. Although there had been numerous cases of supply disruptions and of bilateral pricing disputes, such conflicts had been limited to countries within the Commonwealth of Independent States. And they had been largely dismissed as mere technical problems. In January 2006, that image was badly shattered, as gas flows to Europe were interrupted for four days due to the previously mentioned pricing conflict between Moscow and Kiev. Given the considerable damage that this event would cause to Gazprom's reputation, it is important to consider the broader political context.

In the run-up to the 2004 presidential election in Ukraine, Moscow was clearly bent on supporting Viktor Yanukovich, who was considered friendly to Russia. The Kremlin in consequence launched a powerful campaign that not only included strong personal endorsement from Putin himself but also featured the signing, in August 2004, of a five-year deal for Ukraine to purchase Russian gas at no more than $50 per thousand cubic meters. As pointed out by Andrei Illarionov, following his resignation as Putin's chief economic adviser, it was no coincidence that the span of the agreement covered the five years of the anticipated Yanukovich presidential term. Illarionov was highly critical of how Russian national interest was thus sacrificed to dangerous ideas of "national greatness."[20]

The campaign turned out to have been a gross miscalculation. As noted in Chapter 1, a public uproar against massive vote-rigging brought about the Orange Revolution, which in turn forced a rerun of the election. And the latter was won by the strongly pro-Western candidate Viktor Yushchenko. This outcome was a humiliating defeat for Putin, who clearly viewed the whole process as a personal effrontery, allegedly orchestrated by foreign intelligence services. Following months of contemplation, by the fall of

2005 he seemed to have arrived at the conclusion that the time had come to stop subsidizing countries like Ukraine via low energy prices. If they wanted to cultivate relations with the Americans, they would have to pay the price.[21]

In December 2005, Gazprom, claiming that it was merely striving for adjustment to "market" levels, a notion that has little relevance in the case of piped natural gas and that has little accord with the highly discounted prices charged to some of its politically more malleable customers, announced a hike in the price of gas from $50 to $230 per thousand cubic meters. Strongly negative reactions resulted, both from Ukraine and from those EU member states that would become hostages to the conflict.

Following some backroom dealing, it was agreed that the conflict could be resolved via a very special form of compromise that would allow Gazprom to sell gas at $230 per thousand cubic meters to a newly created intermediary, the previously mentioned RosUkrEnergo, which would then add cheaper gas from Turkmenistan and resell the lot to Ukraine at $95 per thousand cubic meters.[22]

While Russia appeared publicly baffled at the negative reactions from its European customers, in Brussels anxiety over energy security provoked a strong response. Concluding that the main threat comes from unstable countries and from countries that use energy as a means of pressure, a policy document was issued making a pointed statement about "the effects on the EU internal energy market of external actors not playing by the same market rules nor being subject to the same competitive pressures domestically."[23] There could be little doubt that the point was aimed squarely at Gazprom. Although the cat was now out of the bag, the member states remained far too divided for there to be any concerted action.

The renewed conflict that flared up between Russia and Ukraine toward the end of 2008 was different. What again began as a difference over pricing escalated to the point where a two-week supply shutoff left several of the "new" EU member states freezing in the midst of a very cold winter.[24] Given that all metering stations are located on Russian territory, it has been impossible for outside observers to ascertain exactly what happened and who was mainly at fault.[25] What is known is that Gazprom sustained major financial losses. On January 12, 2009, Prime Minister Putin announced that the company had lost $800 million since the beginning of the crisis, and three days later President Medvedev noted that Gazprom had failed to collect $1.1 billion in export payments under contracts for gas deliveries to Europe.[26]

The very fact, however, that both sides were seemingly happy to allow the conflict to drag out, and to accept substantial damage in relations between Russia and the EU, indicates that there were other issues involved than simply the price of gas. The murky nature of Ukrainian domestic politics not only had resulted in complete gridlock on both the gas sector and other reforms but also had combined with the equally murky nature of links between major players in Moscow and Kiev to produce a situation whereby rational solutions to a seemingly simple infrastructural transport problem were in effect blocked.[27]

An important part of the still ongoing conflict is related to the fact that the lion's share of what is commonly known as "Russian" gas exported to Europe has in reality been gas from Central Asia transited to Europe via Ukraine. For as long as producing countries like Kazakhstan and Turkmenistan lacked alternative routes for their energy exports, the Kremlin was able to pocket a substantial margin between prices paid to Caspian Basin producers and prices charged to European customers. As we have seen, by 2009 this was no longer true. The agreement that was reached in 2008, for Gazprom to pay "European prices," had the unanticipated effect of turning the previous cash cow into a major liability.

The main political impact of the lengthy crisis that marked the beginning of 2009 was to provide renewed impetus for the European Union's stalled ambitions to diversify its energy sources and to reduce its vulnerability to future conflicts. This time it would proceed along two tracks, one aimed at reenergizing Nabucco, now referred to as the Southern Energy Corridor, and the other at becoming more heavily involved in Ukrainian energy politics.

The first step on the latter path was taken on March 23, 2009, when at a joint EU-Ukraine conference on international investment a "master plan" to modernize Kiev's gas transport system was agreed.[28] The ambition was comprehensive, aiming to achieve a much needed upgrade and capacity expansion. But even more important was the fact that in return for a €2.5 billion investment, the Ukrainian side agreed to a detailed gas-sector reform program based on EU legislation. If implemented (and this was greatly uncertain), the latter would not only ensure transparency and equal access but hopefully also put an end to the massive corruption that for so long had marked this sector.[29]

Moscow reacted strongly, threatening to "review" its relations with the EU.[30] The formal reason was that it had not been invited to take part in the project. A more likely reason was the implied threat that by upgrading Ukrainian transit capacity from 120 billion cubic meters to at least 140 billion cubic meters and perhaps as much as 180 billion cubic meters, the EU would render the favored Russian bypass options of Nord Stream and South Stream less attractive and thus perhaps also preclude much needed financing from Europe.

A month later, on April 22, 2009, the European Parliament approved a set of new rules for the European gas market that spelled even greater trouble for Gazprom. Quite in line with EU competition policy and with the earlier-mentioned 2006 policy document, the main thrust was that energy companies should not be allowed to combine production and transmission of gas. The ambition to achieve "unbundling" was to proceed beyond *legal* unbundling, which was already ensured, to *ownership* unbundling, which would prevent a producing company from owning assets in a distribution company, and vice versa.[31]

Because this necessarily required Gazprom to divest itself of its pipeline assets, the unbundling constituted a powerful challenge also to the Kremlin. The message was driven home by the introduction of a reciprocity clause banning the involvement of companies or individuals from third countries in liberalized EU infrastructures, unless reciprocity were provided in unbundling and liberalization.[32] In effect, this meant that unless EU companies were allowed access to the Russian upstream, which the Kremlin had firmly opposed, Gazprom would not be allowed access to the EU downstream.

It was beginning to appear that Moscow, by its own assertive behavior, had finally succeeded in baiting the EU into taking concerted action to advance its own collective interest, thus jeopardizing the Kremlin's ambition to lock in the European energy market. And there was much more bad news to come.

As mentioned earlier, in April 2008 the Turkmen president had used an energy security conference in Ashgabat to proclaim energy independence. In line with this setback, on April 24–25, 2009, the Bulgarian capital, Sofia, was host to a European energy summit, captioned "Natural Gas for Europe." With Prime Minister Putin conspicuously absent, Gazprom was forced to note South Stream's exclusion from the list of EU priority projects and Bulgaria's flat refusal to accept its offer to buy a 50 percent equity stake in the country's pipeline network.

In early May, two meetings in Prague, hosted by the Czech EU presidency, added insult to injury. The first, held on May 7, saw the launch of a new "Eastern Partnership," joining all of the EU-27 members with Ukraine, Belarus, Moldova, Georgia, Azerbaijan, and Armenia. Setting aside €600 million over 2010–2013, the program aimed at securing pan-European energy security, together with a free trade agreement, a relaxed visa regime, and support for political reform.[33] Absent from the list, Russia was unhappy indeed over what it regarded as an unfriendly action.

The following day, on May 8 at a conference held to promote the Southern Energy Corridor, it was announced that a deal had finally been reached with Turkey regarding conditions for the transit pipeline that would cross its territory. Hailed as a major breakthrough for Nabucco, Gazprom at least could derive some consolation from the fact that the key players in the Caspian Basin persisted in refusing to make a firm commitment on gas supply for the project.

At the annual summit between Russia and the EU, held on May 21–22, 2009, in the Far Eastern city of Khabarovsk, there were numerous items on the agenda on which little if any progress was to be expected. There was continued disagreement on renewal of the 1997 partnership and cooperation agreement, which had expired in 2007. There was also continued disagreement on Russia's signing of the Energy Charter Treaty, which was held up by President Medvedev as outdated, and there was substantial Russian dissatisfaction over the new Eastern Partnership. Above all, however, the meeting was marked by further saber-rattling over gas transit via Ukraine, with President Medvedev frankly noting that "Russia cannot guarantee that there will be no halts in gas supply to Europe."[34]

The main source of conflict this time was related to the underground storage facilities for gas that had been built in the western parts of Ukraine. At times of peak demand, these facilities allow Kiev to take gas entering in the northeast for its own consumption and to compensate by exporting gas from storage to European customers. For this to work, gas must be pumped into the storage tanks during summer, when demand for transport capacity is low. Due to the financial crisis, however, Kiev lacked the $4 billion needed to purchase 19.5 billion cubic meters of gas, and Gazprom was not willing to supply on credit.[35]

Following intense political wrangling, on July 31, 2009, it was announced that agreement had been reached on a loan package of up to $1.7 billion from the World Bank, the European Bank for Reconstruction and Development, and the European Investment Bank, aimed to support gas-sector reform and to increase the security of gas supplies to Europe.[36] Since only $300 million would be available to pay for gas imports, Ukraine was still far short of the financing needed to ensure sufficient buildup of storage reserves.

Gazprom, despite the chokehold it was in the process of applying on Ukraine, was now in full retreat. Faced with falling demand and deepening financial trouble due to the global financial crisis, on June 17 Gazprom had announced that it would need to postpone concluding the deal on the Kovytka gas field, which it had fought so hard to wrest from TNK-BP.[37] On June 25, in an additional announcement, Gazprom declared that its fixed capital investment for 2009 would need to be slashed by 30 percent.[38] (This investment had been revised upward to $29.4 billion as late as December 2008.)[39]

Against this background, it must have been somehow bittersweet when Gazprom revealed that on June 29 it had achieved a breakthrough in negotiations with Azerbaijan, agreeing to begin accepting deliveries of Azeri gas in 2010. Although the political implications could be substantial, the modest volume—500 million cubic meters—reflected that the very last thing Gazprom needed at the moment was more gas imports, especially so if bought at premium "political" prices, estimated at \$290–\$300 per thousand cubic meters.[40] While Moscow touted the deal as a breakthrough in securing gas from the Shah Deniz field, Baku insisted that such negotiations were still ongoing and open to all interested parties, meaning that the race between Nabucco and South Stream was still on.

On July 13, 2009, years of negotiation finally resulted in a signing ceremony in Ankara where Austria, Bulgaria, Hungary, Romania, and Turkey agreed to launch the project of actually building Nabucco. At an estimated cost of €7.9 billion, it was envisioned that the pipeline, with a capacity of 31 billion cubic meters annually, would be operational by 2014 and reach full capacity by 2020. At the ceremony, EU Commission president José Manuel Barroso described the project as being of "crucial importance for the EU's and Turkey's energy security," and indicated his belief that "this pipeline is now inevitable rather than just probable."[41]

Adding to the Kremlin's troubles, elections held in Bulgaria in early July 2009 had brought to power a man, former Sofia mayor Boyko Borisov, who was committed to getting Bulgaria out of the South Stream consortium.[42] It was also reported that former German foreign minister Joschka Fischer had been recruited as consultant by the Nabucco consortium, mimicking the highly controversial decision of his former boss, Chancellor Gerhard Schröder, to join Nord Stream.[43] To the proponents of Nabucco, only one small thing remained: to find sufficient gas for the venture to become commercially viable.

Although by now we have moved far ahead of the chronology of the presentation, which treats the impact of the global financial crisis in Chapter 7, for the sake of keeping the argument flowing let us now turn to the role of China in creating new sources of confrontation. Beijing's entry into the great game would not only present a serious challenge to Russia's dominance in Central Asia but also, in a broader and more serious context, raise questions concerning Moscow's grip over energy resources in the Russian Far East.

China on the Move

Reflecting the classic insight that at times of economic crisis cash is king, in the spring of 2009 China went on the offensive to capitalize on Russian financial weakness. For simple geographical reasons, if nothing else, both China and Japan have major reasons to prefer Russian energy to imports from the Middle East. Over and above the obvious savings on transport cost, China also has a strategic interest in avoiding the risk that at a time of conflict the US Navy might easily block the Malacca Straits and so cause an acute energy shortage. Similarly, Russian oil and gas companies would stand to gain from exporting Eastern Siberian energy toward the east rather than the west.[44]

The seemingly obvious win-win solution to all of these problems had long been to construct a pipeline to join Russian oilfields in Eastern Siberia with markets in China and Japan. Talks between Moscow and Beijing on building a crude oil pipeline from Angarsk in Irkutsk Oblast to the Chinese oil hub at Daqing had begun already in the mid-1990s. In 1998, Yukos Oil reached an agreement with the China National Petroleum Corporation, and in 1999 Russia and China agreed on a feasibility study. At a summit meeting in Moscow in July 2001, where President Putin and President Jiang Zemin signed the Sino-Russian Treaty of Good-Neighborliness and Friendly Cooperation, agreement was reached on proceeding with the Daqing route. The pipeline would be 2,300 kilometers long and designed to export 20 million tons of oil annually beginning in 2005, and then 30 million tons annually after 2010.[45]

The ensuing events would provide ample illustration of what has been said here about multiple and often conflicting agendas. Fearing erosion of its transport monopoly, Transneft responded by contributing a rival plan for a 3,900-kilometer pipeline from Angarsk to Nakhodka in the Russian Primorsk Oblast. It would have a capacity of 50 million tons annually, and would be destined for the Japanese market. The argument was that this would avoid the dangers inherent in creating a buyer's market for China. It was the start of a long process of intense political infighting between rival interests in Moscow.[46]

The Russian government, under Prime Minister Mikhail Kasyanov, was at first inclined toward the Daqing route, but President Putin was hesitant. At a December 2002 Sino-Russian summit in Beijing, he refrained from committing to the project. Instead, during a visit to Moscow in January 2003 by Prime Minister Junichiro Koizumi of Japan, he noted interest from Tokyo in supporting a pipeline, provided it ran to Nakhodka. Thus was added also a high-level game of rivalry between Tokyo and Beijing.

In May 2003, following intense lobbying by Transneft, the two projects were combined, with Transneft placed in charge of the pipeline and Yukos slated to deliver the oil.[47] On May 29, Russia and China signed an agreement on construction of a $2.5 billion branch pipeline to Daqing, and in a parallel deal Yukos agreed with the CNPC to supply 6 million tons of crude oil annually by rail between 2003 and 2006.[48] In February 2004, Transneft announced a revised route for the proposed pipeline. The origin was moved to Taishet in Irkutsk Oblast, about 130 kilometers northwest of the prior point of departure at Angarsk. From there, it would run north of Lake Baikal, along the Baikal-Amur Mainline railway via Skovorodino in Amur Oblast, and terminate at Perevoznaya Bay in Primorsk Oblast. But then Yukos was dismantled and the game board was transformed. Having taken over Yukos's assets, Rosneft entered into the game, with an agenda of its own.

In February 2004, the Russian government, now under Prime Minister Mikhail Fradkov, officially approved the Eastern Siberia–Pacific Ocean (ESPO) pipeline as a national project. It would run from Taishet to Perevoznaya Bay, with an annual capacity of 80 million tons. In April 2005, the responsible minister, Viktor Khristenko, authorized the construction, splitting the project into two stages. The first would run from Taishet to Skovorodino, with an annual capacity of 30 million tons. Awaiting full capacity in the Eastern Siberian oil fields, backup supplies would be pumped from fields in Western Siberia. An oil export terminal at Perevoznaya Bay was also planned, with an annual capacity of 30 million tons. No mention was made of the spur to Daqing. The second stage would extend the pipeline from Skovorodino to Perevoznaya Bay, with added capacity of 50 million tons. The total capacity of the ESPO would thus come to 80 million tons annually. Subsequently, Transneft announced that the export terminus would be moved from Perevoznaya Bay to Kozmino Bay near the busy port of Nakhodka, south of Vladivostok.[49]

The rather uncontroversial first stage of the project was completed by Transneft in 2009. Although cost overruns tend to be a natural ingredient in projects of this magnitude, the first stage of the ESPO was remarkable in that construction costs grew from $6.6 to $14.5 billion.[50] It is also striking that allegations have been made that $4 billion was stolen from the project.[51] Although Transneft has vehemently denied such allegations, the rumor persists.

The core of the controversy regarding the second phase long concerned what should come first, completing the additional 2,100 kilometers from Skovorodino to Nakhodka or running a branch to Daqing in China. As noted earlier, the project as a whole was surrounded from the outset not only by intense infighting in Moscow but also by rivalry between Tokyo and Beijing. What followed was a high-level game of short-term rent-seeking. Determined to seek maximum contributions toward the investment cost by playing Beijing and Tokyo off against each other, Moscow ended up with poor relations with both.[52]

Given the stakes involved for the Chinese and Japanese governments, it is easy to understand that they could allow themselves be drawn into rival bidding on financial contributions for their own respective routes to be placed at the top of the agenda. What is less intuitively obvious is that Moscow could allow the bargaining to drag out for so long that the end result, in the words of the Japanese scholar Shoichi Itoh, would be that of "scoring on its own goal."[53]

The trigger for the final stage in the process was the global financial crisis, which, as we shall see in Chapter 7, hit Russia very hard. Under severe fiscal pressure, Moscow was suddenly becoming more malleable, and more amenable to renewed Chinese proposals regarding the provisions of loans in return for secure deliveries of energy. Importantly, there was some precedence for this.

When the Kremlin proceeded, back in 2005, to auction off the assets of Yukos, Gazprom had been the designated beneficiary of the deal. But due to threats of international litigation, as discussed earlier, there was a last-minute rearrangement. With less to fear from foreign courts of law, Rosneft stepped in as buyer, having somehow managed on short notice to raise $10 billion for the purpose. Persistent rumors indicated that the source of that loan was Chinese, and that in return China managed to walk away with a contract for deliveries of oil at cheap 2005 prices. The full details emerged only when Rosneft published its accounts for 2005, acknowledging that the bulk of the cash had been received as prepayment for future oil exports to China.[54]

The first move by Beijing to benefit from the financial crisis was made in April 2009, when a deal was struck on "loans for oil." A preliminary agreement to build a pipeline with an annual capacity of 15 million tons had been reached already in October 2008, but disagreement over various conditions had caused it to be postponed.[55] According to the deal signed in April, the Development Bank of China would advance credits of $10 billion to Transneft and of $15 billion to Rosneft. In return, a pipeline through which China would receive 300 million tons of oil over a period of twenty years, starting in 2011, would be built. The pipeline route would be from Skovorodino to Petro China's Daqing oil field, which was to be upgraded with ten new storage tanks, boosting capacity by nearly 10 million barrels per day.[56]

When the pipeline became operational in January 2011, it was clear that China had scored a major gain. In addition to China's upstaging of Japan, the twenty-year deal had greatly reduced its dependence on oil from the Middle East. There was a snag, however, in the form of a failure to agree on the price. The agreement stipulated a price based on delivery at Kozmino Bay, which is the endpoint for the ESPO and a potential bench-mark for pricing regional oil. The conflict concerned the estimate of Transneft logistics costs, which is an important part of the price formula.

Claiming that the CNPC was underpaying by $13 per barrel, the Russ-ian side estimated that the loss over the twenty-year period would come to $30 billion. Following unilateral supply reductions by Transneft, partial debt payments by the CNPC, and attempts to shift the burden onto the shoulders of Rosneft, which supplies the oil, in February 2012 the two sides finally agreed on the price. In return for full payment by the CNPC of its outstanding debt of $130 million, Rosneft and Transneft agreed to a discount of $1.50 per barrel, implying a loss over the full period of the contract of about $3 billion as compared to the original agreement.[57]

Because the pipeline deal implied that China had also secured a foothold in upstream developments of Russian energy resources in the Far East, one may understand how a Stratfor analyst could arrive at the harsh conclusion that "the Russians have essentially locked in the fate of their Far East Strategy to the whims of Chinese energy policy, and this is a compromise that could reveal how financially desperate Russia is."[58] According to a Russian commentator, the implication of the deal was that the Kremlin is "building a pipeline to China that will turn Russia into a raw materials appendage to its huge neighbor in the east."[59]

In the wake of the deal on loans for oil, during a visit by Chinese president Hu Jintao to Moscow in June 2009, the two sides signed a memorandum of understanding to cooperate on natural gas as well.[60] The deal was finalized during a visit by Prime Minister Putin to Beijing in October as part of a $3.5 billion package of trade agreements. According to Gazprom chief executive officer Aleksei Miller, the agreement envisaged two possible routes for supplying China—one from fields in Western Siberia and another from fields in Eastern Siberia and Sakhalin. While the western route could be put in place very quickly, because Gazprom had ready-to-tap gas fields and the entire necessary infrastructure in place there, the eastern route would require the creation of gas-processing facilities. Given the associated investment needs, it was logical that markets expected a second deal on Chinese loans, this time in return for gas. As in the case of the deal on loans for oil, the expected deal on gas had a prehistory that was marked by debilitating Moscow infighting. A deal signed in 1994 had envisioned exports of 20–30 billion cubic meters per year from the Kovytka field in Eastern Siberia. The deal was confirmed in 1997, during a visit to Beijing by Russian prime minister Viktor Chernomyrdin. But Kovytka was controlled by Rusia Petroleum, which was a subsidiary of Sidanco. As Gazprom still did not have any gas resources of its own in Eastern Siberia, in 1998 it instead proposed the link between Altai in Western Siberia and Xinjiang province in the west of China.

As James Henderson puts it, the "anomaly" of Gazprom having a monopoly on gas export but not control over a major supply source in the region would be "one of the key elements in the frustration of a final gas agreement between the two countries." In 2004, the company made it clear to TNK-BP, which had then taken over the license, that support for development of the Kovytka field would not be forthcoming unless Gazprom too was involved. As discussed earlier, in June 2007 TNK-BP was forced to yield. But due to the ensuing financial crisis, Gazprom did not follow through on the purchase.[61]

In addition to such "domestic" trouble on the Russian side, the gas deal has also been held up by serious disagreement on the pricing formula. An agreement to build two pipelines—with a total capacity of up to 80 billion cubic meters annually—had been reached already in March 2006, during a visit by then-president Putin to Beijing, but then the process stalled.[62] Given the structural similarity between the respective deals on loans for oil and for gas, it might have seemed appropriate to suspect that by 2009 the pressures of the global financial crisis had caused the Russian position to become more malleable on the issue of gas as well.

As pointed out by Stephen Blank, however, several reasons called for skepticism. One was the simple fact that the agreement in October 2009 was very much a restatement of that from March 2006. Adding signatures without agreement on the pricing formula would not inspire confidence. In addition, there was also tension over which route should come first. Moscow clearly prefers the western route of a pipeline with a capacity of 30 billion cubic meters annually, leading from Altai to northwestern China. Beijing, however, already has secure supplies from Turkmenistan to that region and would much prefer the eastern route of a pipeline with a capacity of 38 billion cubic meters annually, leading from Eastern Siberia and Sakhalin to northeastern China.[63]

But perhaps the most important reason behind the delay was that Gazprom had failed to agree with the CNPC on how the price should be calculated. Russia insisted on a price for gas that would yield the same level of profitability as sales to Europe. China offered a price that would be based on extraction costs in Eastern Siberia, presumably at Kovytka. In 2007, the two sides were reportedly $50 apart in the price per thousand cubic meters. By 2010, the difference had widened. It was now reported that Russia was demanding $300 per thousand cubic meters, while China was prepared to offer no more than $200–$210.[64]

At a meeting in Moscow in November 2010, an agreement was reached to begin pumping 30 billion cubic meters of gas annually through the Altai pipeline by 2015, but agreement on the pricing formula remained outstanding.[65] Meanwhile, oil had already started flowing through the Skovorodino-Daqing sideline, and cooperation on trade in other areas was booming. Perhaps it is in the latter context that the gas deal should be viewed, as a part of a broader offensive by China to gain a more substantial presence in the region that stretches from Central Asia to Russia's Far East.

The latter understanding is supported by the fact that Beijing's hoard, at the time, of close to $2 trillion in international reserves, was sufficient to support operations on a broader scale than simply Russia. In April 2009, a $10 billion loan was extended to Kazakhstan, in return for stakes in the Kazakh energy complex,[66] and in June a $4 billion credit was provided to Turkmengaz, aimed at financing the capacity upgrade, from 30 to 40 billion cubic meters, of the gas pipeline from Turkmenistan to China that was promised by Berdymukhammedov at the Beijing Olympics.[67]

The agreement with Kazakhstan, signed in Beijing in the presence of President Hu Jintao and his Kazakh counterpart, Nursultan Nazarbaev, was composed of two parts. One was a $5 billion credit from the CNPC to the state corporation KazMunaiGaz, provided in return for a right to purchase a 49 percent minority stake in AO Mangistaumunaigas. The other was a $5 billion credit from the Export-Import Bank of China to the Development Bank of Kazakhstan, aimed at supporting infrastructure projects.[68] The deal with Turkmengaz should be viewed within the same framework of broader Chinese ambitions to provide loans in return for equity and other forms of involvement in national energy sectors.

What has come to be generally known as the Central Asia–China gas pipeline had an important precursor in the form of a pipeline to transport oil from Kazakhstan to China. Agreed already in 1997, construction of the pipeline was undertaken in three stages, with the final leg being completed in 2009. It travels 2,228 kilometers from the Kazakh oil hub at Atyrau on the north Caspian shore to Alashankou in Xinjiang province in the west of China. It has a maximum annual capacity of 20 million tons and is owned jointly (fifty-fifty) by the CNPC and KazMunaiGaz.[69]

When the project to build a gas pipeline from Central Asia to China was first discussed, it was presented as a China-Kazakhstan gas pipeline, intended to follow the same route as the China-Kazakhstan oil pipeline. Initial talks were held in 2003, during a visit to Kazakhstan by Chinese president Hu Jintao. Then, as previously noted, Turkmenistan began talks that resulted in a major deal involving Uzbekistan as well. Construction was started in 2007, and in December 2009 the presidents of the four countries met at Samandepe in eastern Turkmenistan for a valve-opening ceremony.[70]

The initial project was to build two parallel pipelines traveling 1,833 kilometers from Turkmenistan through Uzbekistan and southern Kazakhstan to Horgos in the Xinjiang region of China, where they would connect to the domestic network. The first pipeline was completed in only twenty-eight months, becoming operational in December 2009. The second pipeline became operational in October 2010. In September 2011, the CNPC and KazMunaiGaz signed an agreement for construction of an added 529-kilometer third pipeline in Uzbekistan, with an annual capacity of 25 billion cubic meters. Construction was begun in December 2011 and is expected to be completed in 2014. The total transmission capacity of the Central Asia–China pipeline will then amount to 55 billion cubic meters annually.[71]

In June 2010, an agreement was also signed between China and Kazakhstan to construct a 1,480-kilometer branch pipeline from Beyneu in the western gas fields at Tengiz, Karachaganak, and Kashagan to Shymkent on the border with China, where it will connect with the Central Asia–China pipeline.[72] The first stage was completed in September 2013, and the second stage will come on line in 2015, bringing total capacity to 10–15 billion cubic meters annually.[73]

On the whole, the role of designated winner of the great game over energy resources in Central Asia clearly appears to be moving in the direction of Beijing rather than Moscow.[74] It is especially instructive to contrast the speed with which China has negotiated and implemented its pipeline projects against the complete absence of any progress with the Russian Pre-Caspian pipeline, hailed in 2007 as the final victory of Russia in the great game. The fact that China is evolving a strategy to provide loans not only in return for secure deliveries of oil and gas but also to pursue acquisitions of equity will have far-reaching implications for Moscow's policy to develop its Far East.

As Stephen Blank notes, "Russian spokesmen have long acknowledged the intimate link between developing the [Russian Far East], particularly its energy and energy-related assets, and Russia's power position in Asia."[75] In 2006, Foreign Minister Sergei Lavrov found that "Russia can join the integration processes in the vast Asia-Pacific region only through the economic growth of Siberia and the Russian Far East; in other words, the modernization of these regions is an axiom."[76] In a speech in Kamchatka in September 2008, newly elected president Dmitry Medvedev joined numerous other voices in warning that if Russia fails to develop its Far East, the latter could become a base for raw materials for more developed Asian countries; he concluded that "unless we speed up our efforts, we can lose everything."[77]

Blank's own conclusion is rather to the point. Noting that the rise of China and the current economic crisis had forced Moscow to reassess the Russian Far East and its energy potential, he claims that two insights emerged. First, Moscow would need to stop dithering about building pipelines to China and the Far East. Second, and more important, Moscow would need to "reverse its long-held policy of barring foreign equity investment in Russian energy companies, especially in Siberia and the Far East."[78] The latter insight in particular has a great deal of relevance to Russia's ambition of using energy as a means to recapture its lost stature as a great power.

The problem that Moscow faces has two supplementary dimensions. One is that deals on loans in return for secure deliveries of oil and gas will lock Russia into increasing dependence on a single buyer, and in consequence wreck the previous ambition to build a diversified market consisting of China, Japan, and South Korea. The other concerns the increasing role of equity purchases as part of loan packages. Whether one prefers to talk of Russia's willingness to swap debt for equity as a colonial pattern is a matter of taste. What is irrefutable, however, is that in the wake of substantial Chinese investment, commercial and eventually also political influence will follow.

Possible further developments include roles for China as a partner with Gazprom to develop gas infrastructure in the Far East, and as a partner with Rosneft to develop East Siberian oil fields. The bottom line of the story is captured by Dmitry Trenin: "China is emerging as the state driving the bilateral agenda. For the first time in 300 years, China is more powerful and dynamic than Russia—and it can back up its economic and security interests with hefty infusions of cash."[79]

While the energy game as a whole must not be viewed as a zero-sum game, there is an element of precisely that involved here. Bearing in mind the long tug-of-war between Tokyo and Beijing over the route of the ESPO pipeline, we may conclude that Japan has suffered a serious setback. What remains to be seen is how this will affect its willingness to embark on further cooperation with Russia. Moscow is in need of huge investments to finance further prospecting, field development, and other forms of infrastructure that are needed to revitalize Eastern Siberia and the Far East. Japan could have been a valuable partner in such ambitions, but to date Moscow has not been playing a winning game.

From a diplomatic perspective, it is hard indeed to see the rationale behind Dmitry Medvedev's two visits to the Kurile Islands, first as president and then as prime minister. No other issue has come even close to being such a problem in relations between Moscow and Tokyo as has the status of this tiny territory, which was occupied by Stalin at the very end of World War II. Medvedev's first visit, in November 2010, was the first visit ever by a post-Soviet Russian leader to the islands. It provoked Japan's prime minister at the time, Naoto Kan, to call the event an "inexcusable rudeness." When Medvedev returned for a second visit, in July 2012, he was unrepentant, claiming to have urged members of his government to visit the Kuriles as "it is an important part of the Russian territory." And he added that "this practice will definitely be continued by the new Cabinet."[80]

The crux of the matter is that Moscow has invited participation by Japan in developing the Russian Far East, but only on condition that Tokyo drops its claims to the Kuriles. What is beginning to transpire is that Moscow has overplayed its hand, even grossly so, and that it may have succeeded in alienating both political and business circles in Japan.

Expanding on his previously cited conclusion that Russia had succeeded in scoring on its own goal, Shoichi Itoh suggests that the Russian strategy of playing Japan and China off against each other ended in failure mainly because Moscow did not know when to stop the game. Moscow not only failed to understand the essence of Sino-Japanese relations, banking too much on bad relations between Tokyo and Beijing, but also grossly overestimated the Japanese economy's dependence on energy, failing to note a drive toward increased efficiency and supply diversification. The combined outcome was unwarranted arrogance: "Russia increasingly took a high-handed approach to foreign capital while its resource nationalism was enhanced by oil prices that kept hitting historical highs until the summer of 2008."[81]

Before speculating about the broader implications of these various developments, let us first turn to the impact on Russia of the global financial crisis and the process of postcrisis adjustment.

Notes

1. Richard Galpin, "Energy Fuels New 'Great Game' in Europe," *BBC News*, June 9, 2009, http://news.bbc.co.uk/2/hi/europe/8090104.stm.

2. Socor, "Russia to Increase Purchase Prices."

3. On prices for Turkmen gas exports to Russia, see Pirani, *Russian and CIS Gas Markets*, pp. 292–293.

4. "Average Gas Price for Europe Could Rise to $400 in 2008—Gazprom," *RIA Novosti*, March 14, 2008, http://en.ria.ru/russia/20080314/101336197.html.

5. "Turkmenistan: Will Berdymukhammedov Commit to the Trans-Caspian Pipeline During His Turkey Visit?" *Eurasianet*, March 19, 2008, http://www.eurasianet.org/departments/insight/articles/eav032008.shtml.

6. "Caspian: Azerbaijani-Turkmen Summit Marks Potentially Lucrative Thaw in Relations," *Eurasianet*, May 20, 2008, http://www.eurasianet.org/departments/insight/articles/pp052108.shtml.

7. Rovshan Izmayilov, "Azerbaijan: Baku Likely to Reject Russian Offer to Buy Natural Gas," *Eurasianet*, June 2, 2008, http://www.eurasianet.org/departments/insight/articles/eav060308a.shtml.

8. Kjaernet, "The Energy Dimension of Azerbaijani-Russian Relations," p. 2.

9. Ibid., p. 3.

10. Sergei Blagov, "Russian Ties with Azerbaijan Reach New Lows," *Eurasianet*, January 24, 2007, http://www.eurasianet.org/departments/insight/articles/eav012507.shtml; and Diana Petriashvili, "Gazprom Makes the Georgian Government Pay," *Eurasianet*, January 8, 2007, http://www.eurasianet.org/departments/insight/articles/eav010907.shtml.

11. Stephen Blank, "Turkmenbashi in Beijing: A Pipeline Dream," *Eurasianet*, April 9, 2006, http://www.eurasianet.org/departments/business/articles/041006a.shtml.

12. Bruce Pannier, "Independent Audit Shows Turkmen Gas Field 'World-Class,'" *Eurasianet*, October 18, 2008, http://www.eurasianet.org/departments/insight/articles/pp101908.shtml.

13. BP, *BP Statistical Review of World Energy, 2011*, p. 20.

14. Pannier, "Independent Audit Shows Turkmen Gas Field 'World-Class.'"

15. "Turkmenistan: Ashgabat Sends Shot Across Gazprom's Bow," *Eurasianet*, April 2, 2009, http://www.eurasianet.org/departments/business/articles/040309.shtml.

16. Deirdre Tynan, "Turkmenistan: The Bell Tolls for Gazprom's Dominance of Caspian Energy Market," *Eurasianet*, April 23, 2008, http://www.eurasianet.org/departments/business/articles/eav042409.shtml.

17. "Turkmenistan: Gazprom Plays Hardball with Ashgabat on Pricing," *Eurasianet,* June 1, 2009, http://www.eurasianet.org/departments/news/articles/eav 060209b.shtml.

18. "Turkmenistan, Russia Agree to Resume Gas Supplies in 2010, Ending Impasse," *IHS,* December 23, 2009, http://www.ihsglobalinsight.com/SDA/SDA Detail18049.htm.

19. Ben Farey, "Gaffney Cline Defends Estimates of Turkmen Natural-Gas Reserves," *Bloomberg News,* February 24, 2010, http://www.bloomberg.com/apps /news?pid=newsarchive&sid=aFgRH_Qt6_Ws.

20. As cited in Baev, *Russian Energy Policy and Military Power,* p. 193.

21. Ibid., pp. 149–153.

22. Peter Schwarz, "The Gas Conflict Between Russia and Ukraine," January 5, 2006, http://www.wsws.org/articles/2006/jan2006/gazp-j05.shtml.

23. EU Commission, *An External Policy to Serve Europe's Energy Interests,* p. 1.

24. See further Pirani, "The Russo-Ukrainian Gas Dispute, 2009."

25. See further Balmaceda, "Background to the Russia-Ukrainian Gas Crisis."

26. Mohit Joshi, "Gazprom Lost 1.1 Billion Dollars in Gas Crisis," *Top News,* January 14, 2009, http://www.topnews.in/gazprom-lost-11-billion-dollars-gas-crisis -2109822.

27. For a broad account of the role of Ukraine in post-Soviet energy politics, see Balmaceda, *Energy Dependency, Politics, and Corruption.*

28. The text of the declaration may be found at http://ec.europa.eu/external _relations/energy/events/eu_ukraine_2009/joint_declaration_en.pdf.

29. Alan Riley, "EU-Ukraine Gas Deal Is No Pipe Dream," *Wall Street Journal,* April 23, 2009, http://online.wsj.com/article/SB124043755044245165.html.

30. "Putin Warns EU over Ukraine Pipeline Deal," *EurActiv,* March 24, 2009, http://www.euractiv.com/en/energy/putin-warns-eu-ukraine-pipeline-deal/article -180577?_print.

31. Meulen, "Gas Supply and EU-Russia Relations," p. 851.

32. Nies, *Oil and Gas Delivery to Europe,* p. 25.

33. For more official detail, see http://ec.europa.eu/external_relations/eastern /index_en.htm.

34. Nadia Popova, "No Kremlin Guarantee of Gas to EU," *Moscow Times,* May 25, 2009, http://www.themoscowtimes.com/news/article/no-kremlin-guarantee-of -gas-to-eu/377366.html.

35. Ibid.

36. Ewa Krukowska, "Ukraine May Get $1.7 Billion from International Lenders for Gas," *Bloomberg News,* August 1, 2009, http://www.bloomberg.com /apps/news?pid=newsarchive&sid=aaakquyYMJxk.

37. "Gazprom May Delay Kovykta," *Moscow Times,* June 18, 2009, http:// www.themoscowtimes.com/business/article/gazprom-may-delay-kovykta/378873 .html.

38. Anatoly Medtsky, "Gazprom Considers 30% Investment Cut," *Moscow Times,* June 26, 2009, http://www.themoscowtimes.com/business/article/gazprom -considers-30-investment-cut/379071.html. Total investment for 2009 was planned at 920 billion rubles, with 637 billion for exploration, development, production, and pipeline construction, and the remainder for asset purchases. The 30 percent cut would apply to the lower number, bringing that expenditure down to 446 billion rubles, from 531 billion rubles spent on the same purposes in the previous year.

39. Dmitry Zhdannikov, "Gazprom Debt Burden to Speed Up Gas Crisis End," *Reuters,* January 12, 2009, http://www.reuters.com/article/GCA-Oil/idUSTRE50B4 JR20090112?pageNumber=2&virtualBrandChannel=0.

40. Shahin Abbasov, "Russia Scores Double Match Point with Azerbaijani Gas Deal," *Eurasianet,* June 29, 2009, http://www.eurasianet.org/departments/insightb /articles/eav063009a.shtml.

41. "Nabucco Pipeline Deal: Independence Day for European Gas," *Spiegel Online International,* July 13, 2009, http://www.spiegel.de/international/business /0,1518,635921,00.html.

42. "Caspian Basin: Nabucco Moves Ahead of South Stream in Regional Energy Race," *Eurasianet,* July 19, 2009, http://www.eurasianet.org/departments /insightb/articles/eav072009a.shtml.

43. "Fischer Goes for Gas: Ex-Foreign Minister to Become Nabucco Consultant," *Spiegel Online International,* June 26, 2009, http://www.spiegel.de /international/europe/0,1518,632827,00.html.

44. For an account of Chinese versus Russian strategic perspectives on the energy issue, see Blank, *Russo-Chinese Energy Relations.*

45. Itoh, *Russia Looks East,* p. 22.

46. For a detailed account, see Itoh, *The Pacific Pipeline at a Crossroads.*

47. John Helmer, "China Ties Up Russia's Crude—Again," *Dances with Bears,* October 30, 2008, http://johnhelmer.net/?p=580.

48. "China, Russia Sign Oil Pipeline Agreement," *China Daily,* May 29, 2003, http://www.chinadaily.com.cn/en/doc/2003-05/29/content_166888.htm.

49. Itoh, *Russia Looks East,* pp. 24–25.

50. Poussenkova, "The Global Expansion of Russia's Energy Giants," p. 112.

51. This revelation was the first really major challenge to high-level corruption in Russia. It was fielded by lawyer and anticorruption activist Aleksei Navalnyi, who would figure prominently as an opposition leader during the mass rallies that shook Moscow during the winter of 2011–2012. See Tai Adelaja, "Grand Theft Pipeline," *Russia Profile,* November 18, 2010, http://russiaprofile.org/business /a1290102813.html.

52. For a background on Russia's strategic involvement in developing its own Far East, and on conflicts with other powers in the region, see Blank, "At a Dead End." Russia's role in Asia more broadly is scrutinized in Rutland, "Russia's Economic Role in Asia."

53. Itoh, *Russia Looks East,* p. 30.

54. Gustafson, *Wheel of Fortune,* p. 348.

55. "Moscow-Beijing Sign ESPO Pipeline Deal," *Oil and Gas Eurasia,* October 28, 2008, http://www.oilandgaseurasia.com/news/p/0/news/3086#.

56. "Petro China Increases Storage for Russian Oil," *Oil and Gas Eurasia,* April 28, 2009, http://www.oilandgaseurasia.com/news/p/0/news/4699.

57. China International Oil and Gas Exhibition, "CNPC Receives Discount of Oil Price from Russian Companies," February 29, 2012, http://www.ciooe.com.cn /2012/en/News//ExhibitorsNews/316.html.

58. As cited by Blank, "Loans for Oil, the Russo-Chinese Deal, and Its Implications," p. 23.

59. Yulia Latynina, "Giving China a Piece of Russia," *Moscow Times,* July 1, 2009, http://www.themoscowtimes.com/opinion/article/giving-china-a-piece-of -russia/379201.html.

60. Anatoly Medetsky, "Medvedev, Hu to Speed Up Gas Talks," *Moscow Times,* June 18, 2009, http://www.themoscowtimes.com/news/article/medvedev-hu -to-speed-up-gas-talks/378856.html.

61. Henderson, *The Pricing Debate over Russian Gas Exports,* pp. 6–10.

62. "Russia Signs Gas Deal with China," *BBC News*, March 21, 2006, http://news.bbc.co.uk/2/hi/asia-pacific/4828244.stm.

63. Blank, "Russia's New Gas Deal with China," pp. 23–24.

64. Henderson, *The Pricing Debate over Russian Gas Exports,* pp. 8, 10.

65. "Russia, China Inch Close to Gas Supply Deal," *Commodity Online,* November 24, 2010, http://www.commodityonline.com/news/Russia-China-inch -close-to-gas-supply-deal-33752-3-1.html.

66. "China, Kazakhstan Ink $10 bln Loan for Oil," *Oil and Gas Eurasia,* April 16, 2009, http://www.oilandgaseurasia.com/news/p/0/news/4604.

67. "Turkmens Get $4Bln Loan," *Moscow Times,* June 26, 2009, http://www .themoscowtimes.com/business/article/turkmens-get-4bln-loan/379069.html.

68. Wenran Jiang, "China Makes Strides in Energy 'Go-out' Strategy," July 23, 2009, http://www.jamestown.org/programs/chinabrief/single/?tx_ttnews%5Btt_news %5D=35309&tx_ttnews%5BbackPid%5D=25&cHash=1828d2cfe2.

69. Hydrocarbons Technology, "Kazakhstan-China Crude Oil Pipeline, Kazakhstan," http://www.hydrocarbons-technology.com/projects/kazakhstan-china-crude -oil-pipeline.

70. Socor, "Three Central Asian Countries Inaugurate Gas Export Pipeline."

71. Hydrocarbons Technology, "Central Asia-China Gas Pipeline, Turkmenistan to China," http://www.hydrocarbons-technology.com/projects/centralasia chinagasp.

72. "Kazakhstan Commits $130M to Gas Pipeline," *United Press International,* September 16, 2011, http://www.upi.com/Business_News/Energy-Resources/2011 /09/16/Kazakhstan-commits-130M-to-gas-pipeline/UPI-56621316168700.

73. "First Section of the Phase-II Kazakhstan-China Gas Pipeline Operational," *Pipelines International*, September 12, 2013, http://pipelinesinternational.com/news /first_section_of_the_phase-ii_kazakhstan-china_gas_pipeline_operational/083431.

74. Blank, "The Turkmenistan-China Pipeline," p. 25.

75. Blank, "Russia's New Gas Deal with China," p. 16.

76. Lavrov, "The Rise of Asia and the Eastern Vector," p. 70.

77. Cited from Blank, "Russia's New Gas Deal with China," p. 17.

78. Ibid., pp. 16–17.

79. Trenin, "Russia Reborn," p. 73.

80. "Medvedev Visits Kurile Islands," *RIA Novosti,* July 3, 2012, http://en.rian .ru/russia/20120703/174372986.html.

81. Itoh, *Russia Looks East,* pp. 33, 44–50.

7

Global Financial Crisis

The impact on Russia of the global financial crisis was in many ways deeply revealing. It is certainly true that most of the industrialized economies within the Group of 20 (G-20) suffered more serious damage, above all so in the fiscal dimension. Yet to the Kremlin it was still a rude awakening, putting an abrupt end to the complacency of the early Putin era. By exposing a series of fundamental weaknesses, the crisis provided a firm indication of the true role and place of the Russian economy in the global economic landscape.

The most visible of these weaknesses included a crucial dependence on hydrocarbon exports, the tenuous nature of the domestic financial system, and the associated risks of sudden bouts of massive capital flight. But these were only the tip of the iceberg. Under the surface lurked the kinds of institutional conflicts and shortcomings alluded to earlier, as rooted in deeper Russian history.

Although it is in these latter dimensions that we may find the true reasons why Russia was so badly hurt by the crisis, at the time there was little interest in exploring explanations of that kind. The mainstream of policy analysis remained beholden to the view of Russia as a "normal country," where the possible roles of cultural and historical legacies could be safely set aside.

Market analysts in particular were firmly convinced of the supremacy of generality over specificity. Until 2008, a favored ambition of the Moscow spin-doctors had been to portray Russia as a solid member of a four-nation team of fast-growing BRIC economies: Brazil, Russia, India, and China. Introduced by analyst Jim O'Neill at Goldman Sachs in 2001,

145

the moniker was suggestive and speculation had abounded that by 2050 the combined economic might of the BRIC economies could actually eclipse the combined economic might of the richest countries of the world.[1]

At their first formal summit meeting, held in the Russian city of Yekaterinburg on June 16, 2009, the leaders of the four BRIC economies had much to say about the importance of their group as a whole— they accounted for 15 percent of global GDP and 40 percent of global population—and about their prospects for taking a joint lead in achieving global economic recovery.[2] The sordid truth of the matter, however, was that the hosting nation no longer qualified as a member of this illustrious company.

In a provocative comment, made in the spring of 2010, Dmitry Trenin concluded that "Moscow ought to forget about trying to undermine America's global hegemony and concentrate instead on retaining its place in the 'top league' of world powers. China, India, and Brazil are candidates for membership in it. Russia is a candidate for exit."[3]

There were striking grounds for such a harsh verdict. Both China and India maintained solid growth throughout the crisis, recording increases in GDP during 2009 of 9.1 and 5.7 percent, respectively, and Brazil succeeded in holding the line, at a drop in GDP of merely 0.2 percent. Russia in sharp contrast recorded a drop in GDP for 2009 of 7.9 percent.[4]

Considering that Russia's GDP had grown by a respectable 5.2 percent in 2008, the extent of the contraction came to 13.1 percent. (More detail on Russian economic performance may be found in Appendix 1.) Russian fiscal performance took a similar hit. Having recorded a surplus of 4.1 percent of GDP in 2008, in 2009 the federal budget balance swung to a deficit of 5.9 percent, making for a 10 percent deterioration. While 2010 would bring a rebound in GDP, the fiscal situation would remain strained, mainly but not exclusively due to the upcoming election cycle.

This chapter takes a broader look at what lessons can and should be learned from these experiences. The most immediate question concerns what would happen if there were to be another sharp fall in the price of oil. Although the crisis did provide fundamental support for the wisdom of building precautionary reserves while the going was good, as the Kremlin came out of the crisis it would be singularly committed to heavy fiscal spending. Consequently, a renewed crisis would likely cause much more severe damage than that of 2008–2009.

But more important in a longer-term perspective is the question of potential lessons for economic growth strategy. Would the revelations of hydrocarbon vulnerability prompt a reorientation of economic policy, aiming to reduce the role of the energy complex, or would it simply be a question of returning to business as usual? And of course there is the question of what implications the crisis may have had for Russia's ambitions to use energy to reclaim its influence within the international community.

This chapter lays the groundwork for subsequent discussion of these questions. It begins by looking at the immediate macroeconomic impact of the subprime mortgage crisis. Next it addresses why the regime was concerned about the latitude for fiscal spending, emphasizing how differently the crisis affected the country's elites compared to the population. Finally, the chapter maps out the respective roles of rebounding energy prices and the government's anticrisis program in the ensuing recovery.

Impact of the Financial Crisis

The global financial crisis arrived in Russia via three main channels. The first and by far the most important, powerfully reflecting Russia's hydrocarbon dependence, was via a sharp drop in the price of oil. From a peak of $142.50 per barrel in July 2008, the price of Urals crude dropped to a low of $32.34 per barrel in December, wreaking substantial havoc on the financial as well as the real sectors.[5] The second channel was via a general downturn in global demand for commodities, which compounded the damage to the Russian metals sector. And the third was via a "flight to safety" that caused a substantial capital outflow from Russia. Whereas 2007 had shown a net inflow of $83 billion, 2008 brought a net outflow of $130 billion. Reflecting the impact of the crisis, the fourth quarter alone saw a record-breaking outflow of $130.5 billion.[6]

The first signs that Russia was about to take a beating, and a severe one at that, were beginning to show in the final quarter of 2008. In October 2008, there was still growth in GDP, up by 2.6 percent compared to October 2007. In November 2008 growth was down by 4 percent, and in December 2008 down by 6.7 percent, compared to the same months in 2007. Commodity exports over the same period recorded continued growth in October 2008, up by 12.4 percent compared to October 2007, followed by decreases in November and December 2008 by 16.1 and 25.8 percent, respectively, compared to the same months 2007. Despite the suffering during these months, for the year as a whole Russia's economic performance was still respectable, with growth in GDP of 4.3 percent and a trade surplus of $179.7 billion.[7]

As the year drew to a close, Moscow was in denial, claiming the financial crisis to be a US phenomenon that would have no impact on Russia. In December 2008, Russia's deputy minister of economic development, Andrei Klepach, received a reprimand from Prime Minister Putin for having warned that the economy was about to enter recession. Faced with his superior's insistence that growth would continue in 2009, Klepach retracted his statement.[8] At the World Economic Forum in Davos in January 2009, the minister of finance, Aleksei Kudrin, still touted the party line, famously claiming that Russia was "an island of stability."[9]

There was a striking sense of déjà vu here, if we recall how the Krem-lin had responded to the Asian financial crisis that erupted in the summer of 1997. Back then it had remained insistent, far into the spring of 1998, that Russia was sufficiently stable to be able to ignore what in August of that year would cause a complete meltdown of the country's financial markets and a de facto sovereign default on short-term obligations (the notorious GKOs).

To what extent statements of reassurance this time around reflected genuine beliefs will have to remain a matter for speculation. Perhaps it was the case that the initial period of denial did reflect a genuine belief that the Russian economy was no longer hostage to the price of crude and would thus be able to weather the storm with little damage. Perhaps it was simply a case of posturing, or of trying to reassure markets and the general public. Be this as it may, behind the scenes the impact was severe. In the first half of 2009, Russia achieved the dubious distinction of combining double-digit inflation with a double-digit drop in GDP.

While the political spin-games were being played out, the real sector of the economy continued its slide into recession. During the first quarter of 2009, GDP was down by 12.3 percent and industrial production by 14.3 percent compared to the same period in 2008. The sharp fall in the price of hydrocarbons was also reflected in commodity exports, which were down by 47.4 percent compared to the first quarter 2008.[10] By April 2009, with GDP down by 14.9 percent and industrial production by 16.9 percent com-pared to April 2008, the government was no longer able to view the finan-cial crisis as a passing phenomenon.

Federal budget execution provided a stark illustration of just how badly the crisis was impacting government finance. Having remained solidly in the black throughout the first two terms of the Putin presidency, in 2009 the budget balance slid deeply into the red. Whereas the period of January to April 2008 had shown a surplus corresponding to 9.4 percent of GDP, and whereas 2008 as a whole had recorded a surplus corresponding to 4.1 per-cent of GDP, the same period in 2009 showed a deficit corresponding to 3.1 percent of GDP.[11]

The mounting deficit led to a rapid depletion of the Reserve Fund that had been so wisely accumulated during the good years. Having peaked at $142.6 billion on September 1, 2008, by the end of the year it remained nearly the same, at $137.1 billion. But within six months, by early March 2009, it was down to $94.5 billion.[12] The fund was being depleted so rap-idly that by late April 2009, Finance Minister Kudrin predicted that it would be "practically exhausted" in 2010.[13]

The sudden and drastic deterioration in government finance made it plain that Russia, following a decade of financial independence, would now have to return to the global financial markets as a sovereign borrower. By the end of July 2009, the government announced that it was expecting federal budget deficits corresponding to 9.4 percent of GDP for 2009, 7.5 percent for 2010, and 4.3 percent for 2011.[14] The expected deficit of 3.2 trillion rubles ($103 billion) for 2010 was to be partly covered by contributions of 1.6 trillion rubles from the Reserve Fund, which would then be exhausted, and by 680 billion rubles from the National Welfare Fund.[15] In order to cover the shortfall, sales of eurobonds of up to $20 billion were envisioned for 2010 alone, and more were expected to follow.[16] Added borrowing of up to $11.1 billion might also be sought from lenders such as the World Bank.[17]

Moscow's pending return to indebtedness not only signaled an end to the Russian government's time of invigorating independence from international "advice" and political pressure. More seriously, it also raised questions regarding its ability to meet pressing needs for long-neglected investment. Items of particular urgency included needs to engage in restructuring and upgrading of obsolete production facilities, to undertake maintenance and renovation of the country's crumbling infrastructure, and to provide critical support for a poorly equipped national health care system faced with a mounting public health disaster.

While there was consequently no shortage of reasons for the Russian government to be concerned, its formulation of an anticrisis program would be heavily marked by more immediate needs: bailing out the oligarchs and preventing social unrest among the public. The latter needs highlight the crucial role of rents from the energy complex in purchasing systemic stability by way of fiscal spending. The country's vulnerability to swings in hydrocarbon prices consequently entails greater worries than the technical pursuit of fiscal policy.

As we shall see, concerns about the possibility of social unrest have played a crucial role in the formulation of economic policy in Russia during the postcrisis years. Ambitions to preserve political and systemic stability, though understandable, would not be entirely in line with the demands of an effective anticrisis policy. Nor would they leave much room for consideration of alternative paths ahead.

Causes for Concern

Perhaps the most striking feature of the so-called global financial crisis was that it was felt most severely in the most developed of the industrialized economies, notably so in the United States and in the European Union. In countries that were less economically developed, and less integrated into the global financial system, the consequences were less severe. Countries like India and Indonesia appear to have simply sailed through relatively unaffected. A closer look at the case of Russia will reveal a pattern that is vaguely reminiscent of this distinction, with a modern sector that suffered severe damage and a population at large that was, at least initially, largely unaffected. A further parallel between the crises of 1998 and of 2008 may be instructive here.

The 1998 crisis struck at a time when broad sections of the population were in the process of getting jobs, buying apartments, starting families, and saving money in the bank. Hopes for a better future were riding high. The financial meltdown completely wiped out all of this. Banks collapsed, savings evaporated, and jobs were lost. A decade later, the situation was radically different. During the 2008 crisis, the government, having substantial reserves at hand, was able to prevent the financial shock from having an immediate impact on the real sector, ensuring the survival of most banks and preventing the mass closure of enterprises. While the financial shock was severe indeed, to the population at large it amounted to little more than media headlines.

The reason why this was the case may be explained in terms of the emergence and persistence of a distinctly dual Russian financial system. Despite pervasive early imagery of how Russia had rapidly become a market economy, by the time that the 2008 crisis struck, the main role of the banking industry remained limited to servicing the corporate and not the household sector. Most Russians still lived in a cash-based economy, where wages were paid out in envelopes and where even big-ticket consumer goods such as cars were routinely bought with cash. Some 60 percent of all households did not have a bank account, and nine out of ten of all housing transactions were conducted without bank credit. With fewer than 1 million out of a total of more than 50 million households having any real wealth, there was little reason for the household sector to worry when financial markets went into tailspin.[18] This was important above all in the sense that negative popular reactions would take some time to materialize.

In the early months of the crisis, it was the country's oligarchs, previously so brash and self-assured, who took the brunt of the blow from two sides. The first proceeded via a meltdown on the Moscow stock exchange, which was heavily dominated by banking- and energy-related stocks. From a peak of 2,498, reached on May 19, 2008, by October 24 the RTS index (comprising fifty Russian stocks traded on the Moscow exchange) had tumbled by close to 80 percent, to a low of 549. Market capitalization meanwhile had dropped from $221.3 billion to no more than $49.6 billion.[19] Compounding the damage, the sudden deep freeze on global credit markets made refinancing of debts coming due nearly impossible. The combined result pushed the oligarchs into a process of what Stalin might have referred to as an "eradication as class."

According to calculations by *Bloomberg News,* during the initial phase of market meltdown the twenty-five richest Russians lost a joint total of $230 billion.[20] In the 2009 edition of the *Forbes* list of billionaires, only thirty-two of the eighty-seven Russians who had made it into the 2008 edition would remain.[21] Reflecting that it was not only the super-rich who were suffering, a subsequent calculation by Merrill Lynch and Capgemini Group would show that the number of high–net worth Russians, those with more than $1 million in assets, declined in 2008 by 28.5 percent, or almost double the global pattern.[22]

An important reason for the government to worry about the plight of the wealthy was related to the fact that so many of the oligarchs were so highly leveraged. During the good times they had happily assumed foreign credits to support purchases of assets that in turn were immediately mortgaged for further credits and further acquisitions. Given that Russian sovereign debt had meanwhile been paid down to a trifle, foreign creditors had implicitly assumed that lavish lending to corporate entities was somehow guaranteed by the state.

Oleg Deripaska's business empire provided a case in point. According to information on its website, the total debt of companies controlled by his holding company Basic Element in 2009 amounted to as much as $20 billion. As global credit markets dried up, Deripaska faced imminent margin calls that were impossible to meet, and in the case of bankruptcy his assets would have been transferred to the ownership of foreign creditors. Given that he was far from alone in this predicament, the Russian government found itself being pushed into a tight corner. A series of spectacular defaults and asset takeovers would have caused a fundamental transformation of the game for control over Russian resources. But as we shall see, the Kremlin was both ready and able to ride to the rescue.

Turning to the plight of the citizenry at large, we are faced with a very different picture. In the Yeltsin era, poverty and deprivation had been rampant, caused by a combination of inflation, unemployment, and a general breakdown of the Soviet-era system of social services. Over the first two terms of the Putin presidency, much of this had taken a turn for the better. Wages and pensions in particular had both increased and been paid out with greater regularity. The high approval rates enjoyed by President Putin in no small part derived from this.

Although at first it was not the Russian population at large who felt the impact of the financial crisis, a quick look behind the scenes will show that the government was clearly worried about the specter of pending social unrest. As one of many indications that it felt a need to take preemptive action, already in January 2009 the minimum wage was increased by no less than 88 percent, from 2,300 to 4,330 rubles per month.[23]

To what extent such fears may have been motivated at the time is hard to know. The experience of the mass eruption of discontent from below that marked the winter of 2011–2012 may serve to provide hindsight, suggesting that danger had been afoot already in 2009. Nevertheless, evidence of trouble from below had indeed been both present and mounting.

To begin with, the Kremlin surely must have borne in fresh memory how its 2005 ambition to modernize the system of social security, by replacing Soviet-era benefits in kind with cash payments, had brought masses of irate pensioners into the streets. Arriving in the wake of the Orange Revolution in Ukraine, it had been seen by some as a harbinger of worse to come.[24] In November 2008, as the dark clouds of crisis were gathering, the Russian sociologist Yevgeny Gonthmakher had even stoked the fires of fear by raising the specter of Novocherkassk, the hushed-up incident in 1962 when Soviet armed forced had used machine guns against protesting workers.[25] This said, there was little real evidence to indicate that serious disturbance was pending.

There were some incidents during 2009, the most famous of which was played out in the small town of Pikalyovo in June. Faced with a real danger of rioting, triggered by factory closures, Prime Minister Putin himself arrived on scene to promise that grievances would be addressed. For good measure, he undertook a public chastising of billionaire Deripaska, who was compared to a "cockroach" and ordered to ensure that his local cement factory resume production and orderly wage payments.[26] Throwing his pen on the desk, Putin ordered Deripaska to approach and sign an agreement that would help restart production. Adding insult to injury, following the signing he charmingly added: "Do not forget to return my pen."[27]

The first potentially serious incident arrived at the end of January 2010, in the western enclave of Kaliningrad. Following a rally in December 2009 that had gathered some 5,000 people, the January event saw perhaps 12,000 angry protesters take to the streets. Inflamed by opposition leader Boris Nemtsov's statement "We have had enough!" the masses joined in an appeal for Putin to resign.[28] The event was followed by an Internet campaign that gathered signatures in support of that same appeal.[29] While rumors have it that the Kaliningrad event caused repercussions within the Kremlin, aimed at those who had "allowed" it to happen, it must also be recognized that it was something of a special case.

An important driving force was linked to the financial bailout package. While it was successful in the sense that more or less all of the banks survived, as in many other countries it left domestic automakers hanging. In a bid to protect this important sector, the Russian government imposed a stiff duty on imported cars.[30] In an enclave economy such as Kaliningrad, which was crucially dependent on imports of used cars, this was a severe blow that added to general feelings of discontent. The same held for Vladivostok, where a brisk trade in used Japanese cars had been under way. Thus these cases must be viewed as rather special.

The true test of the seriousness of discontent from below arrived on March 20, 2010, proclaimed a "Day of Wrath" in some fifty cities across Russia. Although thousands did take to the streets, this was far short of the tens of thousands that the authorities had feared and the organizers had hoped for.[31] As there can be little doubt about the actual hardship, in some cases even hunger, that afflicted and continues to afflict the poor and the unemployed, the main question here concerned the limits of legendary Russian endurance.

As it turned out, the mounting groundswell of discontent ended in what could only be referred to—prior to the winter of 2011–2012—as a broad fizzle. Although they were harshly dealt with, members of the liberal opposition did continue their critique against the government, and they kept repeating their calls for Putin to resign. Participating in an antigovernment rally on December 31, 2010, opposition leader Boris Nemtsov was arrested and jailed for fifteen days. Following his release, he urged the West to introduce restrictions on Putin's travel.[32]

While Putin's actions did receive sporadic media attention, they did not succeed in arousing much of a following in broader segments of the Russian population. Thus, the shelving of all fears of an emerging threat to the stability of the regime might have seemed reasonable at the time. But what might have seemed reasonable to outside observers may not have been viewed in the same sanguine way by an extremely risk-averse Russian political leadership. By all indications, the outburst of anger against the regime that was provoked by the rigging of the December 2011 Duma election did arrive as a sudden shock to the regime. Yet the evolution of fiscal policy from 2009 onward was marked by latent fears of social unrest.

In preparations for the 2010 federal budget, the government quite clearly viewed the situation as sufficiently serious to warrant maintaining an unprecedented level of deficit social spending. As mentioned earlier, fiscal performance in 2009 had deteriorated to the extent of turning a surplus of 4.1 percent of GDP for 2008 into a deficit of 5.9 percent. In the draft 2010 budget that was approved by the Duma in October, spending was projected at 9,887 billion rubles, which was about the same as in 2009. With projected revenues increasing only slightly, from 6,713 to 6,950 billion rubles, the projected deficit came to 2,937 billion rubles (about $100 billion), or 6.8 percent of a much smaller GDP.[33] Given that the Reserve Fund had been more than halved over 2009, from $137.1 to $60.5 billion, 2010 would prove to be the year of Russia's return to international debt markets.[34]

Despite Finance Minister Kudrin's ambitions to warn against further deficit-enhancing spending programs, Prime Minister Putin demonstrated great resolve in living up to his promise that 70 percent of spending in the budget for 2010 would have a pronounced social character.[35] He proceeded with a promised raise of pensions, which had increased by a fourth on average in 2009 and increased by almost half again in 2010.[36] In April 2010, he added a further burden by announcing a major increase in health care spending by $16 billion over the coming two years. That increase was to be financed via an increase in the payroll tax, a move generally regarded by economists as a threat to economic recovery. Kudrin responded by claiming to be "disappointed," hoping that the hike might be reconsidered.[37]

While Putin did acknowledge that the mounting fiscal deficit was a problem, he also argued that substantial social spending was necessary in order to prevent unrest of the kind evidenced in Greece. Looking further down the road, however, he was in complete agreement that major cuts in spending would eventually be necessary. That was little more than a year before the eruption of mass protests.

Signs of trouble ahead had been evident already by early 2011, when Putin's popularity ratings began to slip.[38] As we shall see, as Russia emerged out of the crisis, global energy markets would yet again have a major impact on Russian politics. This time, however, the impact would be to generate complacency and a sense that substantial reserves were available to support a massive increase in social spending.

Energy Rides to the Rescue

What helped bring the Russian economy out of the crisis was very clearly linked to a sudden rise in hydrocarbon prices. Contrary to expectations in the early stages, the period of very low energy prices proved to be short. Over 2009, the price of Urals crude rose from $34.40 to $76.60 per barrel, and in 2010 it continued climbing, ending the year at $91.10 per barrel.[39] Given that every $1 change in the price per barrel is estimated to bring a change of about $2 billion in federal budget revenue, this was a significant transformation.

Added support was provided by the fact that the physical output of oil was also on the rise. Due to the general dislocation of the Yeltsin era, Russian oil production had slumped from a high of 11.4 million barrels per day in 1987 to an annual average during the 1990s of around 6 million barrels per day.[40] In 2000, it remained about the same, at 6.5 million barrels per day. Then output began to climb, driven by improved efficiency in operations by the privatized Russian oil companies. As noted earlier, much of this "creaming" of reservoirs that had been neglected during the Yeltsin era was for short-term gain. But it did bring a rise in output. By 2008, when

Putin handed over the presidency to Medvedev, Russian oil production had risen by more than half, to 9.9 million barrels per day.[41]

The size of the fiscal deficit, however, was such that some foreign borrowing was still required, albeit on a scale far less than had been anticipated. In April 2010, the Russian government returned to the eurobond market for the first time since the 1998 meltdown, successfully placing two issues for a joint total of $5.5 billion. Given that the federal budget had set a limit of $17.8 billion for such borrowing, the issue was rather modest, and with offers totaling $25 billion it was greatly oversubscribed.[42]

Noting that the Reserve Fund still contained funds to cover more than half of the projected deficit for the year as a whole, and that the deficit was projected on the assumption of a per-barrel oil price of $58, the initial return to sovereign borrowing was clearly a matter of choice rather than of necessity. Finance Minister Kudrin also indicated that 2010 would see no further sovereign borrowing.[43]

But it must still be recognized that it was not the rise in energy prices alone that took Russia out of the crisis. As most observers would likely agree, the government formulated and implemented an anticrisis program that according to Pekka Sutela "rightly earned accolades" from several international organizations—"one has to agree with the IMF and the World Bank's assessment now that Russia's anti-crisis policy was a major success overall: timely, consistent, and effective."[44]

The bedrock for the anticrisis policy was provided by the drastic shift in the federal budget balance. With revenue falling from 23.6 percent of GDP in 2008 to 18.8 percent in 2009, and with expenditures rising from 18.1 to 24.7 percent of GDP, the budget balance shifted by 11.3 percent of GDP. This in itself provided a powerful fiscal stimulus. Three more specific policy decisions may be identified. Serving to qualify somewhat the impression of a policy that was designed to achieve recovery, they all placed systemic stability above combating the fiscal crisis.[45]

The first was to refrain from rapidly lowering interest rates. Although lowering prime rates was the preferred action of central banks in most other afflicted economies, in the Russian case the need to stem capital outflow was allowed to take precedence. The implication was that the burden of stimulating the economy was shifted from monetary to fiscal policy.

The second policy decision was to undertake a stepwise devaluation of the currency. Although normally advised against, as it tends to generate expectations for a spiral of devaluations, in the Russian case the dangers of a substantial onetime devaluation, which might have provoked a banking crisis, were deemed to be larger. The implication here was that ample time was provided for economic actors to transform rubles into foreign currency holdings, at highly advantageous exchange rates.

The third policy decision was to provide targeted assistance to large Russian enterprises, including those in the notorious company towns. Although such support was recognized to be inefficient, as many of these enterprises really should have been allowed to fail, the risk of an avalanche of closures leading to social and political instability was deemed to be more serious. The implication was that the much-needed restructuring of the Russian economy was yet again pushed further into the future.

Regarding the more specific impact of the crisis, in the short term the need to bail out billionaires was clearly felt to be the most pressing. The rescue operation was devised to proceed along two lines. One was the provision of emergency credits that helped keep foreign banks at bay, and the other was the gradual devaluation that allowed for an orderly transformation of rubles into foreign currency at favorable rates. As the latter was the more controversial, it may be useful to elaborate.

If the Central Bank of Russia had followed the standard recommendation of undertaking a substantial onetime devaluation of the currency, this would have produced an equally substantial increase in the ruble value of foreign debts. For many of the oligarchs, that would have been the final straw, and a wave of defaults would have been unavoidable. There was no question that the currency was greatly overvalued and that a substantial devaluation was necessary. The alternative would have been a sharp surge in imports and an equally sharp contraction of exports. The controversy concerned the actual choice of slow adjustment, staggered over several weeks. What made this choice possible was that the Central Bank had such abundant reserves of foreign currency that it could afford to intervene in the market with operations that ensured a gradual devaluation of the ruble.

There can be little doubt that its decision to use $100 billion of its reserves for this purpose during the fourth quarter of 2008 was intended to provide protection for large corporations. And it worked. Over the period from October 3 to December 19, when the price of oil dropped by 64 percent, the ruble lost only 6 percent of its value against the dollar.[46] As Sutela points out, the price for this operation was paid in terms of a de facto privatization of a large part of the nation's foreign currency reserves.[47] This was, however, quite consistent with what Clifford Gaddy and Barry Ickes have presented as "Putin's protection racket."[48] While the going was good, the oligarchs acted as loyal clients of Putin. When they fell on hard times, the patron had to live up to his part of the bargain, which was to offer protection.

The other dimension of the rescue operation was more straightforward. At the time that the crisis erupted, the corporate sector was estimated to have a total foreign debt of about $500 billion, of which $39 billion would come due in the final months of the year. In an ambition to prevent defaults on these loans, the government introduced a special credit facility of $50 billion to help refinance debts coming due. As disbursements began, it quickly transpired that the largest beneficiaries would be companies belonging to some of the country's richest men, and by implication also big foreign banks that had provided those companies with lavish credits. Included here was Deripaska's RusAl, which received a $4.5 billion loan to repay a syndicated loan from banks including Merrill Lynch, the Royal Bank of Scotland, and BNP Paribas, and Mikhail Fridman's Alfa Group, which received $2 billion to pay off Deutsche Bank.[49]

Quickly realizing, however, that there would be other demands made on the country's international reserves, this credit line was soon to be frozen and only $11.8 billion was actually disbursed.[50] The main competing claim was related to the effort to prevent the ruble from going into tailspin, as Russians began to convert their rubles into dollars and as foreign investors began to withdraw their funds.[51] Having peaked at $598.1 billion on August 8, 2008, by November 21 the country's international reserves were down to $449.9 billion, representing a drop of $148.2 billion, or 24.8 percent.[52] Since July 31, the ruble had slid by 15 percent against the dollar and by 5.5 percent against the Central Bank's reference-currency basket.[53] By the end of 2008, the international reserves would be down to $426 billion, and the ruble would lose 20 percent of its value against the dollar.

As 2009 dawned, the Russian government was faced with the disturbing fact that while the country's sovereign debt had dropped to a mere $29.4 billion, or less than 2 percent of GDP, corporate debt remained at $452 billion.[54] According to the Central Bank's calculations, $128 billion of the latter would come due in 2009. To this should be added the $11.8 billion in bailout loans that had been granted by the government in the fall of 2008 and would come due by the end of 2009.[55]

Realizing that they would simply not be able to meet these obligations, some of the most highly leveraged of the oligarchs had begun cautiously courting their foreign creditors for extensions, but found that this was not well received. In January 2009, a group of metals executives instead came up with a previously unthinkable proposal, in effect representing a reversal of the controversial 1995 loans-for-shares scheme that had basically created the oligarchy. At a meeting with President Medvedev, they proposed merging their assets, including some of Russia's largest mines and factories, into a state-controlled conglomerate. In return, the government would—hopefully—accept to refinance their debt.[56]

Although nothing would come of this proposal, it did provide a stark illustration of just how vulnerable Russia's economic structure was to sudden external shocks. Had it not been the case that in 2008 the Kremlin had at its disposal vast financial reserves, then the edifice built by men like Deripaska and Fridman would have simply come tumbling down. A rerun of the insider rescue operations that followed in the wake of the collapse in 1998 would then have been hard to avoid.

The initial attitude of the Russian government was less than clear, and perhaps deliberately so. At the time that the metals barons made their plea, it surely must have anticipated that in the end it would have to undertake a massive bailout, or accept that many of the country's strategic assets would slip into foreign ownership. Yet it showed no immediate interest in the proposal. Perhaps it simply decided to hold out and hope for repatriation of some of the many billions in oligarch wealth that had been stashed away in offshore accounts, affectionately known in Russian parlance as *offshorki*.

In March 2009, the first deputy prime minister, Igor Shuvalev, told *Bloomberg News* that he preferred foreign banks to assume ownership of defaulted assets, rather than have the government do so. In April, however, Prime Minister Putin told the Duma that shares would be taken over by the state if loans were not repaid on time.[57]

What really served to transform the game was the fact that the drastic rebound in the price of oil also brought about a recovery of the Moscow stock exchange. Demonstrating its independence from the real side of the economy, during the crisis year 2009 the RTS index more than doubled, rising from 637 to 1,445.[58] By 2010 the oligarchs would be back, or at least some of them would. According to *Forbes* magazine, in 2010 the number of Russian billionaires had risen to sixty-two, from merely thirty-two in 2009, and their joint worth had more than doubled, from $142 billion to $297 billion.[59]

While the selective favors that were provided by the Kremlin to its cronies provide an interesting story in itself, the telling of that story shall have to be left for elsewhere.[60] Here let us turn to some implications of the economic recovery. Going beyond fiscal stabilization, they highlight the tenuous nature of the recovery and the broader consequences for a longer-term growth strategy.

Implications of the Recovery

As point of reference, let us recall the portrayal of Russia as one of four fast-growing BRIC economies. Leaving Brazil aside, it should by now be quite clear that among the troika of the Bear, the Dragon, and the Elephant, it is the Bear that is the odd one out. India is in the process of cashing in on a massive wager on the role of mathematics in basic education, which has provided a broad and solid base for developing a globally highly competitive information technology industry. China is approaching a rough par with the United States in manufacturing technology and efficiency, and is widely deemed to be on the cusp of gaining a substantial presence on the global high-technology market. It has already overtaken Japan for the number two slot, much as Japan once overtook Great Britain, and it is poised to overtake the United States to become the world's largest economy. According to IMF predictions, the latter may happen (at purchasing power parity) by 2016.[61]

The core question is where all of this leaves Russia. Will it be possible for a continued dominant position for the country's energy complex to combine with a much-needed drive for modernization? Does the Kremlin really view a wager on energy as a way toward regaining lost power and influence, or does it all boil down to little more than a reach for the easy money? Perhaps most important of all, would a failure to achieve modernization, with or without diversification, be tantamount to leaving Russia with a future as a frozen Venezuela, or as a Kuwait with permafrost, in effect serving as a source of raw materials for the fast-growing and rapidly modernizing economy of China? There does appear to be quite a lot at stake here.

The most intuitive lesson to be drawn from the recovery is that in a narrow sense the problem was shown to be quite manageable. Russia has proven that it may very well adjust to living with the boom-and-bust pattern associated with inevitable swings in hydrocarbon prices. Although vulnerability will remain, Russia has proven its ability to devise a fiscal policy that prudently accumulates reserves in the good years. As shown in 2008–2009, such reserves may absorb shocks and help tide the country through lean years.

But there was also a downside. The sense of complacency that began to return as the economy was coming out of the crisis reflected that living high off the proceeds from resource rents was viewed as much preferable to engaging in the complex and painful reforms that would be necessary for any serious change in course.

This is not to say that fiscal adjustment is without costs and complexities of its own. Although Russian fiscal policy during the early Putin era did receive high marks for maintaining a solid surplus, it was also the case that the windfall of petrodollar revenues allowed a fourfold expansion of federal spending. Measured as share of GDP, federal budget expenditure increased from 14.6 percent in 2000, to 16 percent in 2006, to 17.8 percent in 2008. In the crisis year 2009, expenditure in absolute terms rose to 9,636 billion rubles, from 7,566 billion rubles in 2008, or by 27.4 percent. With a parallel contraction in output by 7.9 percent, the share of expenditure in GDP was pushed to a high of 24.7 percent.[62]

The reason why this development has to be taken so seriously would be manifested during the cycle of elections to the Russian Duma in December 2011 and to the presidency in March 2012. The mainstay of fiscal conservatism during the good years had been to project federal revenue based on a conservative estimate of the average price of oil. For as long as the actual price of oil exceeded the budget projection, the excess revenue could be stashed away in sovereign wealth funds, first the Stabilization Fund and then the Reserve Fund. Until 2008, the combined growth in GDP and in government revenue was so strong that a steady expansion of expenditure could take place without jeopardizing fiscal balance. The inherent dangers in this development came to the fore when the price of oil suddenly collapsed and the economy went into tailspin.

With such heavy emphasis being placed on maintaining political and social stability, it was clear that federal budget expenditure would have to remain high through the elections. In order to avoid a sharp rise in the projected deficit, in preparations for the 2011 federal budget Prime Minister Putin ordered an increase in the projected price of oil, from $58 to $75 per barrel.[63] This was tantamount to allowing for an extra $34 billion in spending, without affecting the projected deficit. Needless to say, actual budget performance will not be directly affected by such creative accounting. The point here relates to the political ambition of creating more leeway for spending.

The problem concerns what is known as the breakeven price of oil—the actual price of oil at which federal revenue suffices to cover federal expenditure. As expenditure keeps increasing, so does the breakeven price of oil. Over the period 2000–2006 it was kept in the range from $20 to $40 per barrel. In 2008 it rose to $62; in 2009 it reached $99; and in 2010 it was estimated at $105. While actual developments until the spring of 2012 demonstrated that the price of oil could both exceed and remain above that level, in the postcrisis years the budget was clearly being squeezed to the hilt. In June 2012, former finance minister Aleksei Kudrin warned that the breakeven price had reached $117 per barrel.[64]

By thus removing the option of a return to the previous policy of prudent accumulation of reserves during good times, the Russian economy was made increasingly vulnerable to a renewed financial crisis, yet again highlighting the fundamental dilemma of vulnerability to swings in hydrocarbon prices.

At the outset of 2011, the Reserve Fund had been reduced to $25.4 billion.[65] With a federal budget that projected revenues for the year of 8,844 billion rubles and expenditures of 10,658 billion rubles, the projected deficit came to 1,814 billion rubles, or about $60 billion.[66] Given, moreover, that planned budgets for 2012 and 2013 were expected to bring in deficits of about the same size, and that the run-up to the presidential election was marked by a strong reluctance to cut politically sensitive social spending, the stage was set for a major return to borrowing.

This in itself would not meet with any trouble. As the Russian economy emerged from the financial crisis, its fundamentals remained strong. Compared to other industrialized economies, Russian debt as a share of GDP was a mere trifle. Markets would consequently be happy to extend credit, even substantial credit. The core of the problem lay elsewhere. It rested in the link between sovereign and corporate borrowing, on the one hand, and the impact on the high-profile ambition of undertaking modernization, on the other. As neither the state nor the corporate sector could be expected to put up the quite substantial resources that would be needed for serious modernization, the prospects did not look good.

This brings us back to our core question concerning the relationship between energy and long-term growth strategy. The next chapter looks at the prospects, more narrowly, for achieving sustainable growth in output of oil and gas, and for placing this development on a sound, nonconfrontational, commercial footing. The final chapter will then place these reflections into a broader context to reconnect with Russia's strategy for long-term development and growth.

Notes

1. See further Jim O'Neill, "Building Better Global Economic BRICs," November 30, 2001, http://www.goldmansachs.com/our-thinking/archive/archive -pdfs/build-better-brics.pdf, which introduces the original concept; and Jim O'Neill, *BRICS and Beyond*, 2007, http://www.goldmansachs.com/our-thinking/archive /archive-pdfs/brics-book/brics-full-book.pdf, which provides an in-depth look at the matter.

2. Andrew E. Kramer, "Emerging Economies Meet in Russia," *New York Times*, June 16, 2009, http://www.nytimes.com/2009/06/17/world/europe/17bric .html?_r=0.

3. Dmitry Trenin, "Cost of the Matter," *Kommersant,* May 14, 2010.

4. International Monetary Fund, "World Economic Outlook Update: Restoring Confidence Without Harming Recovery," July 7, 2010, http://www.imf.org/external /pubs/ft/weo/2010/update/02/index.htm.

5. "Oil Prices Push Trade Surplus Past $200Bln," *Neftegaz*, February 9, 2009. http://neftegaz.ru/en/press/view/5614.

6. "UPDATE 1-Russia 2008 Capital Outflows at Record $130 bln," *Reuters,* January 13, 2009, http://in.reuters.com/article/asiaCompanyAndMarkets/idINLD 44860120090113.

7. Central Bank of Russia, "Key Economic Indicators in 2008," http://www .cbr.ru/eng/statistics/print.aspx?file=macro/macro_08_e.htm&pid=macro&sid=oep. Numbers given here for GDP reflect changes in output volumes for what the Central Bank refers to as the "key economic sectors."

8. "Klepach Says GDP Plunged by 9.5%," *Moscow Times,* April 24, 2009, http://www.themoscowtimes.com/news/article/klepach-says-gdp-plunged-by-95 /376549.html.

9. "Russia Is an 'Island of Stability': Finance Minister," *RT News*, January 24, 2008, http://rt.com/business/russia-is-an-island-of-stability-finance-minister.

10. Central Bank of Russia, "Key Economic Indicators in 2009," http://www.cbr .ru/eng/analytics/macro/print.asp?file=macro_09_e.htm.

11. Economic Expert Group, "Federal Budget Execution," http://www.eeg.ru/pages/148.

12. Ministry of Finance of the Russian Federation, "Aggregate Amount of the Reserve Fund," http://www1.minfin.ru/en/reservefund/statistics/amount/index.php?id4=5817.

13. "Kudrin Says Reserve Fund to Be Spent by '10," *Moscow Times,* April 23, 2009, http://www.themoscowtimes.com/business/article/kudrin-says-reserve-fund-to-be-spent-by-10/376518.html.

14. "State to Sell $20Bln of Eurobonds," *Moscow Times,* July 28, 2009, http://www.themoscowtimes.com/news/article/state-to-sell-20bln-of-eurobonds/379903.html.

15. "Russia May Seek Loans of $18Bln," *Moscow Times,* July 27, 2009, http://www.themoscowtimes.com/business/article/russia-may-seek-loans-of-18bln/379849.html. These two sovereign wealth funds were created in 2008, by way of splitting the Stabilization Fund, originally established in 2004.

16. "State to Sell $20Bln of Eurobonds," *Moscow Times,* July 28, 2009, http://www.themoscowtimes.com/news/article/state-to-sell-20bln-of-eurobonds/379903.html.

17. Ibid.

18. Sutela, "Russia's Response to the Global Financial Crisis," p. 2.

19. Moscow Exchange, "Daily History of the RTS," http://moex.com/en/index/stat/dailyhistory.aspx?code=RTSI.

20. "Oligarchs Lose $230Bln in Collapse," *Moscow Times,* October 13, 2008, http://www.themoscowtimes.com/business/article/oligarchs-lose-230bln-in-collapse/371599.html.

21. For the rankings, see Luisa Kroll, "The World's Billionaires," *Forbes,* March 10, 2010, http://www.forbes.com/2010/03/10/worlds-richest-people-slim-gates-buffett-billionaires-2010_land.html?boxes=listschannellatest.

22. Courtney Weaver, "Number of Russian Millionaires Plummets 28.5%, Report Finds," *Moscow Times,* June 25, 2009, http://www.themoscowtimes.com/business/article/number-of-russian-millionaires-plummets-285-report-finds/379050.html.

23. World Bank (in Russia), "Jobless Recovery?" March 2010, http://www-wds.worldbank.org/external/default/WDSContentServer/WDSP/IB/2010/03/30/0003330 38_20100330000444/Rendered/PDF/537060NWP0RER21eng0Box345623B01 PUBLIC1.pdf.

24. Nikolay Petrov, "Social Benefits Crisis: Domestic Policy Change for Putin," February 2, 2005, http://carnegieendowment.org/2005/02/02/social-benefits-crisis-domestic-policy-change-for-putin/ifb.

25. Yevgeny Gonthmakher, "Stsenarii: Novocherkassk-2009," *Vedomosti,* November 11, 2008, http://www.vedomosti.ru/newspaper/article.shtml?2008/11/06/167542).%20.

26. Nadia Popova, "Pikalyovo Wants More Help from Putin," *St. Petersburg Times,* June 19, 2009, http://www.sptimes.ru/index.php?action_id=2&story_id=29296.

27. Zarakhovich, "Putin Resolves Protest in Pikalevo." A video clip of this much-publicized event may be viewed on YouTube at http://www.youtube.com/watch?v=VrRHM-oSHlw.

28. Alexandra Odynova, "Thousands Decry Putin as Public Anger Swells," *Moscow Times,* February 1, 2010, http://www.themoscowtimes.com/news/article/thousands-decry-putin-as-public-anger-swells/398704.html.

29. See http://www.putinavotstavku.org.

30. Subsequent ambitions to support automakers would produce a $20 billion support package, including a "cash for clunkers" program worth 11.5 billion rubles. See "Russia Launches 'Cash-for-Clunkers' to Revive Car Market," *The Independent*, March 8, 2010, http://www.independent.co.uk/life-style/motoring /russia-launches-cashforclunkers-to-revive-car-market-1918269.html.

31. Alexandra Odynova, "Rallies Calling for Putin's Ouster Fizzle," *Moscow Times*, March 22, 2010, http://www.themoscowtimes.com/news/article/rallies -calling-for-putins-ouster-fizzle/402264.html.

32. "Nemtsov Urges West to Place Restrictions on Putin's Travel," *Moscow Times*, January 18, 2011, http://www.themoscowtimes.com/news/article/nemtsov -urges-west-to-place-restrictions-on-putins-travel/429025.html.

33. "Russian State Duma Approves 2010 Draft Budget in First Reading," *RIA Novosti*, October 21, 2009, http://en.rian.ru/business/20091021/156545994.html; and "Infographics," *RIA Novosti*, October 22, 2009, http://en.rian.ru/infographics /20091022/156557588.html.

34. Ministry of Finance of the Russian Federation, "Aggregate Amount of the Reserve Fund."

35. Nadia Popova, "2010 Budget Protects Social Outlays," *Moscow Times*, July 31, 2009, http://www.themoscowtimes.com/news/article/2010-budget-protects -social-outlays/380014.html.

36. Sutela, "Forecasting the Russian Economy," p. 3.

37. Anatoly Medetsky, "Putin Promises $16 Billion for Healthcare," *St. Petersburg Times*, April 23, 2010, http://www.sptimes.ru/story/31273.

38. In March 2011, according to the Levada Centre, Putin's approval rating dropped below 70 percent for the first time since July 2005. See the website Russia Votes, at http://www.russiavotes.org/president/presidency_performance_trends.php #190.

39. Top Oil News, "Urals, Brent and Light Sweet Crude—2009," http://www .topoilnews .com/wp-content/oilprice2009.xls; and Top Oil News, "Urals, Brent and Light Sweet Crude—2010," http://www.topoilnews.com/wp-content/oilprice2009.xls.

40. Soviet oil production reached a peak of 12.4 million barrels per day in 1987. Of this, 11.4 million barrels per day was produced in the Russian Federation. Grace, *Russian Oil Supply*, p. 65.

41. BP, *BP Statistical Review of World Energy, 2011*, p. 8.

42. "Russia Returns to Global Capital Markets with $5.5 bln Eurobond Issue," *RIA Novosti*, April 22, 2010, http://en.ria.ru/business/20100422/1587 01158.html.

43. "Russian Eurobond Successful, but No More This Year—Kudrin," *RIA Novosti*, April 22, 2010, http://en.rian.ru/business/20100422/158706236.html.

44. Sutela, "Russia's Response to the Global Financial Crisis," p. 4.

45. For a concise summary, see further ibid., pp. 6–8; and Sutela, "Forecasting the Russian Economy," p. 3.

46. Gaddy and Ickes, "Russia After the Global Financial Crisis," p. 301.

47. Sutela, "Forecasting the Russian Economy," p. 3.

48. Gaddy and Ickes, "Russia After the Global Financial Crisis."

49. Sergei Balashov, "Oligarchs Bite the Dust," *Russia Profile*, March 11, 2009, http://russiaprofile.org/business/a1236791034/print_edition.

50. Andrew E. Kramer, "The Last Days of the Oligarchs?" *World Affairs Board*, March 8, 2009, http://www.worldaffairsboard.com/nato-russian-resurgence /50116-last-days-oligarchs.html.

51. In November 2008, when the Central Bank began to ease up its defense of the ruble, it was reported that since the beginning of August foreigners had with-

drawn more than $180 billion from Russia. Emma O'Brien, "Russia Scales Back Ruble Defense As Oil Drop Spurs Depreciation," *Bloomberg News,* November 24, 2008, http://www.bloomberg.com/apps/news?pid=20601083&sid=adS9Usc9GdEk &refer=currency.

52. Central Bank of Russia, "International Reserves of the Russian Federation," http://www.cbr.ru/eng/hd_base/default.aspx?Prtid=mrrf_m.

53. O'Brien, "Russia Scales Back Ruble Defense."

54. Central Bank of Russia, "External Debt of the Russian Federation," http://www.cbr.ru/eng/statistics/print.aspx?file=credit_statistics/debt_e.htm&pid =svs&sid=ITM_38104.

55. Kramer, "The Last Days of the Oligarchs?"

56. Ibid.

57. Fortescue, "The Russian Oligarchs and the Economic Crisis."

58. Moscow Exchange, "Daily History of the RTS," http://moex.com/en/index /stat/dailyhistory.aspx?code=RTSI.

59. For the full list, see "The World's Billionaires," *Forbes,* March 10, 2010, http://www.forbes.com/2010/03/10/worlds-richest-people-slim-gates-buffett -billionaires-2010_land.html?boxes=listschannellatest.

60. See further Boris Nemtsov, "No More Welfare for Russia's Oligarchs," *Radio Free Europe/Radio Liberty,* February 19, 2009, http://www.rferl.org/article printview/1495217.html.

61. Michael Dolgow, "The Last Years of America's Historic GDP Reign," *Bloomberg Businessweek,* July 17, 2012, http://www.businessweek.com/articles /2012-07-17/the-last-years-of-americas-historic-gdp-reign.

62. Bank of Finland Institute for Economies, "BOFIT Russia Statistics, 1990– 2007," http://www.suomenpankki.fi/bofit_en/seuranta/venajatilastot/Documents /BOFIT_RussiaStatistics_1990_2007.pdf; and Bank of Finland Institute for Economies, "BOFIT Russia Statistics," http://www.suomenpankki.fi/bofit_en/seuranta /venajatilastot/Pages/default.aspx.

63. "UPDATE 2-Russia Gov't to Base 2011 Budget on $75/bbl Oil," *Reuters,* June 2, 2010, http://uk.reuters.com/article/idUKLDE6511RI20100602.

64. Andrew E. Kramer and David M. Herszenhorn, "Former Russian Minister Warns of Economic Ebb," *New York Times,* June 23, 2012, http://www.nytimes .com/2012/06/24/world/europe/former-russian-finance-minister-warns-of-recession .html?_r=0.

65. Ministry of Finance of the Russian Federation, "Aggregate Amount of the Reserve Fund."

66. "Federal Budget for 2011 and Planning Period for 2012 and 2013," *RIA Novosti,* http://en.rian.ru/infographics/20101126/161511100.html.

8
Picking Up the Pieces

As Russia was emerging from the global financial crisis, and as oil prices once again began to spiral skyward, driven by the spread of the Arab Spring across North Africa, a by now familiar sense of complacency was yet again beginning to lull the Russian elite. What in the midst of the crisis had looked like a pending return to persistent deficits in the federal budget, and to a renewed accumulation of politically troublesome sovereign foreign debt, was suddenly beginning to appear as no more than a mere market correction.

From a narrow perspective of fiscal stability, there were ample grounds for the positive change in mood. After all, the government had demonstrated that it was capable of building reserves that could help withstand even substantial drops in hydrocarbon prices. And it had pursued an anticrisis policy that was widely perceived to have been highly successful. Yet the future of the Russian economy, and of Russia more generally, will not hinge on fiscal policy alone. The country's increasingly heavy dependence on rents from hydrocarbon resources has a number of other dimensions as well, all with serious implications for future developments.

The main issue at hand has been succinctly formulated by Michael Ellman: "The negative experience of certain other countries raises the question of what will be the long-run effect of Russia's enormous energy riches on the structure of the economy and the welfare of the population." His specific questions concern whether the substantial incomes that are derived from hydrocarbon exports will "undermine manufacturing and agriculture and swell the ranks of civil servants, the military and the unemployed," or be used "to develop an internationally competitive tradables sector that generates well-paid market-sector employment for the population."[1]

There is much at stake here. At a casual glance, it may seem that the Kremlin's urge to recapture Russia's lost stature as a great power has met with a fair bit of success. The sudden bonanza of petrodollar inflow was helpful in several ways. It pulled the Russian economy out of depression. It restored fiscal balance, and it offered an arena of international relations where Moscow could again speak from a position of strength. But the hydrocarbon windfall was also deceptive, providing a false sense of security that relieved pressures to undertake much-needed reforms. The core of the problem concerns whether the current mode of living high off hydrocarbon rents represents a viable course for the future. Is this compatible with the emergence of an "internationally competitive tradables sector"?

If the answer to this question should turn out to be in the negative, and if no policy adjustments are made, then the long-term implications may be serious indeed. Russia will then risk being left with an increasingly backward economy that has little if any chance of achieving global competitiveness, and with an energy complex that is reduced to the rather ignominious role of providing fuel for growth in the more developed economies, notably so for the fast-growing Chinese economy.

In a broader perspective, the truly fundamental question concerns the implied role of the resource sector as a driver of economic growth. In the Russian case, this goes well beyond general arguments on the "resource curse" and the "paradox of plenty." At stake here is not generality but rather specificity, namely, whether Russia can break with its long-term legacy of a dominant role for the state, of weak property rights protection, and of a focus on economic growth based on forced extraction of resources. Our search for an answer to this question shall proceed in two steps.

This chapter will focus, more narrowly, on matters relating to the prospects for a positive further development of the country's energy resources. Assuming that the energy sector will remain dominant, the performance of this sector will be of crucial importance to the economy as a whole. Consequently, this chapter provides a critical assessment of energy policy as pursued since 1992 and an outline of the challenges that lie ahead. I argue here that Gazprom has been badly managed, entailing neglect both of development of new gas fields and of the challenges inherent in shale gas and liquefied natural gas. I suggest that the rise to prominence of Rosneft risks resulting in a process of "restatization" that may cause deterioration in governance similar to that at Gazprom. Finally, I also question the economic rationality of pipeline politics and suggest that motives other than purely commercial ones have been at play.

The subsequent, concluding chapter will then place the energy story into a broader context of prospects for Russia to achieve sustainable economic development and global integration. It details how the country has become dependent on oil, to the point even of what some have referred to as sheer addiction, and discusses the prospects for much-needed modernization, based on rents from the energy complex. I argue there that while multiple and at times conflicting agendas have been at play, institutional inertia from the past is being reasserted, and strikingly so. Vladimir Putin may in this respect be viewed more as a hostage of the past than as a shaper of the future.

Energy Policy in Disarray

Before we proceed to the question of whether Russian energy policy may be viewed as sustainable, it is essential to note that the initial conditions facing the country's first post-Soviet regime were favorable indeed. Massive investment throughout the 1970s and the 1980s had served to build a formidable platform for energy extraction. Although the output of oil had peaked in 1987, by the time of the Soviet dissolution the gas industry still offered great promise. As Matthew Sagers puts it, "Russia entered the 1990s blessed with the world's largest gas producing industry and transmission system." These were assets that would allow the country to simply "coast along," well into the post-Soviet transition period.[2]

Although it should be recognized that the oil and gas industries alike were beset with multiple problems, these were problems that related largely to technological backwardness and to rigidities of the central-planning hierarchy. With a carefully devised energy policy, aimed at clarifying property rights and at creating a market-based tax structure and pricing regime, the government *could* have achieved major improvements. By providing incentives for cost efficiency, and for increased investment in exploration and development of new resources, it *could* have promoted output growth. And with the addition of a policy to promote conservation and increased efficiency in domestic energy use, it *could* have freed up additional and quite substantial energy resources for export. Regrettably, none of this was to be.

In a scathing critique of Russian energy policy during the years 1992–2005, Vladimir Milov, Leonard Coburn, and Igor Danchenko begin by pointing at the introduction of a comprehensive regulatory system, and at the promulgation of a Russian "energy strategy" for the period up to 2020. Noting that the existence of such elaborate frameworks "creates an impression that Russia's national energy policy is both systematic and comprehensive," they maintain that the energy strategy in reality "resembled a manifesto for a planned energy economy." The main gist of their argument is that the making of energy policy was left to the mercy of traditional sector-based energy economists. In consequence, "formal and informal traditional institutions rooted in a planned economy (such as the balance of fuel and energy resources and state control) remained the 'ultimate instruments' for the solution of energy issues."[3]

The simple fact that different parts of the energy complex would develop so very differently may be ascribed to the absence of a consistent and comprehensive policy for energy-sector reform. Quite in line with the government's early policy to undertake "systemic change," deregulation and privatization schemes were implemented in the oil and coal industries. Prices for oil, oil products, and coal were deregulated in 1992–1993, and restrictions on profitability were lifted. As described in previous chapters, breakup and privatization of the oil industry was also introduced at an early stage. Denationalization of the coal industry followed in 1999. As a result, by 2004 the government's ownership share in oil and coal companies had been reduced to below 10 percent.[4]

The Gazprom behemoth, however, not only succeeded in resisting all attempts by the liberal reformers to break it up into competing private enterprises, but also succeeded in retaining full control over the pipeline grid, and long managed to evade all ambitions to implement serious economic reform. By the mid-2000s, it was consequently possible for Milov, Coburn, and Danchenko to conclude that Gazprom's "structure and governance have remained unchanged since the 1980s."[5]

Similarly, Russia's unified system of power generation and transmission long remained concentrated in one "national champion," the RAO Unified Energy System. Following the appointment in 1998 of Anatoly Chubais as the chief executive officer, an ambitious process of reform was introduced. But the ambition was restricted to achieving unbundling of the core activities (generation, transmission, and sales) of vertically integrated power-generating companies. State ownership has remained pervasive, and liberalization of the electricity market has remained stalled. The continued absence of market-based incentives for improvement in performance should be viewed against the background of a rapid deterioration in the generation and transmission infrastructure. By 2005, more than half of the generating capacity was in serious need of renovation and maintenance, and the prevalence of obsolete technology caused the Russian power industry to burn 40–50 billion cubic meters more gas compared to equivalents within the European Union.[6]

Viewed as a whole, the main failure of energy policy during the formative years of post-Soviet development was that so little was done to constrain the predatory instincts of well-placed insiders. By in effect allowing hosts of vested interests to help themselves to the assets and revenue streams of the energy complex, the government was responsible not just for wreaking havoc on property rights and on contractual rights more generally.

By implication, it was also complicit in siphoning off investment resources that could have been put to good use in upgrading both infrastructure and the technological capabilities of the oil and gas industries. The latter in particular would have serious long-term consequences.

The Kremlin's general attitude toward the energy complex, as a secondary economic sphere that could be tasked with servicing and subsidizing other sectors, was clearly reflected in its pursuit of pricing policy. In sharp contrast to the otherwise powerful ambition to liberalize, the domestic energy market would remain heavily regulated.

At the time of the collapse of the Soviet Union, gas was, as it still is, the most widely used fuel in Russia, accounting for 45 percent of total primary energy supply and 49 percent of fuel used to generate power. Because Gazprom in turn produced 94 percent of the country's total output of gas, the company was of overwhelming importance. It was consequently a significant move, both for Russia and for Gazprom, when the government decided that gas prices must be regulated. During most of the 1990s, in the words of James Henderson, "this regulated tariff was the only relevant domestic wholesale price."[7]

A particular feature of this regulation was that gas prices for industrial users were set much lower than for residential users. At the outset of the 1990s, households paid prices thirty times higher than those charged to industry.[8] While that difference would shrink, industrial prices would remain low. In the words of Simon Pirani, it is the industrial price that has consistently been "the key marker for the Russian gas sector, covering more than 85 percent of the country's customer demand."[9] As industrial prices remained far below prices prevailing on the European market, Gazprom was in effect forced to provide gas for domestic users at a substantial discount.[10] This form of implicit and highly burdensome taxation has seriously hampered the company's economic ability to engage in costly development of new gas fields.

Two factors have provided important compensation. One is the company's legal monopoly on export, which has allowed it to capture substantial gains at times of high world-market prices for hydrocarbons. (Denied access to foreign markets, domestic independent producers have instead been allowed to charge whatever prices the domestic market will bear.) The other is Gazprom's retention of control over the Unified Gas Supply System. In addition to providing a means of control over domestic competitors, the latter has also added to the lack of transparency in Gazprom's pricing policies.

Writing in 2006, Milov, Coburn, and Danchenko, noting that the Putin era had brought further regress to the central-planning mentality, reached a rather harsh verdict: "In sum, Russia's energy policy is fragmentary and contradictory. Its structure is dictated by rather short- and medium-term interests that are detached from the functioning of the capital-intensive energy sector."[11]

Regarding the more specific question of gas-pricing policy, 2006 was a potential watershed. If Gazprom were to be able to develop much-needed new fields in the north, it would have to be allowed to charge higher prices to domestic consumers. In November 2006, President Putin in consequence announced the introduction of a "netback parity" target, implying that by the end of 2011 domestic prices would be brought to parity with prices on the European market. This move was coupled also with the introduction of an exchange on which gas could be freely traded. Initially designed for a scope of 10 billion cubic meters, half from Gazprom and half from independent producers, in 2008 the scope of the exchange was increased to 15 billion cubic meters.[12]

These moves toward liberalization did look promising. But they would run into a host of problems. Although domestic gas prices did increase, the subsequent rapid rise in global hydrocarbon prices caused the netback parity target to become ever more elusive. Allowing full adjustment would produce a seriously negative impact on the prospects for economic growth. By the end of 2011, industrial prices consequently remained at about 60 percent of netback target. The gas exchange, moreover, had been closed since January 2009.[13] Ambitions remain that prices and trading will be liberalized, but they are becoming surrounded by increasing caveats and restrictions.[14]

Turning from gas to oil, we may find a set of tax and pricing problems that are of even greater importance to long-term performance. In general terms, every government in a resource-rich country will be faced with a fundamental dilemma. The difference between the cost of extraction and the market price of the resource is known as the ground rent—an income that is unrelated to the operation of extraction as such. In the case of oil and gas, rising world-market prices have caused such rents to become very large. In countries where subsoil resources belong to the state, which is the case in Russia, the ground rent will by definition also belong to the state. Consequently the government will need to reach agreement with operators on how it should be shared.

If the state captures too much of the rent, this will leave operators with insufficient resources for further development. If it captures too little, operators will be left with large windfall incomes. But what is a fair share, and how does one arrive at an acceptable estimate of the actual cost of extraction? As evidenced by the track record of conflicts between resource-rich countries and international oil companies, there are no easy solutions.

The system that was introduced in Russia, following the breakup of the Soviet Union, was geared into overcoming the problems of a weak state.

Private oil companies were faced with a combination of a tax on exports and a tax on production. As both were linked to world oil prices, they were in effect levied on gross income rather than on profits. And the actual rate has been fairly steep. The export tax was set at 65 percent of the export price for Urals crude, and the production tax at an additional 22 percent. The combined tax rate on crude oil thus came to 87 percent, levied on the export price above a threshold of $25 per barrel.[15]

While this system might have made sense in the early days, when the state had insufficient resources to monitor company costs, over time it would come under increasing pressure of highly valid critique. While crude oil prices did increase dramatically, so did the costs of extraction. When the global financial crisis struck, taxation was capturing well over 90 percent of the oil companies' upstream profits at the margin.[16] The consequence was a deep reluctance to commit investment to much-needed development of new oil fields, and to focus instead on "creaming" fields already in production.

In 2005 the government intervened, making a bad situation even worse. Driven by a belief that exporting crude oil is more "backward" than exporting refined products, the tax regime was altered to give a discount on the latter. Producers responded as expected, by increasing the share of processing, and exports of fuel oil in particular boomed. But there was a snag. Due to low quality, Russian-refined products would fetch lower prices than crude exports. The government in consequence ended up subsidizing actual value destruction.[17]

There has been increasing appreciation of the need to undertake fundamental change of the oil tax regime. The preferential treatment of refined products must be phased out, and a move must be made toward taxing profits rather than gross income. But it is a slow-moving process. Powerful vested interests have emerged that advocate maintaining the preferential treatment of refined products, and with respect to introducing a profit tax the devil is in the detail. No serious change on the latter is expected before 2020.[18]

Proceeding to the question of output performance of the oil and gas sectors during the first two terms of the Putin presidency, we may recall the stark contrast that emerged between a state-controlled gas industry that remained flat and a privatized oil industry that scored a 50 percent increase in output. While it may be tempting to ascribe this difference to privatization, and to a more successful implementation of reform within the oil industry, matters are not quite as simple as that, as Leslie Dienes has clearly demonstrated. The numbers he cites as evidence are suggestive indeed.

Having peaked at 569 million tons in 1987, a decade later Russian oil production had dropped by close to half, hovering in 1996–1999 at between 301 and 305 million tons. It then began to soar, reaching 421 million tons in 2003 and close to 440 million tons in 2004. The question concerns where all the additional oil came from. Dienes's unequivocal answer is that it mostly represented oil that had either not been lifted or been simply left behind during the turbulent 1990s.[19]

Based on a conservative estimate, Dienes argues that up to 400 million tons of oil may have been accessible by ways of well restoration, reservoir stimulation, and horizontal drilling, all of which were undertaken by privatized Russian oil companies, assisted by Western service firms.[20] While the volumes that were thus added did contribute toward the Russian economy's image of success, even substantially so, this could be no more than a temporary boost. Noting as "striking" the "meager efforts" that the largest Russian companies had invested in drilling and well completion at new fields, Dienes concluded (in 2004) that the boom was simply not sustainable.[21]

Although the rate of production slowed, the output of oil continued to rise, ensuring that by the end of 2009 Russia would surpass Saudi Arabia to become the world's largest producer of oil. But the latter was due mainly to a sharp reduction in Saudi output. Exercising its role as swing producer, the kingdom reduced output from 10.9 million barrels per day in 2008 to 9.9 million in 2009. In 2010, output was back at 10 million barrels per day, and in 2011 it reached a record high of 11.2 million, thus returning Saudi Arabia to its position as the world's largest producer of oil.[22] Early in 2012, moreover, the Saudi oil minister, Ali Al Naimi, said that if needed, the kingdom could boost output even further, to reach 12.5 million barrels per day.[23]

Russia meanwhile has reached a plateau. The additions to recent growth may be more than explained by output from Rosneft's giant Vankor field in Eastern Siberia, which came online in 2009. According to the company's website, it is the biggest field to have been discovered and brought into production in Russia since 1990. With recoverable reserves that are estimated at more than 3.8 million barrels, it will provide the main supply of oil for the ESPO pipeline.[24] At the outset of 2012, Vankor was already pumping 330,000 barrels per day, and is set to reach peak production of 500,000 barrels per day in 2014.[25] Looking beyond Vankor, the need to make up for declining output in the traditional fields will remain pressing.

Thus there are reasons to question both the purpose and the sustainability of Russian energy policy. A large part of the answer to why we must reach this conclusion and whether it will have lasting significance may be derived from Markku Kivinen's suggestion that what is good for Gazprom may not necessarily be good also for Russia, and from Margarita Balmaceda's account of agency and policy differentiation not only among the recipients of Russian oil and gas but also among the Russian actors themselves.[26] As none of these patterns seem likely to change soon, the prospects for improved efficiency in Russian energy policy do not look very bright.

It may of course be argued that few if any countries in the present world have formulated energy policies that live up to the multiple demands of sustainability, ranging from conservation and emission control to energy-efficient engineering, ecologically sound exploration and extraction practices, and promotion of renewables. The reason why the Russian case must nevertheless be viewed as rather special rests in the overwhelming role played by the country's energy complex in the development of both economy and society.

Sustaining Output Growth

The future of the Russian energy complex will hinge on whether sufficient new discoveries can be made to make up for depletion of old fields. This not only entails serious challenges in developing new technology, but more importantly represents a need to break away from deeply ingrained patterns of overdependence on a small number of fields in Western Siberia that have offered optimal geological and geographical conditions for exploitation.

The gas industry in particular has long been concentrated in a single gas-producing region to the north that has provided close to 90 percent of national gas output. Known as Nadym-Pur-Taz, after the three rivers that border the region, it includes the three previously mentioned supergiant fields Medvezhe, Urengoi, and Yamburg. All of these have now passed peak production and are set in irreversible decline.[27]

The case of oil is similar to that of gas in the sense of being concentrated in a rather small region surrounding the supergiant Samotlor field. But in the short term the case of oil has also been different. As noted earlier, the privatized Russian oil companies were faced with a peculiar opportunity. The Soviet legacy of poor production techniques had left such a negative impact on oil-well management that there was considerable room for compensatory short-term improvement.

One part of this legacy rested in a lack of access to modern technology such as computers and software. Insufficient computing power had restricted the scope of seismic modeling and thus prevented effective drilling. With modern techniques, Western service companies could improve the precision of drilling and thus unlock much oil that had been bypassed and left in the ground.[28]

Another and even more important part of the legacy concerned the practice of water-flooding, which is used as a secondary recovery technique throughout the world. When the natural pressure in a reservoir falls, water may be injected to maintain lift (a technologically more challenging alternative is to inject gas). What made the Soviet/Russian case so problematic may be explained by what the US Central Intelligence Agency referred to as the "Soviet Stakhanovite approach." Given the singular focus on raising output, water was injected to increase rather than maintain pressure, and it was done under a regime of embargo that prevented access to superior Western technology, such as high-capacity submersible pumps.[29]

This essentially represented a road to ruin. When the volume of water injected exceeds the volume of oil extracted, more water than oil will eventually be coming to the surface. In the giant Samotlor field, which by now is 80 percent depleted, the "water cut" has risen to 90 percent, meaning that the requirements of extracting the final 10 percent of oil will include not only pumping water in and out but also separating that water from the oil. In Thane Gustafson's words, the Soviet oil industry has become "the largest water company in the world."[30] To this can be added the need for electricity to drive the pumps, which would strain the net contribution from oil to the energy balance as a whole.

The key to successful water-flooding rests in ensuring that the injected water remains behind the oil, pushing it toward the well. If injection is too aggressive, water will break through the wall of oil and what comes out of the well will be oil mixed with water. Via careful monitoring and aggressive closure of damaged wells, Western service companies succeeded in vastly improving water-flooding and thus in substantially increasing ultimate recovery.[31]

But ultimately these were no more than short-term measures. While they did increase the recovery rate, nothing could alter the fact that oil is a "wasting asset." Once the oil that had been left in the ground had been recovered, which was largely achieved during Putin's first term in office, the Russian oil industry was again faced with the need to find new assets, which meant moving into new regions. At a casual glance, this could be viewed as a continuation of past trends.

From its early beginnings at and around Baku, the Russian oil industry went through several stages of shifting geographical focus. Following severe wartime damage to the Azeri fields, it shifted first to the Volga-Urals region and then to Western Siberia. As Marshall Goldman puts it, Russian oilmen were lucky in the sense that substantial new finds coincided in time with old fields being depleted: "So far, each time output in one major region slackened, the Soviets found a new region. It would be nice if Russian oil operators could continue in this leapfrog manner."[32]

Nice it would certainly be, but that does not make it any more likely. Two-thirds of the still untapped oil resources in Western Siberia are presently deemed to be virtually unrecoverable. The future of Russian oil must consequently be viewed as critically dependent on successful exploration of new frontiers, which in turn poses a new set of highly complex challenges. The latter include extreme Arctic climate and offshore drilling conditions, increasingly complicated geology, and demands for robust new

infrastructure to be put into place. It is estimated that it costs $2.50 to ver-
ify one ton of crude reserves in Western Siberia, and $4.00–$5.60 to do the
same in Eastern Siberia.[33] Thane Gustafson sums up part of the contrast by
noting that while the conditions of geology in the former region have represented "an oilman's dream" those in the latter represent "an oilman's
nightmare."[34]

To date, the Russian government has failed to elicit serious participation by private oil companies in exploring the country's eastern regions.
Further, meeting the challenges that lie ahead will entail a need to enter into
some form of relationship with foreign partners. As already shown by the
cases of Sakhalin, Kovytka, and Shtokman, this will be problematic.

And we must not forget the role of domestic political and bureaucratic
trouble. The story of the Vankor field may serve to illustrate the types of
turf battles that will surround future exploration. Discovered in 1988,
Vankor went through a long series of legal problems before eventually ending up in the hands of Rosneft and being declared commercial in 2009.

All in all, the future prospects for oil as well as gas must now be
viewed as heavily contingent on new fields being brought online and on
cutting-edge technology being made available. As noted by seasoned
observers Arild Moe and Valery Kryukov, this also appears to be well
understood by the political leadership. At a July 2008 meeting in Severo-
dvinsk, Putin frankly observed that "the potential for growth based on the
former resource base and outdated technologies has in fact been
exhausted."[35]

In the case of gas, expanding the resource base will not primarily be a
question of making new discoveries. As previously noted, large new discoveries have already been made, ranging from Kovytka in Eastern Siberia,
to a number of smaller but jointly important fields on the Yamal peninsula,
to the giant Shtokman field in the Barents Sea.[36] If these discoveries are
included, Russia has technically recoverable reserves that are estimated to
last for another eighty years or so, at current extraction levels. The remaining question concerns when and whether these new discoveries will actually be brought online. The track record of poor governance at Gazprom
must in this respect be viewed as a serious problem.

The case of oil is different from that of gas for other reasons as well. In
a downbeat assessment of the prospects for making additional new discoveries, Moe and Kryukov begin by noting that the "Soviet geological complex
was a large, well-supported sector whose mapping and exploration activities
were accorded high political priority." Due to a combination of deliberate
policy and of fiscal pressures brought about by the economic depression,
government financing for geological mapping and exploration plummeted
during the 1990s. In 1990, Russia's geological service employed some
480,000 people. By 2008, the number had dwindled to about 120,000.[37]

The government's initial expectations that private companies would step in to assume the burden of continued exploration were frustrated by a number of factors. Over and above the general chaos that marked the 1990s, in the Putin era private oil companies were also deterred from making longer-term commitments due to battles over subsoil legislation.[38] In a pointed analysis of the policymaking process that surrounded this legislation, Stephen Fortescue documents how the process was "characterized by delay and bitter debate," causing it to become "damagingly ineffective."[39]

The overall conclusion reached by Moe and Kryukov is harsh: "Consequently, our overall assessment of policies related to exploration and renewal of the resource base is negative, and we remain pessimistic about the prospects for rapid improvement."[40] A similarly pessimistic outlook is presented by Dienes, who notes as an "irony" of the production upsurge in the early 2000s that "the most profitable private companies are the ones that have squeezed the cream of their reserves the hardest." The inevitable consequence of this "predatory approach" was a decrease of reserves at the top of the reserve pyramid and an enhanced need for more intensive exploration.[41] Added reason for a downbeat assessment of the prospects for enhanced exploration, and of the prospects for bringing online discoveries already made, may be derived from the fact that both Gazprom and Rosneft are so heavily indebted.

Rosneft's ambition to make it into the energy industry's big league has certainly been highly successful. In 1998, when Sergei Bogdanchikov was appointed chief executive officer, the company produced no more than 11.9 million tons of oil. By 2004, its output had increased to 21.6 million tons, and in 2005, following the absorption of Yuganskneftegaz, it produced 74.4 million tons. By 2010, with the Vankor field online, its output had increased to 115.8 million tons. At that time it was also one of the leading independent gas producers in Russia, with an annual output of natural and associated gas of about 12 billion cubic meters.[42] Following its $55 billion takeover of TNK-BP in 2012, it actually surpassed ExxonMobil to become the world's largest publicly traded oil and gas company.[43] But the company's rise has also been accompanied by heavy borrowing, notably so from China, which renders its prospects for further expansion rather shaky.

Similarly, when the global financial crisis struck, Gazprom was already in such bad shape that, following all its efforts to wrest energy assets from foreign operators, it was forced to put both Kovytka and Shtokman on hold. In 2011 and 2012, the company earned higher profits than any other company in the world. But the money did not go into field development, or even into dividends for shareholders. Much simply disappeared into overpriced deals with contractors, who have turned out to be the real winners. In December 2012, analysts at Rusenergy, a leading consultancy in Russian oil and gas, named Gazprom the "loser of 2012." The company was branded "failure of the year" for the collapse of the Shtokman consortium, and "disappointment of the year" for its decision to launch construction of South Stream before all permissions had been secured and markets in Europe had stabilized.[44]

The failure of Gazprom to begin exploiting all the resources it has on hand is discouraging from the point of view of consumers, many of whom would surely prefer reasonably clean natural gas to less environmentally friendly sources of energy. But moreover, this failure is especially striking if compared to the track record of independent Russian gas producers such as Novatek, Nortgaz, and Itera.[45] From 1998 to 2006, when there was a significant surge in oil output, Gazprom actually registered a slight decline in output, by 0.6 percent, from 553.7 to 550.3 billion cubic meters. Meanwhile, oil companies increased their output of associated gas from 29 to 58.5 billion cubic meters, and independent gas producers scored a huge takeoff, from 1.1 to 46.1 billion cubic meters.[46]

Given that the latter expansion occurred despite the fact that independents were denied access to lucrative export markets, we have added reason to look with concern at the favored position of Gazprom. It comes across as particularly disturbing that following the removal of the Chernomyrdin-Vyakhirev team, the new management inserted by Putin was tasked with clawing back lost ground, rather than with promoting efficiency by allowing room for the independent gas producers to develop. Noting that US companies, enjoying the fruits of the shale boom, presently pay much lower gas prices than do their Russian counterparts, one might think that a policy of increasing competitive pressure to reduce costs would have been preferable to ratcheting up prices.

Let us turn now to the problems entailed in exploration under technologically challenging Arctic and offshore conditions, and the controversial participation by major foreign oil companies in Russian oil and gas exploration. The post-Soviet era has been marked by swings of the pendulum, from an early accommodating attitude that included production-sharing agreements to a later policy of cutting foreigners down to size. More recently, there has been a somewhat surprising reawakening of interest in the much-reviled production-sharing agreements.

In a speech to the Duma in early December 2010, the minister of energy, Sergei Shmatko, predicted a rebirth of such deals: "I think that in the future, [production-sharing agreement] projects may move into new areas. We need to look at our legislation and international experience in the field."[47] Whether seriously meant or not, the statement clearly reflected the imperative need to attract foreign participation in working energy deposits that are hard to extract.

A specific reason that may help explain the seeming about-face is related to the prospects for exploration of the Arctic shelf, which is widely believed to hold vast deposits of still undiscovered oil and gas. According to a study by the US Geological Survey, published in 2008, the area north of the Arctic Circle has an estimated 90 billion barrels of undiscovered, technically recoverable oil, 1,670 trillion cubic feet of technically recoverable natural gas, and 44 billion barrels of technically recoverable natural gas liquids. This accounts for about 22 percent of the undiscovered, technically recoverable resources in the world.[48] As a consequence of global warming, which is causing the ice cover to melt, both governments and energy companies in the region have awakened to the sudden lure of opportunity.

The surprise deal that was struck between Russia and Norway in 2010, to finally settle a four-decade dispute over their common border in the Arctic, must be viewed against precisely this background.[49] The same goes for the previously mentioned and equally surprising announcement, at the outset of 2011, of a deal between Rosneft and BP to develop the Artic shelf. Although that deal subsequently collapsed, the rapid switch to ExxonMobil as the new partner for Rosneft did serve to illustrate the rising importance of the Arctic. While politically significant, the latter developments can have an impact only over the medium to longer term.

Regarding prospects for the more immediate future, the long-standing absence of real cooperation between Russia's oil and gas sectors is problematic. The fact that oil producers also produce significant volumes of associated gas has in the past been viewed as a mere nuisance. Much gas has been wasted due to flaring and venting in the field. Reasons why this has remained the case also in the post-Soviet era include bottlenecks in gas-processing facilities, troubles accessing the trunk pipeline grid, and the fact that the most lucrative export markets have been reserved for Gazprom.[50]

The exact size of Russia's emissions is hard to measure, mainly because of a lack of metering, but according to a 2008 study by the World Bank, using satellite images, Russian oil producers flared some 40 billion cubic meters of associated petroleum gas. Exceeding the combined volumes of gas flared by Nigeria, Iran, Saudi Arabia, Algeria, and Indonesia in 2008, this caused losses to Russia of nearly $13 billion.[51]

Given the combined problems of economic losses and an embarrassingly high Russian contribution to the global emission of greenhouse gases, the question of associated gas has developed into an increasingly important issue. Recognizing that a quarter of the country's output of associated gas was wastefully flared, in 2007 President Putin announced that associated gas utilization would increase to 85 percent of production by 2011, and to 95 percent by 2015.[52] By 2011, political pressure and increased fines had succeeded in reducing flaring by an impressive 28.5 percent, from 52.3 to 37.4 billion cubic meters. But Russia still remained the most wasteful country in the world, flaring more than the 36.3 billion cubic meters jointly contributed by Nigeria, Iran, Saudi Arabia, Algeria, and Indonesia.[53]

Another cause for concern about the future prospects for development of the Russian energy complex is the development of domestic demand. The availability of exportable energy resources, and thus of much needed revenue, will depend not only on Russia's ability to sustain output growth but also and perhaps more crucially on its ability to deal with the gross inefficiencies that have long marked domestic energy use. While a real breakthrough on the latter count would be of major importance, it does not seem to be in the cards, at least not in the near term.

From a global perspective, the Russian economy stands out as being highly energy-intensive, not to mention wasteful. According to World Bank data, in 2010 it consumed 0.335 kilograms of oil equivalent per US dollar of GDP produced (measured at purchasing power parity). Although this was a significant improvement over 2000, when Russia's consumption was 0.492 kilograms of oil equivalent, its 2010 consumption, compared to other major industrialized economies, was still very high. In comparison, in 2010 the United States, an inveterate energy guzzler, consumed 0.172 kilograms of oil equivalent, or just about half of Russia's consumption. The United Kingdom consumed 0.101 kilograms of oil equivalent, Germany 0.121, and France 0.134. Even Canada, with a burden of Arctic climate similar to that of Russia, consumed only 0.212 kilograms of oil equivalent.[54]

The reasons why Russia's consumption is so high have a lot to do with its failures to overcome the Soviet legacy of wasteful energy use. Insulation remains poor, modern technology remains to be developed, and prices still do not really favor energy conservation. The auto industry in particular presents the discouraging prospect of rapidly rising demand that will be met by a supply of highly energy-inefficient vehicles. Continued economic growth will consequently be accompanied by continued growth in domestic demand for energy.

Thus the prospects for sustained growth in output of exportable Russian energy look bleak indeed. While geological reasons will cause oil production to stagnate and likely decline, bureaucratic and political reasons cast doubt over the future of a revival in gas. Bearing in mind the assumption that over the foreseeable future the energy complex will remain the dominant sector in the Russian economy, this is bad news. And there is more to come.

Foreign-Market Development

Deriving gain from exports requires access to markets. In the case of oil, this is not a major problem, but in the case of gas it is. While oil may be freely sold on world markets, at spot prices or according to contractual agreements, in the case of Russia, with its weakly developed capacity for

LNG, gas export has been almost fully dependent on pipelines and long-term contracts. The reason why this is problematic relates to the fact that once a pipeline has been built, the parties will be locked in and pricing disputes are bound to follow. As we have seen, overly optimistic forecasting of Turkish demand for gas caused the initial euphoria around the Blue Stream pipeline to be transformed into pricing disputes and a shelving of plans for a Blue Stream II.

Demand for Russian gas from the European Union has long formed the bedrock of Russian exports, and consequently also the bedrock of export revenues. Of total Russian energy exports, about 80 percent of the crude oil and two-thirds of the gas flow to the EU.[55] While the global financial crisis resulted in a sharp contraction in overall energy exports, which was bad enough in itself, the sudden rise to prominence of unconventional gas, especially shale gas, may well have changed the game.

As detailed in Chapter 5, the combination of a rapid buildup of LNG export capacity and the sudden emergence of the United States as the world's largest producer of gas produced a substantial diversion of LNG exports from the United States to the European Union. Expectations for continued growth in US import demand had caused installed regasification capacity to reach 130 billion cubic meters. Yet actual imports of LNG to the United States in 2009 and 2010 were limited to 13.1 and 12.3 billion cubic meters, respectively.[56] This transformation in turn caused the emergence of a European gas glut. The short-term impact on Gazprom was severe. Having tried in vain to dissuade Qatar from flooding the European market with lower-priced LNG, Gazprom was faced with a downward pressure on prices and with a drop in market share, from 28 percent in 2009 to 23 percent in 2010.[57]

At the time, there was still a fair amount of consensus that the gas glut would be temporary only, and that over the medium term gas consumption within the EU would rise substantially. This was especially so after the March 2011 nuclear disaster in Japan, which caused many politicians to have second thoughts about the use of nuclear power. The decision by the German government, in June 2011, to finally conclude its nuclear era drove the point home. According to most observers, the demand for gas will continue increasing over time. But the picture is complicated.

In its *World Energy Outlook 2010,* the International Energy Agency predicted that demand for gas would increase by 1.4 percent annually until 2035, for an accumulated growth of 44 percent from 2008, making gas the only fossil fuel that would be in greater demand in 2035 than in 2008.[58] To countries producing natural gas, this was good news. Yet it was not clear how the envisioned growth in demand for gas would be met, and at what prices. The problem for Gazprom is that much of the increase in demand will be covered by unconventional gas. In its "Golden Age of Gas" scenario, the International Energy Agency envisioned that 35 percent of the global increase in gas production over 2008–2035 would be unconventional gas.[59] This brings us back to the implications of the shale boom.

An immediate consequence of the increasing role of spot sales of LNG in Europe was a widening gap in prices. The rather logical consequence was that European customers began to demand an increasing role for hub-based spot-market pricing.[60] And it was not a temporary problem. By mid-2012, with oil prices on the rise, the difference between spot-market prices and contracted Gazprom prices for gas rose to $150 per thousand cubic meters: while pressure from US imports drove the former to a low of $300, Gazprom's oil-linked contract prices rose to $450.[61]

The implications were not limited to a downward pressure on prices. Far more important was the impact on the European gas-market structure. Traditionally, gas in Europe has been sold under long-term bilateral contracts with clauses on take-or-pay that require payment for minimum levels of deliveries irrespective of whether the gas is accepted or not. Faced with the new realities, big suppliers like Statoil did agree to renegotiate, from long-term contracts to spot-price indexation. By 2011, just over half of all long-term contracts in Europe, with durations of up to twenty-five years, were still indexed.[62] From a global perspective, Korea also moved quickly and successfully to renegotiate with the United States; it now buys US gas on a cost basis (meaning cost of extraction, liquefaction, and transport), paying only about half of what Japan pays for US gas.[63]

At the beginning of 2010, Gazprom was faced with similar proposals from its European customers, who demanded lower prices as well as reductions in contractual take-or-pay volumes. The outcome was an agreement that a 15 percent share of the price indexation would be moved to hub-based prices for three years, beginning in October 2009. Most companies were also allowed to "roll over" volumes not taken below minimum contracted levels.[64] Although Gazprom chief executive officer Aleksei Miller made it abundantly clear that Russia would prefer to stick to oil-price linkage, accepting only minor spot-market concessions, this may not turn out to be a winning strategy.

The impact on the market provides clear evidence. As customers pressed home their demands, the proportion of Europe's gas bought on the spot market rose dramatically, from 15 percent in 2008 to 44 percent in 2012. By early 2014, it had reached more than half, and in northwest Europe it stood at 70 percent. Gazprom's contracted prices in consequence were revised downward. Having peaked at 70 percent above spot prices in 2009, during the first half of 2013 the margin had been squeezed to 5–6 percent.[65]

In concluding their detailed study of the prospects for hub-based pricing of gas in Europe, Jonathan Stern and Howard Rogers suggest that there is no commercially viable alternative. It is simply not sustainable to have a dual price structure whereby utility companies pay oil-linked prices under long-term contracts while their customers and competitors have the opportunity to buy at hub-based prices. It is not a question of which price will be higher but of a need to harmonize pricing into one formula. Although the departure from oil-linked prices will be painful for some, and may have to proceed via litigation, Stern and Rogers are convinced that the transition to spot-market pricing will proceed.[66] This has mainly involved arbitration over gas-price revision clauses, with differences settled out of court.

Another and potentially more serious cause for Gazprom to be concerned about its European market relates to the previously mentioned potential for shale gas production within the European Union. Although this will take a decade or more to develop into a serious alternative, the very thought of Poland being transformed from importer to exporter should give pause to Russia's ambition of building a "ring fence" around the European market. And perhaps it should place Russian pipeline diplomacy in a different light. Yet Gazprom's leadership appears to be in denial.

In June 2010, Gazprom chief executive officer Aleksei Miller tried to debunk what he called "the shale myth," by claiming that shale gas is nothing more than a local natural resource that can only be used to compensate for shortages of conventional gas in the regional markets. In 2011, he elaborated on his point by arguing that "shale gas is a well-planned propaganda campaign, similar to those for global warming or biofuels." And he referred to the rapid rise in US shale gas production as a "bubble," similar to the prior dot-com bubble in the information technology market.[67] What may turn out to work in Gazprom's favor is that grave environmental concerns may yet cause the shale boom to lose some of its force.[68] Symptomatically, Gazprom has found a new role for itself as an advocate for ecological concerns in Europe.

Perhaps the most important implication, however, as pointed out by Robert Orttung and Indra Overland, is that uncertainties over what the future may bring have made it rational for Russia to hold back on such major investments that are required in order to bring Shtokman and Yamal online.[69] This has resulted in a rather strange combination of new fields being put on hold, while massive new construction of pipelines to Europe continues apace.

To the east, Russia has a potential market for both oil and gas in China that is bound to grow quite substantially. The spectacular growth of the Chinese economy has caused a rapid growth also in energy demand. Between 2000 and 2008, Chinese demand for primary energy more than doubled, rising from 872 to 2,131 million tons of oil equivalent. In 2009, it became the world's largest consumer of primary energy, surpassing the United States. From 2008 until 2035, Chinese demand for primary energy is expected to increase about 1.8 times. Driven by an expected sixfold increase in the number of private passenger vehicles between 2008 and 2035, China is expected to account for 57 percent of the growth in global demand for oil over the period.[70]

The outlook for gas is even more striking. In its *Energy Outlook 2030*, BP predicts that Chinese gas demand will grow by 7.6 percent annually, to reach a level of gas use in 2030 that is equal to that of the European Union in 2010. China is expected to account for close to a quarter of the global increase in demand for gas over the period.[71] Given Russia's needs to develop its energy resources in Eastern Siberia and the Far East, it would consequently seem logical indeed for the previously mentioned 2009 agreement on "loans for oil" to be followed by an agreement also to bring Russian gas to the Chinese market.

Part of the reason why talks over the proposed pipeline deal have remained stalled is that in the short term Beijing clearly feels it can negotiate from a position of strength. It has secured major imports of pipeline gas from Turkmenistan and Myanmar, and of LNG from Malaysia, Indonesia, Qatar, and Australia. This is expected to cover projected demand at least until 2020.[72] But projections of increasing demand indicate that at some point a deal with Russia will likely have to be made.

Continuing disagreement over pricing obviously forms an important part of the reason for the project being stalled. But as suggested by Shoichi Itoh, this may in part be no more than strategic camouflage for other and more fundamental disagreements. More important, perhaps, are remaining differences on where the gas will be sourced, where pipelines will be drawn, and what China may be offered in terms of rights to participate in the Russian upstream.[73]

Symptomatically, in June 2012, Russia's newly appointed energy minister, Alexander Novak, announced that Gazprom had proposed swapping production assets with China, in a long-term deal that would allow China to participate in Russian field development, in return for allowing Gazprom to do the same in China. It was explicitly said that the proposed swap formed part of the ongoing price negotiations.[74] We thus have continued reason to view Chinese interest in Russian gas as part of a larger ambition on the part of China to become a major player in its own right.

Pipeline Politics

Let us turn now, finally, to the broader role of pipeline construction as a vital part of the development of the Russian energy powerhouse, recalling the rather heavy-handed way in which Gazprom has used its control over the Unified Gas Supply System and its legal monopoly on gas export. This has not only constrained the growth of potentially more efficient domestic gas producers but also caused foreign backlash. The latter has included the previously mentioned ambitions by the EU to diversify away from Russian sources, and to introduce legislation to counter the allegedly hegemonic ambitions of Gazprom. It was symptomatic that European leaders, at their first-ever energy summit, held in Brussels on February 4, 2011, agreed to launch a trillion-euro bid to slash dependency on gas from Russia, and on oil from the Middle East, by linking national and regional electricity grids and gas pipelines by 2014.[75]

The impact of such backlash is clearly being felt by the Kremlin. The spat that erupted between then–prime minister Putin and European Commission president Barroso at a meeting in Brussels at the end of February 2011 indicated that Moscow no longer may have sensed it was acting from a position of real strength. Commenting on the changes in EU legislation that were intended to achieve "unbundling"—that is, to prevent oil and gas producers from also managing pipelines—Putin tersely noted that "we're talking about the confiscation of property here." Barroso countered that the legislation was nondiscriminatory and that the rule applied to Russian as well as European companies.[76]

Subsequent events would show that Gazprom, and the Kremlin, had good reasons to be apprehensive. In September 2011, surprise "dawn raids" were conducted on twenty sites across ten countries in Central and Eastern Europe, including Gazprom operations in Germany and the Czech Republic. In a statement on the event, the European Commission said that the investigation was focused on "the upstream supply level, where, unilaterally or through agreements, competition may be hampered or delayed."[77]

As previously mentioned, a year later, on September 4, 2012, a probe was launched by the EU's antitrust agency, the DG Competition, into alleged anticompetitive activities by Gazprom in several of these countries. If found to be in breach of EU competition rules, the company would face a fine of up to $14.5 billion, corresponding to 10 percent of annual revenue. Putin responded by issuing a decree prohibiting Russian "strategic" companies from disclosing information to foreign agencies without prior permission.[78]

In a comment on the matter, Alan Riley suggested that the antitrust case brought against Gazprom may well turn out to be the antitrust case of the decade, comparable to the prior high-profile case against Microsoft. The allegations, concerning resale clauses, denial of third-party access, and unfair pricing, not only concern the core features of EU competition policy, but also go to the very heart of the business model that the Kremlin has developed for Gazprom. Riley consequently anticipates a drawn-out battle in which every step along the road will be contested. Although the Kremlin may be expected to apply considerable pressure on "friendly" capitals within the EU to intervene in its favor, there will be little room indeed for such intervention, likely causing added frustration and disbelief on the Russian side. Riley expects that Gazprom will severely damage its reputation during the legal process and ultimately lose this battle.[79]

The stubborn intransigence that marks both Gazprom and the Kremlin suggests that the future may bring more bad news for Russia. With the EU market remaining the bedrock for Russian gas export, it was disturbing that total EU demand dropped from 502.9 billion cubic meters in 2010 to 443.9 in 2012. And Gazprom's refusal to adjust to the new realities of shale and LNG gas made a bad situation even worse. Total supply to the EU declined from 150 billion cubic meters in 2008 to 130 in 2011. And in 2012, Norway for the first time overtook Russia as the largest supplier of gas to the EU, with Gazprom imports decreasing by 10 percent and imports from Norway increasing by 12 percent.[80]

The causes for this may be reflected in the willingness of Norway's Statoil to adjust to hub-based spot-market pricing—it has renegotiated 80 percent of its contracts away from oil-linkage since 2009—and the unwillingness of Gazprom to do the same. As a result of this unwillingness, Gazprom was forced to pay out $3.2 billion in refunds to its European customers in 2012 alone. In April 2013, Gazprom's market capitalization dropped below $100 billion, and by the summer it was down to $90 billion. Though the impact was being felt, the future risks of a substantial inflow of LNG from Australia, the United States, and East Africa, combined with a reduced demand from Japan as nuclear plants reopen, paradoxically seemed not to worry the Gazprom management. In the words of a Western oil banker, "They were asleep at the wheel."[81]

Moving from the case of gas to that of oil, we may note that although the Russian oil industry was broken up and privatized, almost to the hilt, this did not apply to the national oil pipeline grid. As was the case with the old Soviet Ministry of Gas, the Soviet Ministry of Oil had a separate administration, known in this case as Glavtransneft, which was in charge of oil transport. In 1993, the Russian government transformed this administration into a state-owned enterprise named Transneft. Designated as legal successor to Glavtransneft, it absorbed all the latter's assets and went on to assume a position of real power over the oil industry as a whole. As of 2014, Transneft transports 93 percent of all Russian crude oil and petroleum products. And it controls a pipeline network that is 70,000 kilometers long, with over 500 pumping stations and over 20 million cubic meters of reservoirs.[82]

Transneft, though it differs from Gazprom in not having a legal monopoly on exports, has been quite successful in blocking plans by private oil companies to build their own pipelines. Most important, in 2002 it defeated ambitions by Yukos to build a pipeline to China, and by LUKoil, Sibneft, Yukos, and TNK to build a pipeline from Western Siberia to the ice-free port in Murmansk. The only case where Transneft has had to accept being shut out was when the Caspian Pipeline Consortium built its pipeline to transport oil from Tengiz in Kazakhstan to the Russian export port at Novorossiisk. And even here, recent developments have indicated that Transneft has become the unexpected front-runner to ship the bulk of the flow from the Kashagan field. The route would be via its existing Atyrau-Samara pipeline that links Kazakhstan with Russian trunk pipelines.[83]

But the case of Transneft is similar to that of Gazprom in the sense that both have engaged in costly pipeline construction that defies purely commercial logic. Gazprom has developed a strategy of constructing pipelines for gas export that is aimed at cutting out transit countries. The Blue Stream pipeline to Turkey was built in order to bypass Ukraine and Moldova. The Nord Stream pipeline to Germany was built in order to bypass Poland and the Baltic States. And the planned South Stream pipeline is intended to prevent the EU from constructing its Nabucco pipeline, which in turn would bypass Russia.

In the 1990s, Russia's oil pipeline infrastructure was marred by serious bottlenecks. Russian producers had to export over 50 million tons of oil annually via more costly railroads and internal waterways. The added transport cost has been estimated at $5–$7 per barrel.[84] This is no longer the case. Nor do the future prospects for Russian oil production indicate any need for capacity enhancement. Why, then, is Transneft involving itself in major new pipeline projects in all directions? As suggested by Adnan Vatansever, it is hard not to believe that there are strategic political motives involved.[85] A quick look at developments during the first decade of the twenty-first century will bring the point home.

In 2000, Russia produced 324 million tons of crude oil, of which 145 million tons were exported. The remainder was refined into petroleum products, of which 63 million tons were exported. By 2009, crude oil production had increased to 494 million tons, crude exports to 247 million tons, and exports of refined products to 124 million tons. Domestic consumption meanwhile had remained almost flat, increasing from 116 to 123 million tons. What made it possible to accommodate this surge in export volumes was an increase in export capacity that entailed new pipelines as well as a new export terminal at Primorsk, just outside St. Petersburg. Viewed in isolation, each of these projects may seem rational, but viewed as a whole, as argued by Vatansever, the economic rationality is subject to doubt.[86] The first step toward building pipelines for strategic purposes was taken in 2001, when the first stage of the Baltic Pipeline System (BPS-1) was launched. Linking Western Siberia with the new Russian port at Primorsk, it allowed Moscow to bypass its traditional Baltic Sea export ports at Ventspils in Latvia and at Butinge in Lithuania.

In 2000, the main route for export of Russian crude oil to markets outside the Commonwealth of Independent States remained that of the previously mentioned Druzhba pipeline, which in that year carried 52.4 million tons. Other routes were the Black Sea ports, which carried 43.1 million tons in 2000, and the Baltic Sea ports, which carried 20.8 million tons in 2000. In 2009, with a substantially higher export of crude, only 55.7 million tons were shipped via Druzhba and 46.7 million tons via the Black Sea ports. The real game changer was that exports via the BPS-1 and Primorsk had grown to 70.1 million tons in 2009, while the traditional Latvian and Lithuanian export ports stood idle.[87]

Several further projects for capacity enhancement are presently ongoing or have been recently completed. One is the second stage of the Baltic Pipeline System (BPS-2), whose construction was suggested in the aftermath of a transit dispute with Belarus in 2007. Hooked up with the Druzhba at Unecha, close to the Russia-Belarus border, it runs to a new terminal in Ust-Luga on the Russian coast just west of St. Petersburg. Construction of the pipeline was completed in October 2011, but problems at the export terminal caused the launch to be delayed until September 2012.[88] Maximum capacity of 50 million tons annually is to be reached in 2014. Of this, 12 million tons will go to a refinery at Kirshi, east of St. Petersburg.[89]

Another is the second stage of the previously mentioned ESPO pipeline to the Pacific. As noted earlier, the first stage, from Taishet to Skovorodino, was launched in 2009, with an annual capacity of 30 million tons. Awaiting completion of the second stage, half of this was exported to China, via the spur to Daqing, and the other half was transported on rail to the export terminus at Kozmino Bay. The launch of the second stage, which took place at the end of December 2012, will add another 20 million tons, bringing annual capacity to 50 million tons. And it is expected that the project as a whole will eventually reach an annual capacity of 80 million tons.[90]

Two additional projects to enhance Russian crude oil export capacity even further are the Burgas-Alexandropoulos Pipeline (BAP) and the Samsun-Ceyhan Pipeline (SCP). Both have been designed to bypass the congested and ecologically sensitive Bosporus and Dardanelles Straits. The BAP is to begin at Burgas on the Bulgarian coast of the Black Sea and run to Alexandropoulos on the Greek coast of the Aegean. It would have an initial annual capacity of 35 million tons, to be increased to 50 million tons. In December 2011 the Bulgarian government said it was pulling out, but the response from Transneft was that according to the mutual agreement, no party can withdraw until "after the pipeline has paid for itself."[91] Consequently the project was placed on hold.

Controversy has surrounded the SCP as well. Designed to cross Turkey from the Black Sea port at Samsun to the southern export outlet at Ceyhan on the Mediterranean, it would have an initial annual capacity of 50 million tons, to be increased to 75 million tons. The oil would come from Kazakhstan, delivered to Samsun from the Russian port at Novorossiisk. In September 2011, Transneft announced that it no longer considered the project economically feasible and that negotiations had been frozen.[92] Given Turkey's pronounced ambition to become an energy hub for the region, the latter was unwelcome news. But it was clearly not the end of the story.

Noting that the second stage of the ESPO and the BPS-2 will jointly add an annual capacity of 70 million tons (later 100 million tons), and that the BAP and the SCP could add a further 85 million tons (later 130 million tons), one wonders where all the additional oil destined to flow through these pipelines will come from. According to Russia's *Energy Strategy 2030,* which was approved in 2009 and published in 2010, Russian oil production was envisaged to increase by only 42–47 million tons, from 488 million tons in 2008 to 530–535 by 2030.[93] According to the "New Policy Scenario" in the International Energy Agency's *World Energy Outlook 2010,* Russian oil production will actually decline, by 50 million tons by 2030.[94]

Beginning with the ESPO, the motives at play here seem entirely rational. From a purely commercial point of view, the pipeline is important to Russia in securing that Kozmino Bay blend can be established as a benchmark for crude in the region. By establishing substantial overcapacity, the pipeline may also enable Russia to play its "Asia card," putting customers in its European markets on notice that Moscow does have other options for export. From a strategic foreign policy point of view, the ESPO is important in promoting Russia's ambitions in its relations to China, Japan, and Korea. And from a strategic domestic political perspective, it ensures that Transneft will have a more dominant presence in the Far East, where oil to date has been transported via channels outside its network.

The main problem that runs through all such explanations, however, rests in the simple fact that recoverable oil reserves in Eastern Siberia will not be sufficient to fill the pipeline. Three fields come into question: Vankor in the Krasnoyarsk region, Verkhnechon in the Irkutsk region, and Talakan in the Sakha Republic. In 2010, Vankor produced 12.7 million tons and the other two jointly produced 7.2 million tons. As mentioned earlier, Vankor is expected to reach peak production, of 25 million tons annually, by 2014; peak production at the other two fields, jointly, will not exceed 15 million tons annually.[95] In sum, this means an export capacity of 50 million tons annually, possibly increasing to 80 million tons, with proven resources of no more than 40 million tons.

It is of course possible to fill the ESPO pipeline by pumping remaining oil from Western Siberia toward the east. This would accord with the presumption of Moscow wishing to play its "Asia card." But it is a debatable proposition. It would result not only in extra transportation costs but also in questions regarding the BPS-2. Will there really be enough oil to fill both the BPS-1 and the BPS-2, which will have a joint annual capacity of 125 million tons, without drawing down quite substantially the flow through Druzhba? Given that the traditional Baltic Sea export ports are already standing idle, also idling a growing part of the capacity of Druzhba would seem to make little commercial sense.

Over and above the saving on transit fees, which is clearly out of proportion to the cost of additional pipeline construction, the main advantage would seem to be the bypass. By gaining direct access to European markets, Moscow will be relieved of its troubled dependence on transit states like Belarus and, in particular, Ukraine. To Kiev, the prospect of being cut out of its role as transit partner must be rather unsettling. Among conspiracy theories, it has been suggested that the building of bypass capacity is a way of devaluing the Druzhba, making it cheaper for Moscow to realize its long-standing ambition of assuming control over energy infrastructure in Belarus and Ukraine. We cannot wholly ignore the worries of governments in Poland and the Baltic republics that the bypass has strategic political motives, nor can we dismiss suggestions that major public infrastructure investments, with grossly inflated price tags, serve as vehicles for well-placed insiders to line their own pockets. Previously mentioned allegations that $4 billion went missing during the first stage of the ESPO project would accord with the latter. All in all, it is difficult to view the boom in pipeline construction, for oil as well as gas, as being motivated by commercial reasons alone.

Turning, finally, to the BAP and the SCP, it may seem even more questionable what the motives are. If capacity for export of oil to Europe is already abundant, why engage in building even more? Here the answer may be more distinctly commercial. In anticipation of the coming online of the Kashagan field, which would bring large volumes of additional oil from Kazakhstan, Russia was clearly aiming to position itself to profit from offering an export outlet via Turkey. The implied ambition to retain a firm hold on exports of Kazakh oil may also help explain pressure from Moscow on the members of the Caspian Pipeline Consortium to double the capacity of the export pipeline from Tengiz to Novorossiisk, to 65 million tons annually.[96]

Beyond this commercially plausible explanation, we may also consider the fact that pipeline construction has become part of a bigger game between Moscow and Ankara. Noting Turkey's interest in having a pipeline to Ceyhan for crude oil, Russia has seen an opportunity to introduce linkage with approval for its high-priority South Stream gas pipeline. When work on the Samsun-Ceyhan pipeline was frozen in 2011, it was suggested that the freeze was linked to pending approval by Ankara of South Stream.[97]

It is also from this perspective that we may view the prospects for the previously mentioned Blue Stream II pipeline for gas to actually be built.

During a visit to Ankara in August 2009, Prime Minister Putin combined talks on South Stream with a suggestion to revive the Blue Stream II. Instead of running east to west, the pipeline would now run north to south across Anatolia to the Mediterranean coast. It would also be a Russian-Turkish venture, without participation by Italian oil and gas company ENI.[98] During a visit to Turkey in June 2010, Prime Minister Putin added that the gas would be offered to Syria and Lebanon but not to Israel.[99] Although Russian sources have remained insistent that this is a "live project," it remains to be seen what will materialize in the end.

A completely new twist to the game was added in March 2012, when Turkey and Azerbaijan suddenly announced that they had reached agreement to build the Trans-Anatolian Pipeline (TANAP), to transport gas from the Shah Deniz field in Azerbaijan to a point on the border between Turkey and Bulgaria. The annual capacity would be 70 billion cubic meters, of which 60 billion cubic meters would be for Turkey. As the TANAP would replace Nabucco on Turkish territory, it caused a flurry of activity to reconfigure the fundamentals of pipeline competition between Russia and the European Union.[100] Again, what the final outcome will be remains shrouded in mystery.

Adding to certainty, however, in July 2012 the long-standing guessing game over the actual size of gas reserves in Turkmenistan received substantial new input. In its annual and highly respected *Statistical Review of World Energy,* BP estimated Turkmenistan's proven reserves of gas by the end of 2011 at 24.3 trillion cubic meters. This was almost double the number given for the end of 2010 (13.4 trillion cubic meters), which in turn had been a substantial increase from 9 trillion cubic meters at the end of 2009. It was indicative of the rapid emergence of Turkmenistan as a major player in the world of gas that BP opted to present its annual report in that republic. Turkmenistan is now very close to bypassing Qatar, with proven reserves of 25 trillion cubic meters.[101]

On Shaky Foundations

Russian energy policy to date has been a veritable battleground for hosts of vested interests, all with their own short-term agendas. Perhaps the best characterization has been offered by Pavel Baev, suggesting that the "diffuse nature of interactions" over resources in the Caspian Basin has not been reflective of the "great game" model, but rather involved a great many "small games and petty intrigues played by state, sub-state and non-state actors."[102] What he sees in the Caspian context has arguably been true also in the overall context of Russian energy policy.

The outcome has been very far removed from the market-based ideal of sustainable output growth, of energy efficiency combined with conservation, and of commercially sound pipeline management. Exactly what the balance has been between commercial and other forms of motivation will remain controversial. What should be clear, however, is that the games that have been played around Russian energy resources have been detrimental to the publicly pronounced ambition to achieve diversification, modernization, and global economic integration.

Simply put, the Russian energy complex rests on shaky foundations. And it is on these very foundations that Russia's future must be built.

Notes

1. Ellman, *Russia's Oil and Natural Gas,* pp. 4–5.
2. Sagers, "Developments in Russian Gas Production," pp. 651–652.
3. Milov, Coburn, and Danchenko, "Russia's Energy Policy," pp. 285, 287.
4. Ibid., p. 286.
5. Ibid., p. 292.
6. Ibid., pp. 290–291.
7. Henderson, *Domestic Gas Prices in Russia,* p. 5.
8. Stern, *The Russian Natural Gas "Bubble,"* p. 36.
9. Pirani, *Elusive Potential,* p. 4.
10. In 2004, the Organization for Economic Cooperation and Development (OECD) estimated this discount at up to $2.3 billion per year; see OECD, *Economic Survey: Russian Federation,* p. 135. The discount is defined as the difference between the prevailing tariff and the long-run marginal cost of production. As Henderson emphasizes, there are many complications here; see Henderson, *Domestic Gas Prices in Russia,* p. 8.
11. Milov, Coburn, and Danchenko, "Russia's Energy Policy," p. 287.
12. Henderson, *Domestic Gas Prices in Russia,* p. 10. As in the case of determining the size of the Gazprom subsidy to other industries, calculating the "netback parity" price would be complex. The technical formula for the calculation is simple: Gazprom export price in Europe, less transport cost from the Russian border, less export tax (30 percent), less the cost of transport from the market in Russia (normally Moscow). But the lack of transparency causes every step to be shrouded in uncertainty.
13. Henderson, *Domestic Gas Prices in Russia,* p. 11.
14. Following intense lobbying by Gazprom, the government approved a 15 percent hike in domestic tariffs, to take place on July 1, 2013. On top of this, the company wanted an additional hike of 26 percent in the fall, in its aim to achieve netback parity in 2014. But in September, President Putin instead approved a price freeze on utilities for 2014. The message to Gazprom was that it should work more efficiently. See "UPDATE 1-Russia Domestic Gas Tariffs to Rise 15 pct in 2013," *Reuters,* April 26, 2012, http://www.reuters.com/article/2012/04/26/russia-gazprom -tariff-idUSL6E8FQBH420120426; and "Russian Price Freeze Decision Boosts Rate Cut Chances," *Reuters,* September 12, 2013, http://www.reuters.com/article /2013/09/12/russia-economy-cbank-idUSL5N0H817V20130912.

15. Gustafson, *Wheel of Fortune,* p. 370.

16. Ibid., p. 371.

17. Ibid., p. 372.

18. Ibid., p. 477.

19. Dienes, "Observations on the Problematic Potential of Russian Oil," pp. 320–321.

20. It may be added that the most successful Russian oil companies developed very different approaches to "brownfield" development, reflecting very different roles of the Western service companies. The most aggressive, and controversial, of the lot was Yukos Oil. See further Gustafson, *Wheel of Fortune,* chap. 5.

21. Dienes, "Observations on the Problematic Potential of Russian Oil," pp. 321–322.

22. US Energy Information Administration, "Countries," http://205.254.135.7 /countries. In terms of crude oil production, which does not include liquids from gas production, Russia remained the top producer in 2011 as well, with 9.77 million barrels per day as compared to 9.46 million barrels per day for Saudi Arabia. The two datasets are at times not kept separate, generating confusion.

23. Carole Nakhle, "OPEC Oil Production Outlook Uncertain," *Geopolitical Information Service,* July 13, 2012, http://www.geopolitical-info.com/en/energy /opec-oil-production-outlook-uncertain, p. 2.

24. Rosneft, "Vankorneft," http://www.rosneft.com/Upstream/ProductionAnd Development/eastern_siberia/vankorneft.

25. Henderson, *Rosneft: On the Road to Global NOC Status?* p. 40.

26. Kivinen, "Public and Business Actors in Russia's Energy Policy"; and Balmaceda, "Russia's Central and Eastern European Energy Transit Corridor."

27. Sagers, "Developments in Russian Gas Production," p. 652.

28. Gustafson, *Wheel of Fortune,* pp. 38–41 and chap. 5.

29. Central Intelligence Agency, "Intelligence Memorandum: The Impending Soviet Oil Crisis," March 1977, http://www.foia.cia.gov/sites/default/files/document _conversions/89801/DOC_0000498607.pdf.

30. Gustafson, *Wheel of Fortune,* p. 191.

31. Ibid., pp. 209–210.

32. Goldman, *Petrostate,* p. 39.

33. Itoh, *Russia Looks East,* pp. 4, 9–10.

34. Gustafson, *Wheel of Fortune,* p. 466.

35. Moe and Kryukov, "Oil Exploration in Russia," p. 313.

36. The Yamal peninsula has long been what Matthew Sagers refers to as the Holy Grail of the Russian gas industry, "forever pursued, but forever receding." Of the twenty-six fields that have already been discovered there, only two— Bovanenkovo and Kharasaveyskoe—are slated for commercial exploitation in the near future. Sagers, "Developments in Russian Gas Production," p. 670.

37. Moe and Kryukov, "Oil Exploration in Russia," pp. 315, 318.

38. See further Adachi, "Subsoil Law Reform in Russia."

39. Fortescue, "The Russian Law on Subsurface Resources," pp. 161, 177.

40. Moe and Kryukov, "Oil Exploration in Russia," p. 326.

41. Dienes, "Observations on the Problematic Potential of Russian Oil," p. 325. See also Bradshaw and Bond, "Crisis amid Plenty Revisited"; Gaddy, "Perspectives on the Potential of Russian Oil"; and Dienes, "Observations on the Russian Heartland."

42. Rosneft, "History," http://www.rosneft.com/about/history.

43. Kenneth Rapoza, "Russia's Rosneft Surpasses ExxonMobil to Become World's Biggest Oil Co.," *Forbes,* March 21, 2013, http://www.forbes.com/sites /kenrapoza/2013/03/21/russias-rosneft-surpasses-exxonmobil-to-become-worlds -biggest-oil-co.

44. Igor Booth, "Unlearned Lessons of State Capitalism: What Is Good for Gazprom Is Not Good for Russia," November 26, 2012, http://imrussia.org/index .php?option=com_content&view=article&id=338%3Aunlearned-lessons-of-state -capitalism-what-is-good-for-gazprom-is-not-good-for-russia&catid=54%3A economy&Itemid=97&lang=en.

45. For a broad account, see Henderson, *Non-Gazprom Gas Producers in Russia.*

46. Sagers, "Developments in Russian Gas Production," p. 658.

47. "Russia May Revive Production Sharing Agreements for New Oil and Gas Projects," *Energy-pedia News,* December 8, 2010, http://www.energy-pedia.com /article.aspx?articleid=143326.

48. More specifically, the Arctic accounts for about 13 percent of the undiscovered oil, 30 percent of the undiscovered natural gas, and 20 percent of the undiscovered natural gas liquids in the world. About 84 percent of the estimated resources are expected to occur offshore. See further US Geological Survey, "90 Billion Barrels of Oil and 1,670 Trillion Cubic Feet of Natural Gas Assessed in the Arctic," July 23, 2008, http://www.usgs.gov/newsroom/article.asp?ID=1980.

49. The initial announcement that an agreement on demarcation had been reached was made in April 2010, with actual signing of the treaty taking place in September 2010. See "Russia, Norway Reach Agreement on Demarcation of Maritime Borders—Norwegian Premier," *RIA Novosti,* April 27, 2010, http://en.rian .ru/russia/20100427/158767092.html; and "Russia and Norway Sign Maritime Border Agreement," *BBC News,* September 15, 2010, http://www.bbc.co.uk/news /business-11316430.

50. Sagers, "Developments in Russian Gas Production," pp. 667–670.

51. Kupchinsky, "Russian Gas Flaring."

52. "Russia May Fail to Meet Gas Flaring Target by 2011," *Reuters,* October 9, 2007, http://uk.reuters.com/article/2007/10/09/russia-gas-flaring-idUKL09592968 20071009.

53. World Bank, "Estimated Flared Volumes from Satellite Data, 2007–2011," http://web.worldbank.org/WBSITE/EXTERNAL/TOPICS/EXTOGMC/EXTGGFR /0,,contentMDK:22137498~pagePK:64168445~piPK:64168309~theSitePK:57806 9,00.html.

54. World Bank, "Energy Use (kg of Oil Equivalent) per $1,000 GDP (Constant 2005 PPP)," http://data.worldbank.org/indicator/EG.USE.COMM.GD .PP.KD.

55. US Energy Information Administration, "Russia," http://www.eia.doe.gov /countries/cab.cfm?fips=RS.

56. Stern and Rogers, *The Transition to Hub-Based Gas Pricing,* p. 8.

57. Frank Umbach, "Energy: Russian Gas—The Changing Global Market," *Geopolitical Information Service,* June 11, 2012, http://www-geopolitical-info.com /en/energy/russian-gas-the-changing-global-market, p. 3.

58. International Energy Agency, *World Energy Outlook 2010,* p. 7.

59. Umbach, "Energy: Russian Gas," p. 3.

60. For a detailed assessment, see Stern and Rogers, *The Transition to Hub-Based Gas Pricing.*

61. Olga Khvostunova, "How Gazprom Snoozed Through the 'Shale Gas Revolution,'" February 5, 2013, http://imrussia.org/index.php?option=com_content&view=article&id=382%3Ahow-gazprom-snoozed-through-the-shale-gas-revolution&catid=54%3Aeconomy&Itemid=101&lang=en.

62. Umbach, "Energy: Russian Gas," p. 3.

63. Stefan Lippert, "Japan's Role in the US Shale Gas Revolution," *Geopolitical Information Service,* July 20, 2012, http://www.geopolitical-info.com/en/energy/japan-s-role-in-the-us-shale-gas-revolution.

64. Stern and Rogers, *The Transition to Hub-Based Gas Pricing,* pp. 25–26.

65. "Paying the Piper," *The Economist,* January 4, 2014, http://www.economist.com/news/business/21592639-european-efforts-reduce-russian-state-owned-companys-sway-over-gas-prices-have-been.

66. Stern and Rogers, *The Transition to Hub-Based Gas Pricing,* pp. 36–37.

67. Khvostunova, "How Gazprom Snoozed Through the 'Shale Gas Revolution.'"

68. See, for example, "Special Report: The Great Shale Gas Rush," *National Geographic,* October 2010, http://news.nationalgeographic.com/news/energy/2010/10/101022-energy-marcellus-shale-gas-rush; and Roger Harrabin, "Shale Gas Moratorium in UK Urged by Tyndall Centre," *BBC News,* January 17, 2011, http://www.bbc.co.uk/news/science-environment-12190810.

69. Orttung and Overland, "Russia and the Formation of a Gas Cartel," p. 64.

70. Itoh, *Russia Looks East,* p. 16.

71. BP, *BP Energy Outlook 2030,* p. 31.

72. Itoh, *Russia Looks East,* pp. 35–37. See also Henderson, *The Pricing Debate over Russian Gas Exports,*" pp. 13–14, 18–19.

73. Itoh, *Russia Looks East,* chap. 5.

74. Gleb Bryanski, "UPDATE 1-Gazprom Offers Field Swap with China to Aid Gas Talks," *Reuters,* June 7, 2012, http://uk.reuters.com/article/2012/06/07/russia-china-gas-idUKL5E8H79OZ20120607.

75. "Europe Launches Trillion Euro Energy Revamp" *EU Business,* February 4, 2011, http://www.eubusiness.com/news-eu/summit-energy.8hl.

76. Andrew Rettman, "Putin and Barroso in Public Scrap on EU Energy Law," *EUObserver,* February 24, 2011, http://euobserver.com/foreign/31869.

77. Alex Barker, Stanley Pignal, and Gerrit Wiesmann, "Gazprom Raided in EU Antitrust Investigation," *Financial Times,* September 27, 2011, http://www.ft.com/intl/cms/s/0/43f9f24c-e92b-11e0-af7b-00144feab49a.html#axzz2BX2fwEIt.

78. "Hands Off from Gazprom: Putin Signs Decree Protecting Gas Giant from EU Probe," *RT News,* September 11, 2012, http://rt.com/business/news/gazprom-putin-decree-protect-eu-investigation-888.

79. Riley, "Commission v. Gazprom."

80. Frank Umbach, "Europe's Gas Market Is Changing Rapidly," *Geopolitical Information Service,* September 10, 2013, http://www.geopolitical-info.com/en/energy/europe-s-gas-market-is-changing-rapidly.

81. Guy Chazan and Neil Buckley, "A Cap on Gazprom's Ambitions," *Financial Times,* June 5, 2013, http://www.ft.com/cms/s/0/75027894-cd24-11e2-90e8-00144feab7de.html.

82. See Transneft's website, at http://eng.transneft.ru/company.

83. "Russia Emerges as Surprise Favourite to Ship Kashagan Oil," *Reuters,* August 8, 2013, http://mobile.reuters.com/article/article/idUSL6N0G92N820130808?irpc=932.

84. Milov, Coburn, and Danchenko, "Russia's Energy Policy," p. 295.

85. Vatansever, *Russia's Oil Exports,* pp. 12–19.

86. Ibid., pp. 6, 12–14.

87. Ibid., pp. 6–7.

88. Anatoly Medetsky, "New $130M Baltic Port Gives Export Flexibility," *Moscow Times*, September 28, 2012, http://www.themoscowtimes.com/business /article/new-130m-baltic-port-gives-export-flexibility/468931.html.

89. Socor, "Russia Completing Baltic Pipeline System Construction."

90. Platts, "Russian Crude Oil Exports to the Pacific Basin—ESPO Starts Flowing," May 2010, https://www.platts.com/IM.Platts.Content/InsightAnalysis /IndustrySolutionPapers/espoupdate0510.pdf.

91. "Burgas-Alexandroupolis Pipeline Agreement Allows Parties to Exit Only After Recoupment," *Russia Beyond the Headlines,* July 16, 2012, http://rbth.ru /articles/2012/07/16/burgas-alexandroupolis_pipeline_agreement_allows_parties _to_exit_onl_16382.html.

92. "USAK Energy Expert Ozertem: 'Good Will & Subsequent Attitudes May Increase Chances of Samsun-Ceyhan,'" *Turkish Weekly,* September 9, 2011, http://www.turkishweekly.net/news/123074/usak-energy-expert-ozertem-good-will -subsequent-attitudes-may-increase-chances-of-samsun-ceyhan.html.

93. "Russia Adopts New Energy Strategy," *RIA Novosti,* November 26, 2009, http://en.rian.ru/russia/20091126/156995275.html.

94. Vatansever, *Russia's Oil Exports,* p. 13.

95. Itoh, *Russia Looks East,* pp. 5–7.

96. Socor, "Samsun-Ceyhan Pipeline Project."

97. "Turkey Diversifying Natural Gas Suppliers," *Eurasian Energy Analysis,* December 5, 2011, http://eurasianenergyanalysis.blogspot.se/2011/12/turkey -diversifying-natural-gas.html.

98. Socor, "Gazprom, Turkey Revive and Reconfigure."

99. "Russia May Exclude Israel from Blue Stream-2 Gas Pipeline Project— Putin," *RIA Novosti,* June 8, 2010, http://en.rian.ru/world/20100608/159345416 .html.

100. Vladimir Socor, "Nabucco Pipeline Takes Another Twist," *Asia Times,* March 30, 2012, http://www.atimes.com/atimes/Central_Asia/NC30Ag01.html.

101. BP, *BP Statistical Review of World Energy, 2012,* p. 20. See also Socor, "BP's Appraisal Doubles the Proven Reserves."

102. Baev, *Russian Energy Policy and Military Power,* p. 56.

9

Backward
into the Future

During Vladimir Putin's first two terms in power, the media hype surrounding the role of energy in Russia contained both positive accounts, of how the sudden inflow of petrodollars had helped stabilize the Russian economy, and negative accounts, of how Russia had begun again to throw its weight around, this time by wielding a newfound "energy weapon." Much of this imagery has by now slipped into history. Yet the contrast does remain reflective of the multiple and at times conflicting roles that have been played by the Russian energy complex during the time since Putin first assumed power.

The energy story as a whole has revolved around four main themes. One concerns the trauma that was caused by the collapse of the Soviet Union. Russia sought to use its sudden accumulation of energy wealth to make itself great again—to become an "energy superpower." Another captures the role of the energy complex in the economic rebound. A growing sense of complacency, driven by Russia's deceptive sense of being able to continue living high off rents from energy resources, caused pressures for reform to be eroded. A third is the form of "wild capitalism" that emerged when the Soviet Union collapsed and formerly state-owned assets were up for grabs. The sheer size of the spoils to be had from energy triggered a scramble for asset-grabs and a spectacular rise in corruption, both of which had seriously negative implications for the rule of law. Fourth and final is the Kremlin's increasing authoritarianism and its ambitions to reimpose control over the country's energy resources. By undermining the prospects for accountability in government and for the emergence of a rules-based market economy, it has reconnected with historical legacies of forced growth that aim to overcome backwardness by focusing on extraction of resources.

These four themes provide important context. Yet as we turn now to look at future prospects and challenges, the key question to address is the role of the resource sector in long-term growth. Will it be possible to combine a continued dominant role for the energy complex with such steps toward institutional modernization that are needed to overcome backwardness and to secure global integration and competitiveness of the Russian economy? The answer to this question requires an argument built in three steps.

The first step expands on the preceding discussion about the dismal outlook for sustainable development of the Russian energy complex, showing that the suggestive imagery of reduced energy dependency that was associated with the economic rebound during Putin's first two terms in power was faulty. Because Russia remains dependent on oil, a "nonoil" Russia is simply not realistic. Consequently, we must view the future of the Russian economy, and thus of Russia as a whole, as being held hostage to the prospects for improved governance of the energy complex.

The second step looks at the program for modernization launched by Dmitry Medvedev. Because true modernization must reach beyond matters such as superficial renovation of the townscape, imports of high-tech consumer gadgetry, and proliferation of social media, the challenge for Russia remains that of achieving improved quality of governance. This entails a call for fundamental institutional transformation, and a break with the multiple legacies of Russia's past. Beyond the rhetoric, there has been little indeed of the latter, which drives home the point that obstacles go far beyond the general problems of the "resource curse." The ongoing struggles over the spoils from energy have reflected just how deeply entrenched these problems are.

The third and final step returns to the argument of the book as a whole. While there have indeed been multiple and at times conflicting agendas at play, we must not altogether forget the role of Vladimir Putin. The point is not to view him as the architect and driver of a return to authoritarianism. The current mode of governance must, on the contrary, be viewed as the result of endogenous institutional adaptation, in the form of a reconnect with important legacies from the past. Briefly put, it is not Putin or the Kremlin but rather the burden of history and patterns of path dependence that have created the current regime.

The dominant pattern in Russian long-term development has been resource-based growth featuring extensive resource mobilization rather than intensive resource utilization. It has been focused on military needs and rationalized by reference to imagery of enemies, both within and without. The controversial ambition to build an energy superpower may from this perspective be viewed as little more than a transitory phase.

As suggested in previous chapters, the massive wager on military modernization that is entailed in the State Armament Program for the period 2011–2020 provides clear evidence of a reconnect with historical legacy. Rents from energy are being channeled not into modernizing the energy complex, which might have been conducive toward modernizing the Russian economy as a whole, but rather into restarting the country's long-neglected military-industrial complex, presently rebranded as a defense-industrial complex. Russia may in this sense be viewed as moving backward into the future. Let us begin with a closer look at Russia's mounting dependence on hydrocarbons.

Hooked on Oil

This book has emphasized the prominent role played by energy in Soviet development. The oil crisis in 1973 provided a massive boost in hydrocarbon revenues, likely prolonging the life of the Soviet Union, and subsequent drops in the price of oil caused severe trouble. There is also Yegor Gaidar's important argument that a sharp reduction in hydrocarbon revenues played a major role in the collapse of the Soviet Union.

Here we take a closer look at energy dependence during the Putin era, which assumed entirely new and even more worrisome proportions. Let us recall Thane Gustafson's portrayal, derived from works by Clifford Gaddy and Barry Ickes, of how dependence has been transformed into addiction, and also Aleksei Kudrin's statement, from February 2011, that "the oil industry, from being a locomotive for the economy, has become a brake."[1] Viewing the Yeltsin era as an exceptional yet symptomatic "time of trouble" allows us to focus on the economic rebound that coincided with Vladimir Putin's rise to power.

Inspired by the rapid turnaround of the Russian economy, from basket case to star performer, observers began projecting imagery of an economy that was also becoming increasingly diversified and increasingly decoupled from its previous dependence on oil. In 2008, Peter Rutland could still find that, "unlike the typical Third World petro-state, Russia has a diversified economy with a substantial manufacturing sector."[2] It was a happy story, generating great hopes for modernization and global integration. Regrettably, it was largely an illusion, generated by statistical misrepresentation.

In its *Russian Economic Report* for November 2004, the World Bank expressed great surprise that official numbers could claim energy to account for less than 9 percent of Russian GDP, with a presumably vibrant service sector contributing 60 percent, while those same official numbers claimed that oil and gas exports accounted for no less than 20 percent of GDP.[3] As had already been shown by Masaki Kuboniwa, the simple answer was that for reasons of tax avoidance and evasion, Russian oil companies had been using elaborate transfer pricing schemes to shift revenues out of their core businesses and into trading companies, which in some instances were quite nebulous. While this made taxation more difficult to enforce, it also gravely distorted the image of where Russian GDP was being produced. Once the bogus trade margins had been reassigned, it was seen that the energy sector accounted for no less than 25 percent of the country's GDP.[4]

The continued dominance of the energy sector logically also entailed continued vulnerability to swings in the price of oil on the world market. In suggestive graphs covering the decade beginning in 2000, Gaddy and Ickes show how closely movements in a range of important indicators tracked changes in the price of Urals crude, which is the main Russian export blend. It may not be all that surprising that this was the case for the RTS index of the Moscow stock exchange, which is heavily dominated by energy companies. More important, however, this was also the case for the annual sales revenue of Russia's top 100 non–oil and gas companies, reflecting that the impact of fluctuations in oil price is pervasive even outside the oil and gas sector. Driving the message home, the same close fit could be found also for the production of railway freight cars, for retail sales, and for imports. All in all, Gaddy and Ickes present convincing empirical evidence to back their claim that "everything is oil."[5]

The logic behind this claim is that the rise in revenue from oil and gas exports caused not only rising profits and rising government revenue but also rising household incomes. Over the period from mid-2000 until mid-2008, when the global financial crisis struck, real wages and incomes almost tripled. The latter in turn produced a rapid rise in household spending. Given the uncompetitive nature of Russian-made consumer goods, this was bound to translate into rising imports. What may have looked like a bubble was in fact a consumer boom sustained by a transfer of real value away from oil- and gas-importing nations. It was, however, a boom that rested on a fragile foundation. When the price of oil collapsed, so did the fundamentals of the Russian economy.[6]

It is important here to draw a line between the impact of changes in the price of oil on revenues, which is straightforward, and the impact of the same on economic growth, which is a highly complex issue. The existence of such a link is not in question. As Rudiger Ahrend notes, "while Russian growth was increasingly driven by consumption, it was largely sustained by rising oil exports."[7] The main problem is that different theories on economic growth place different emphasis on different drivers and that it will be difficult to separate causes in a chain of events. While it was clearly the case that the boom in household spending during the Putin era did provide a boost to economic growth, it is not easy to know how much of this boost could or should be viewed as autonomous from the rise in oil prices.

The main reasons, however, why Russia's dependence on hydrocarbons has proven to be so tenacious, and why it must be taken so seriously, go beyond volatility in prices. They are lodged in fundamental features of economic geography and of deeply entrenched patterns of informal institutions that emerged under the Soviet order. As phrased by Gaddy and Ickes, the "big problem for Russia is not what is missing, but rather what is there—as a result of 70 years of misallocation."[8]

This book has repeatedly referred to problems of harsh climate and complex geology that will arise when exploration moves deeper into Eastern Siberia and the Far East. These problems are clear and present, and they will prove hard to deal with. Yet they make up only part of what Fiona Hill and Clifford Gaddy have referred to as the "Siberian curse."[9] While many countries in the third world are struggling to formulate policies to promote industrialization, Russia's problem is that Soviet economic planners achieved what has been alternately known as both overindustrialization and misindustrialization. The problem, as phrased by Hill and Gaddy, is that "the system produced the wrong things. Its factories produced them in the wrong way. It educated its people with the wrong skills. Worst of all, communist planners put factories, machines, and people in the wrong places."[10]

A crucial step on this road was taken in the 1970s, when the wager on the energy complex in Western Siberia was accompanied by a broad ambition also to achieve industrialization of these areas. The urge by the resource lobbies to build cities and associated infrastructure became simply overwhelming. By the 1980s, Siberia had been transformed into a sinkhole, a massive drain on the economic resources of the Soviet Union. Following the collapse of the Soviet system, the Russian Federation was left with what Hill and Gaddy refer to as a "costly gift that can neither be easily maintained nor adapted to the market."[11]

Part of this "gift" was given by nature. Russia has twice as much territory north of the Arctic Circle as does Canada, and has some of the coldest places in the world outside Antarctica. In sharp contrast to other Arctic countries, however, Russia has failed to concentrate its population, and the main part of its economic activity, in the warmer parts of the country. The latter constitutes the human-made part of the gift.

The essence of the "Siberian curse" is that too many large cities, of a million or more inhabitants, have been built in places that suffer from extreme cold and from having little or no access to vital transport infrastructure. The costs of dealing with the cold are quite substantial, including insulation, special-purpose machinery, and low labor productivity, as well as wear and tear of both human and physical capital.[12] To this may be added the costs of maintaining life in places that—in extreme cases—may be reached only by helicopter. None of this would have been possible in a functioning market setting. Yet the ambition to maintain cities and population across Siberia has been happening for so long that it has become part of Russia's self-image and will thus be all the more difficult to reverse. It is at the core of this conundrum that we may find the energy complex and the associated lobbies of mineral extraction.

What comes out of all this is a fairly obvious recommendation: Russia must "shrink." While there is little to be done, at reasonable cost, about the country's physical geography, its economic geography may be transformed by deliberate political action. Investment may be channeled into warmer areas of the country, where the transport infrastructure also is more supportive, and internal migration may be encouraged toward those areas.

During Putin's first term in office, actual development did feature some ambitions, notably so by the World Bank, to support programs that were designed to shift population away from the country's cold and remote areas. Subsequently, however, the president would demonstrate growing commitment to supporting the "monotowns" and to keeping Siberia populated. While the latter would seem to make little economic sense, it can be given solid political and bureaucratic explanations.

In a paper about the prospects for Russia to achieve sustainable economic growth, published in 2010, Gaddy and Ickes take issue with the broad understanding that if Dmitry Medvedev were to be successful in his ambition to implement a modernization program, "it would be wonderful for Russia." Their counterargument is that this type of enthusiasm rests on a faulty understanding of the true problems that face present-day Russia. Unless the real causes of stagnation and backwardness are fully recognized, policies that appear to lead to the goal of modernization may actually lead the country into what Gaddy and Ickes suggestively characterize as "bear traps."[13]

The main reason for this, which the authors have explored elsewhere, is that the resource-dependent Russian economy has evolved a distinct form of "addiction" to resource rents that goes beyond the general resource curse. Due to the peculiarities of Soviet economic planning, resource abundance and resource rents had "a more deleterious, and less easily reversible impact than resource rents in market economies." The driving force was the absence of market signals, which made it impossible to determine whether a given activity added or subtracted value. Consequently, enterprise managers could freely engage in value-destroying activities. In the process of doing so, they became addicted, for survival, to receiving a share of national resource rents. As such rents exploded in the 1970s, the addiction was reinforced, helping explain both the absence of renewal and "how the system could unravel so quickly."[14]

Faced with the challenge of transition, the economics profession in general was beholden to a belief that simply freeing up markets would be conducive toward correcting for previous misallocations and that sufficient political will would help overcome problems such as weak property rights and corruption. Gaddy and Ickes argue that the problem runs deeper: "Russian institutions serve to preserve a legacy of misallocation. They preserve the poor location choices and the poor use of assets that is endemic in Russia. This makes the bad equilibrium self-enforcing."[15] The key to success in dealing with this problem lies in reallocation, in improving the systemic ability to respond to changing circumstances. If this cannot be achieved, major new investment programs will only make prior problems even worse.

If a genuine solution must entail the earlier-suggested "shrinking" of Siberia—a restructuring of Russia's economic geography—it must also be realized that powerful vested interests have emerged that will seek to block any such ambition. In regions that would be targeted for downsizing, company directors have clear personal interests in maintaining the size of their enterprises, and regional governors have equally clear personal interests in helping them make the case for continued support from the federal budget.

It is true that this is a pattern that may be found in many countries. The Russian case, however, is special in the sense that those arguing for subsidies will be supported by those who would have to pay for the subsidies. The simple reason is that governors and company directors in economically strong regions have reasons to prefer paying subsidies rather than accept in-migration that would produce congestion as well as a downward pressure on wages. Policy measures that are aimed at "keeping the lights on" in towns that really ought to be downsized symptomatically include the regime of restrictive residence permits in Moscow.[16]

While the portrayal of "bear traps" is suggestive indeed, capturing ways in which the formulation of Russian economic and energy policy runs the risk of actually making things worse rather than better, it falls a bit short of also suggesting how such risks may be avoided. Gaddy and Ickes themselves acknowledge that "it might appear that we have offered nothing in the way of a positive agenda of what should be done." Given that raw materials extraction represents the only sector where the Russian economy has an undeniable comparative advantage, there is yet again reason to agree with their previously cited contention that "even under optimal conditions for investment, any dream of creating a 'non-oil' Russia that could perform as well as today's commodity-based economy is unrealistic."[17]

Thus it may be said that the problems of Russian resource dependence have two interrelated and equally complicated dimensions. One is the long-term legacy of informal institutions, geared into supporting resource extraction, that have proven to be so resilient over time. As summarized in Chapter 2, this "burden of history" entails path-dependent patterns of unaccountable government, conditional property rights, and a drive to overcome perceived backwardness by resorting to forced growth. It constitutes a powerful obstacle to diversification as well as modernization.

To this we may add the more recent legacy of development of Siberia. Extending beyond the constraints of climate and geology, the "curse" entails vested interests in maintaining a warped economic structure that presents further powerful obstacles to much-needed modernization. National energy champions such as Gazprom and Rosneft, whose operations are based in Siberia, will find themselves in the midst of this conundrum. They will be expected to shoulder what really should be public-sector obligations, and they will be drawn into opaque games of regional lobbying and networking.

Let us now turn to look in more detail at the core question of modernization, recalling not just the need to look beyond superficial signs of modernity, such as modern gadgetry and a townscape of glitzy façades. More fundamentally, we must also bear in mind that our assumption of a continued dominant role for the energy sector indicates that this is where the needs for modernization are most imminent. Yet, whether change is implemented inside or outside the energy complex, the tasks entailed are formidable. At stake are the prospects for a successful introduction of the institutions of a modern society and a high-performance economy.

Medvedev's Modernization

There can be little doubt that Russian elites and government circles have absorbed the message on dangers inherent in a further slide into backwardness, also known in Russia as "primitivization" (*primitivizirovanie*), and in the possibility of Russia being reduced to a raw materials colony to the developed nations. Apprehension about the latter possibility has been growing in tandem with the rise in prominence of energy exports. And it has been focused on a fear that Russia may become a mere "resource appendage" to China.[18]

In a much cited article, titled "Go, Russia!" (*Rossiya, vpered!*), that was published in September 2009, President Medvedev issued a stark and provocative challenge: "Should a primitive economy based on raw materials and endemic corruption accompany us into the future?" Making his case for the need to modernize, he spoke of a "humiliating dependence on raw materials," about how "finished goods produced in Russia are largely plagued by their extremely low competitiveness," and about the need to stamp out "bribery, theft, intellectual and spiritual laziness, and drunkenness."[19]

Although the Medvedev presidency would turn out to be little more than a brief interlude, at the time there were many who did believe that serious change was in the making. Following eight years of focus on achieving an "authoritarian restoration," the Kremlin's rhetoric was suddenly being focused instead on modernization, on combating corruption, and on promoting the rule of law. The new master of the Kremlin was young. He would offer ample proof of his fancy both for modern gadgetry such as iPhones and iPads and for the use of modern social media such as Twitter and micro-blogging.[20] A lawyer by training, he could also credibly lash out at the causes behind the country's abysmal investment climate.

Those who were favorably disposed to his program could recall a symbolically important event that took place on February 17, 2008. Speaking at an economic forum in the Siberian city of Krasnoyarsk, Medvedev, who was then very soon to be (s)elected president, laid out what would be the main goals for his presidency. In summary they were presented as the "four I's": infrastructure, innovation, investment, and institutions.[21]While all four could be viewed as critically important for the future shape and role of the Russian economy, there were good and interrelated reasons why none would prove to be within easy reach.

Most important, perhaps, was the fact that Medvedev's tenure as president in his own right was never seriously intended. In stark reflection of the lack of transparency and accountability in Russian governance, the country's institutions proved sufficiently malleable to allow a range of tricks to be played out. By making a mockery out of all talk about constitutionalism and the rule of law, this drove home a powerful message about regime priorities and intentions.

As the end of Putin's second term in office was drawing near, speculation was rife about what would follow. It was deeply reflective of the nature of the political order of Putin's Russia that much time and energy were spent debating whether he would opt to honor the constitutional ban on serving more than two consecutive terms. Some drew parallels to rumors about how Boris Yeltsin may even have contemplated introducing a state of emergency when it looked as though he would not be able to win reelection in 1996. Others devised fanciful scenarios involving Putin retiring to a position behind the scenes, from which he would continue to wield real power. Some even speculated that Putin might prefer to join the international club of senior statesmen, touring the globe and giving lectures at exorbitant fees. The bottom line was that newly introduced formal constitutional rules of the game had again been trumped by the preferences and highly personalized networks of the ruling elite.

The actual solution was inventive, deemed at the time even to be quite ingenious. In December 2007, with less than three months to go before the scheduled election, Putin announced that, in his opinion, Dmitry Medvedev would be a good successor as president. Appearing on state television, Putin said that "I have known him very closely for more than 17 years and I completely and fully support this proposal."[22] For himself, he would humbly consider the post of prime minister, should he be asked.

To historically conscious Russians, the announcement could not fail to bring to mind the classic statement by Peter the Great, that "to whom I will to him I shall give my throne."[23] The maneuver even caused some to recall an event in 1575 when Ivan the Terrible staged a mock abdication, announcing that his office as Grand Prince of All Rus would pass to a certain Simeon Bekbulatovich, a khan of the minor khanate of Qasim who was not even of the true blood (meaning, not of Rurikide descent). Ivan, for himself, reserved the humble title "Ivan of Moscow." Less than a year later, however, Ivan returned to the Kremlin and his loyal vassal was demoted to Grand Prince of Tver, still a very important post.[24]

Historical analogies aside, the deal was done and Medvedev's path to the Kremlin was clear. Having been duly nominated as a candidate for United Russia, Putin's purpose-built "party of power," in March 2008 he was elected to serve as president of the Russian Federation for the period 2008–2012. Having assumed the formal reins of power, Medvedev immediately appointed Putin to serve as prime minister. What would come to be known as the "tandem" was born.

As Medvedev's first and only term in office was in turn drawing to a close, speculation again was rife about what would follow. Would the caretaker be allowed to serve a second term, or would Putin decide to return? Members of the respective praetorian guards were clearly apprehensive, fearing that positions, revenue streams, and perhaps even personal security were on the line. While the two members of the tandem may well have remained on genuinely friendly personal terms, rivalries and even outright antipathies between members of their respective teams made this an inherently unstable arrangement, prone to far more speculation and infighting than under traditional monocratic rule.

It all came to an abrupt halt on September 24, 2011, when President Medvedev told delegates at a United Russia conference that he and Prime Minister Putin had decided to simply swap jobs.[25] Adding insult to injury, Putin also let it be known that this was a decision the pair had reached prior to Medvedev's election, but had kept to themselves: "I want to say directly: [Medvedev and I] reached an agreement between ourselves long ago, several years ago, on what to do in the future, on who should do what."[26]

Putin may well have believed that his personal standing was so strong that admitting to the ploy would be viewed as little more than the arrogance of power—as an essential sign of strength. But on this occasion he may have been just a bit too smart for his own good, as Russia's subsequent "winter of discontent" would seriously weaken his personal authority and thus also compromise the effectiveness of his rule. Above all, this made it abundantly clear to everyone that the presumed agenda for modernization and a fight against corruption had not been seriously intended.

Regarding Medvedev's "four I's," his first goal was to improve the country's infrastructure. This task was at the same time less controversial and more challenging than the other three. It was less controversial in the sense that there could be no denying the need. Untold numbers of reports have been presented, by official authorities as well as by private market operators, to document the decrepit nature of key infrastructure components ranging from roads, rails, bridges, and harbors to water treatment plants, power-generation facilities, and central-heating systems, not to mention the drilling, pumping, and refining installations that make up the country's energy complex.

In all of these, showcase illustrations may be held up to demonstrate impressive modernization, including state-of-the-art technology, but they are exceptions only. A case in point is the previously mentioned East Siberian Vankor oil and gas field, which has been developed with some of the most advanced technology available in Russia. Included here are "smart wells," equipped with wireless transmitters that send real-time information about well performance to remote data centers.[27] Other fields lag far behind.

The broad variety of estimates that have been presented on how much it would cost to achieve a serious modernization run into the trillions of dollars, to be spent over extended periods of time. It is the latter that also causes this to be such a challenging task. In the short term, the sorry state of Russia's infrastructure may be viewed as the opportunity cost of fiscal conservatism. Since the latter has been viewed as one of the main achievements of the past decade, it has not been easy to argue the case for massive spending. According to some cynical critics, it would have made little sense to abandon fiscal conservatism, only to embark on projects of modernization that would never have been finished anyway.

Perhaps the main reason for pessimism on this count is the ubiquitous corruption that causes so much of state funding for major investment projects to be diverted into private pockets. To the previously mentioned allegations that $4 billion went missing during construction of the ESPO pipeline to the Pacific, we might add allegations of funds lost in preparation for the 2012 APEC summit meeting in Vladivostok.[28] And we must surely not forget the race to turn the beach resort of Sochi into a host venue for the 2014 Winter Olympics, described by critics of the Kremlin as one of the most corrupt projects in Russia's history.[29]

To historically conscious Russians, there is nothing new here. It all represents continuity with the notorious corruption that for so long has figured so prominently in accounts both from and about Russia, from the great Russian novels to present-day hoopla about campaigns against corruption. During a visit to France, the famous Russian nineteenth-century historian and writer Nikolai Karamzin was asked by Russian emigrants to describe what was happening in Russia. His classic answer was formulated in a single word: *Voruyut*—"They are stealing." The time when he lived was one of monumental corruption. Stories about kickbacks in relation to the building of the Trans-Siberian railroad may be viewed as early precursors to present-day accounts of oligarch corruption and wealth creation.[30]

The next of Medvedev's "four I's" regards the need to promote innovation. As is amply evident, this must indeed be viewed as a paramount priority, perhaps as the only way of preventing a reduction of the Russian economy to the status of a raw materials colony to the industrialized economies, including China. Yet although there has been much talk about the latter danger, the only tangible result has been the launch of a Russian version of Silicon Valley, a high-tech innovation center based in the town of Skolkovo in the Moscow region.

While there is nothing inherently wrong with this scheme, one should be wary of betting too much on its potential to act as a driving force in a broad-based process of modernization. Even if it should turn out to be a stunning success, which for systemic reasons is unlikely in the extreme, it is hard indeed to see that it will have the broad impact on the Russian economy as a whole that is critically needed for serious modernization to result.

What Skolkovo does illustrate is that any ambition to undertake serious modernization of the Russian economy will need to entail not just a serious boost in fixed capital investment. It will also and more importantly need to address the sorry state of the country's research and higher education complex. While economic policies may change, and while political elites may alter their ambitions, there is little that can be done even over the medium term to compensate for the neglect of this sector during the post-Soviet era. The legacy of the Yeltsin era in particular was one of utter devastation, caused, in the words of Julian Cooper, by "severe budget constraints, depressed rates of pay, and an economy that until now has generated modest demand for product and process innovations."[31]

The argument on economic structure is perhaps the most important here. The real reason why research and development reached such high standards during the Soviet era was that demand originated from and was funded by the military-industrial complex, which received top priority in resource allocation. In sharp contrast, however, to the experience of Western industrialized nations, there was very little spin-off from this research in terms of civilian innovation and product development. Rather than encourage such proliferation, the authorities made sure that researchers were locked into closed cities that did not even exist on the map, and that consequently had no possibilities to interact with entrepreneurs in a consumer-driven civilian sector. When the Gaidar government decided to more or less terminate the military-industrial complex, the prospects for "conversion" to civilian production consequently were very poor.

Well into the Putin era it remained the case that research and development had a mainly military orientation. The negative outcome reflects that the military had ceased to be a secure source of demand, and by implication of funding. From 1990 until 2005, the number of researchers dropped by more than half, from 993,000 to 400,000, and spending on research and development from just over 2 percent of GDP to 1.2 percent of GDP.[32] The problem was not just that these numbers were falling. Even more serious was the fact that weak recruitment from below was causing the average age of remaining researchers to rise. Already by the time that Putin took over, it was approaching age sixty, above male life expectancy at the time.[33]

The outlook for the future is marked by two patterns. One is that demographic trends point very clearly in the direction of shrinking cohorts of young people, and the other that the glitz and glamour that has marked the Putin era has not been conducive to convincing those who remain to opt for a career in the world of science. The future prospects for modernization and diversification must consequently be viewed as bleak at best. When and if the Kremlin does decide to attempt to reverse the trend, aiming to recapture the role once played by Russia in the international world of science, it will be a long slog indeed.

The next of Medvedev's "four I's" regards the need to promote investment. Clearly, successfully transforming Russia into a modern and competitive player on global markets will require substantial increases in the level of fixed capital investment. And it is far from clear what the sources for such a boost would be. While growth in fixed capital investment under Putin was substantial, it was in no way sufficient to overcome the legacy of the preceding decade. The drop under Yeltsin had been so massive that while the level of GDP by the time that Putin left the Kremlin had been brought back to the status quo before Yeltsin, this was very far from the case when it came to erosion and obsolescence of the capital stock. An international comparison will serve to bring the point home.

According to World Bank calculations, over the period 2000–2005, China invested a staggering 40 percent of its GDP, a number that agrees well with the boomtown image of that country. The eurozone meanwhile came in at 21 percent and the United States at 19 percent, with Russia trailing at no more than 18 percent.[34] Short of comparing Russia with China, which is a very special case, it should be obvious that Russia's investment needs were, and remain, of a different magnitude altogether from those of the United States or the European Union. Its poor performance must hence be viewed as highly worrisome for the future.

To this may be further added that, for reasons of monopoly power, most of the nontradable goods that go into Russian fixed capital investment are sold in Russia at prices that exceed those on world markets. If the resources that are being bought with fixed capital investment outlays were to be counted at world market prices, then Russian investment would come in at a mere 9 percent of GDP, vastly below what would be needed for a serious upgrading and restructuring of the capital stock.[35]

This may be viewed against historical experience from postwar reconstruction in Japan and Western Europe, where successful rebuilding was associated with an investment intensity that, according to Jacques Sapir, was "greater than 20 percent and probably closer to 25 percent."[36] In addition to a high rate of fixed capital investment, which facilitated the rebuilding of damaged infrastructure and production facilities, the respective recovery strategies of Japan and Western Europe also placed heavy emphasis on technological progress and on building cutting-edge human capital. The successes that were scored may be reflected in the transformation of the label "made in Japan" from something of a joke into a distinctive mark of quality.

The remaining question concerns where the funds for a boost in Russian investment would come from. As the government is clearly not going to shoulder the responsibility, beyond selected "mega-projects" and dubious ambitions to create "national champions," this leaves Russian corporate investment and foreign direct investment, neither of which inspires much confidence.

Beginning with the prospects for Russian corporate investment to pick up the slack, let us recall that the Russian government made prudent use of the oil windfall by paying down and almost eliminating its sovereign debt. What many failed to note was that corporate borrowing over the same period of time rose to the extent that total Russian foreign debt in 2009 was more than two and a half times the size it had been in the crisis year 1999.[37]

What made this expansion possible was a combination of a steady improvement in the sovereign credit rating, low interest rates on global credit markets, and a belief that oil prices would remain high, all of which encouraged capital inflow. At the outset there was a general belief that this was a healthy process of "recycling." Assuming that foreign capital would be better invested than domestic capital, it was suggested that public-sector balance-of-payment surpluses converted into US Treasury securities could act as collateral for private-sector borrowing.[38] A similar argument has been suggested with respect to China's massive accumulation of US securities, likening the process to the emergence of a new system—the Bretton Woods II—of a global reserve currency.[39]

In the case of Russia, the oil-price collapse combined with the global credit crunch to throw corporate debtors into serious trouble and the economy as a whole into recession. Given what is known about proceedings in Russian bankruptcy courts, there was little risk of foreign banks actually electing to trigger default on corporate debt. The problem is that, given the tough repayment schedules that face Russian corporations, there will be little room in the future for any form of expansive investment.

Regarding foreign direct investment, what is important here is not just the fact that inflows are relatively small and highly volatile. We must also consider what is known as "round-tripping," that a substantial share of actual capital flows is made up of Russian capital leaving and returning, following a brief stay in some foreign account. It is symptomatic, for example, that until the crisis in 2013, Cyprus was among the top foreign investors in the Russian economy.[40] And it is significant that single events of a mainly political nature have left major marks in the charts.[41]

The causes have been a combination of tax evasion, money laundering, and outright criminal activity. The bottom line, however, is that once account is taken of the bogus nature of these capital flows, the true size of both capital flight and of foreign direct investment will have to be heavily discounted. The reason why this matters is that "true" foreign direct investment will embody precisely such forms of technology and management skills that are needed for serious modernization.

The last of Medvedev's "four I's" regards the need to improve institutions. This is clearly and perhaps even necessarily related to the need to promote innovation. Again, however, though there is a growing awareness of the problem, there has also been a distinct lack of ambition to tackle it with any degree of purpose. Compared to the task of promoting innovation, that of undertaking institutional reform has been surrounded by even more talk, mainly about the rule of law and about a struggle against corruption. In effect, however, it has all been much ado about nothing.

In stark reflection of the steady decline in quality of governance, the Russian investment climate has come to be widely perceived as simply appalling, plagued by what the US State Department euphemistically summarized as "a complicated and fluid set of challenges ranging from corruption to a weak judiciary to excessive red tape." It was somehow symptomatic that at about the same time that Judge Viktor Danilkin was busy reading the 250-page verdict against Mikhail Khodorkovsky, in December 2010, Dmitry Medvedev was addressing a business council on modernization, bemoaning the fact that so few Russian companies had opted to issue equity during the year: "Part of the problem is, of course, our investment climate, which is bad. Very bad."[42] One may legitimately wonder whether the president considered himself to be part of the solution, or perhaps part of the problem.

Agency vs. Evolution

Though both the Yeltsin era and the Putin era were marked by predatory activities that caused great harm, the former was broadly market friendly and featured much pluralism. Perhaps under a different post-Yeltsin leadership Russia could have matured into a liberal democracy with a rules-based market economy, as initially envisioned by the proponents of transition. If so, should Vladimir Putin be held culpable for the contrary outcome?

The empirical evidence is certainly suggestive. With Putin in the Kremlin, the window of opportunity for building democratic institutions and for pursuing a market-friendly economic policy, aimed at securing high value-added and global competitiveness, was slammed firmly shut. As the process of economic reform ground to a halt, economic policy instead was in effect reconnected with the traditional Russian path of statism and market-contrary government. But can this unfortunate turn of events really be explained by the transition of power from Yeltsin to Putin? Thus formulated, the question recalls the classic prior question of whether Soviet power would have evolved differently without Stalin.[43]

This book has repeatedly cautioned against associating Putin and the Putin era with the presence of an early master plan, instead suggesting that Russia's post-Soviet development has been a case of endogenous institutional evolution. As in the case of Stalin, there is a clear limit to this argument. In effect, presenting personality and leadership as unimportant leaves us with historical determinism, which is clearly unacceptable. What is at stake here is the classic question of continuity versus change in Russian development, better formulated, perhaps, as a case of agency versus evolution. What, more specifically, is the latitude for Russian rulers to implement fundamental change by deliberate design?

If we look merely at broad policy agendas, the answer would seem to be that this latitude is rather dismally narrow. Over the centuries, Russian development has been marked by a distinctive pendulum movement between reform and repression, with deeply rooted institutional patterns shaken and then reestablished, to the detriment of prospects for institutional modernization. The Yeltsin era has been characterized here as yet another "time of trouble," an amorphous period evolving in the wake of the collapse of the Soviet Union. Laudable ambitions of Westernizing reform ended up in great disappointment. The ensuing Putin era could be viewed as a reaction akin, perhaps, to the "authoritarian restoration" undertaken by Alexander III, in response to the Great Reforms of his father, Alexander II.

But how much of what actually happened after Putin's ascension to power may be credibly ascribed to an early agenda, or even to deliberate agency by the new leader and his Petersburg entourage? Speculation about what the future may bring must come to terms with this crucial question. Bearing in mind the caution against ascribing to the ruler too much power of agency, if we look merely at rhetoric it would seem that Putin has indeed been quite clear about what he wants.

There is his statement to the Russian Federal Assembly in 2005, portraying the collapse of the Soviet Union as a major geopolitical disaster of the century. There is his hard-line message to a security conference in Munich in 2007, accusing the United States of an almost uncontained use of military force. And there are his more recent portrayals of the customs union with Kazakhstan and Belarus as the most important geopolitical and integration event in the post-Soviet space since the breakup of the Soviet Union, and of further post-Soviet integration as unstoppable.

The message that we may extract from these statements goes beyond resentment over shrunken territory and a loss of global respect and influence. At the heart of Putin's analysis of what had gone wrong, one may sense an implicit understanding that the dissolution of the Soviet Union was accompanied by destruction also of such mechanisms of command and control from above that are vital to ensuring well-ordered economic activity and a functioning society. This would need to be put right again.

Already in his 2000 self-portrait book *First Person,* he indicated a belief that a supercentralized state is in some sense inscribed in Russia's DNA: "But from the very beginning, Russia was created as a supercentralized state. That's practically laid down in its genetic code, its traditions and the mentality of its people."[44] His more recent statements on post-Soviet integration also indicate that his view of Russia is congruent with the shape of the former Soviet Union as a whole, possibly excluding the Baltic republics.[45]

There can be little doubt that Putin's initial ambitions upon assuming power were aimed at restoring domestic order and at reclaiming lost respect in the global arena. It is again symptomatic that his rhetoric would repeatedly recall Stalin's famous statement from 1931 on the inherent dangers of weakness and the imminent need to catch up with the West: "Such is the law of the exploiters: beat the backward and the weak. . . . We have fallen behind the advanced countries by fifty to a hundred years. We must close that gap in ten years. Either we do this or we will be crushed."[46]

A widely cited illustration of Putin's "Stalinist" mind-set in this narrow sense could be found in his otherwise rather odd comment on the horrid terrorist attack on a school in Beslan in September 2004, which left at least 334 hostages dead, including 186 children: "We showed ourselves to be weak. And the weak get beaten (*A slabykh byut*)."[47]

Even more poignant is his commentary on the need for military rearmament, published in *Rossiiskaya Gazeta* during his 2012 election campaign. Again he recalls Stalin's concern about having fallen behind and needing to catch up: "Russia's defense research centers and production facilities have been slow to modernize over the last 30 years. In the coming decade, we need to close this gap." And again Putin repeats the warning against showing weakness: "We should not tempt anyone by allowing ourselves to be weak."[48]

Yet for all the warnings that have been issued about mounting authoritarianism, about a pending police state, and about a return, in effect, both to the Soviet Union and to the Cold War, the actual outcome has fallen far short of the ominous rhetoric. As phrased by Stephen Fortescue, Russia has become a halfway house of sorts, wedged between democracy and authoritarianism: "It is not a democracy in which an opposition and electorate can create and enforce expectations of policy resolution. Nor is it a tyranny in which a dictator with untrammeled power forces policy through with as much brutality as required."[49]

To drive the point home, it will suffice here to note the stark contrast between the Communist Party of the Soviet Union and United Russia, Putin's purpose-built "party of power." While the former wielded real power and was an essential tool of government, the latter has become increasingly discredited and ineffectual. Putin may be harsh and vindictive, but his ability to discipline and control society is clearly limited.

Beyond emphasizing that current Russian authoritarianism represents a pale version of its Soviet predecessor, we may also note that imagery of a reconnect with the past misses one further important point. The traditional pattern of Russian development had been consistently focused on forced mobilization of resources from above for the purpose of supporting a military-industrial establishment. Under Putin, narrow short-term interests in personal enrichment were allowed to take precedence over the traditional longer-term state interest in security and sustainability. This would prove to have seriously negative consequences, measured not just in capital flight and lack of investment in technological development.

By far the greatest problem that would face a reverse transition from free markets to pervasive state control was that so little remained of the once formidable Soviet military-industrial complex. The pronounced ambition to make Russia great again, and to reassert the state interest, would consequently need to proceed along a different path. Attempting to cure superpower hangover by transforming the Soviet military superpower into a Russian energy superpower would, however, be rife with problems. It not only opened up a field of unprecedented opportunity for personal enrichment by hosts of competing clans. It also voided the possibility of maintaining systemic integrity by way of reference to enemies and national security concerns. All of this leads one to question whether Putin and his Petersburg entourage really did have a coherent economic agenda from the outset.

It is true that the discovery that Putin had defended a doctoral dissertation at the St. Petersburg Mining Institute caused a bit of a stir. Presented in 1997, it dealt with planning of the mineral resource base of the St. Petersburg region and it was believed to lay out the need for state control over mineral resources. This could be taken as evidence that assembling an energy powerhouse, upon which a new system of political power could be built, was indeed an important early priority.[50]

Although the text of the dissertation would turn out, once it was made available, to contain little to nothing on energy policy, the intellectual environment at the Mining Institute could still be viewed, as suggested by Thane Gustafson, as an incubator for subsequent strategic thinking. Beginning in the mid-1990s, a small group of officials had formed a discussion group on natural resource policy. Under the leadership of the rector of the Mining Institute, Vladimir Litvinenko, over the period 1997–1999 the participants published several important works, of which Putin's dissertation was the first. Two other prominent members were Viktor Zubkov, who defended a dissertation on tax policy in the natural resource sector, and Igor Sechin, who wrote on conditions in the Russian oil industry.[51]

Putin, following his move to Moscow and his subsequent elevation to master of the Kremlin, would retain firm bonds with these men, and the policies they would implement can be viewed as rooted in their early thinking. The emerging consensus was that the experience of the 1990s had demonstrated that the market cannot work alone, without guidance. Free markets had brought "depression, decline, and disorder." The root cause was a lack of state leadership, and the solution was seen to lie in a state-private partnership. The theses that were presented by Putin and Sechin contain an outline of the main principles of state capitalism that they would later espouse. In the words of Gustafson, "Their outlook, from the first, is resolutely mercantilist, nationalistic, and patriotic."[52]

Expanding on the role of early thinking, Gustafson points at two additional articles published in Putin's name in 1999, when he had already been elevated to the position of head of the FSB (domestic successor to the Soviet KGB), and was soon to be appointed acting president of Russia. The first emphasized the role of the resource sector as the basis for economic growth and pleaded for the need to capture resource rents to be used in rebuilding the rest of the economy, and the second laid out the case for a strong state, condemning the market radicalism of the 1990s.[53]

This is clearly not to say that from the outset the men from Petersburg had a detailed agenda on natural resource and energy policy. On the contrary, Putin would himself show ambivalence on a number of key issues, ranging from the breaking up of Gazprom and the suggested merger of Gazprom and Rosneft into a single "national champion," to the final settling of the score with Yukos Oil. It may be argued that Putin has proven to be a tactician rather than a strategist, but that is precisely what the legacy from the past dictates. True power derives not from repression alone but from a skillful balancing of rival clans.

This said, there are two main priorities that may be viewed as rooted in the early thinking. One is the need to formulate an effective tax policy to capture energy rents. Viktor Zubkov, having defended his thesis on precisely this topic, was well suited to lead the charge against the oil barons.

Supported by his son-in-law, Anatoly Serdyukov, who was appointed to head the federal tax service, he would also be instrumental in the eventual dismantling of Yukos, by way of inflated tax claims. As noted earlier, however, that system of oil taxation has evolved over time into a major problem that remains to be resolved.

The second priority was that of forming "national champions," as a manifestation of the envisioned state-private partnership. Having written on conditions within the Russian oil industry, Igor Sechin was in turn well qualified to take on this task. Following Medvedev's elevation to the presidency, Sechin was appointed deputy prime minister in charge of energy and executive secretary of Putin's newly created Energy Commission. Having served as chairman of the board at Rosneft from 2004 until 2011, in May 2012 he was made president of the company. While there can be little doubt that Rosneft is a rising star, it again remains questionable what this will mean in terms of performance. As suggested earlier, there are grounds to suspect that Rosneft will rather emulate the style of governance that has done so much damage to Gazprom.

Beyond these priorities, many of the events outlined in this book must be viewed as ad hoc responses to emerging conflicts and opportunities. The role of Putin in these events has been unclear and shifting. Gustafson is probably correct in presenting Putin's evolving mind-set as marked by a "consistent bias toward control, a preference for state ownership, an instinct for domination, and an intolerance of opposition."[54] But thinking is one thing. Taking effective action is something very different, especially so when the main challenge is that of maintaining balance between rival interests. The role that Putin has played is reminiscent of what Charles Lindblom once noted about communist systems as having "thumbs where one would want fingers."[55]

There can be little doubt that even within the current Russian system there is room for deliberate intervention to succeed. Yet it will also remain true that such interventions stand a greater chance of success when they are formulated in accordance with informal institutional patterns from the past than when they seek to achieve a fundamental break with path-dependence. This provides part of the answer to the question of whether Putin should be held culpable for "democratic backsliding" and for a return to market-contrary government. His ambitions were simply so well attuned to institutional inertia from the past that he could largely go with the flow. Medvedev's attempted modernization in contrast represented a challenge to traditional institutional solutions and thus stood a much smaller chance of success, even had he been granted a second term.

The main question in a long-term perspective is whether Russia will return fully to the traditional mode of resource extraction for the purpose of defense and security. The massive State Armament Program, launched in

2010, devoting 19.4 trillion rubles to ensuring that by 2020 Russia's armed forces will be 70 percent modern, can be considered evidence that the wager on building an energy superpower was no more than a phase, a temporary substitute for the defunct military superpower.

The renewed wager on the military-industrial complex may indeed be viewed as a logical return to the traditional path of development. It has also been viewed by some as rather worrisome. It is based on assessments of security threats from NATO that border on sheer paranoia, and it allocates resources for rearmament that go way beyond what might be needed for a reasonably dimensioned modern defense force. Yet none of this can be taken as evidence that the Russian Federation will morph into a replica of the Soviet Union, or that fears of a return to the Cold War will prove to have been warranted. Compared to its Soviet predecessor, the Russian Federation is simply too weakened and too conflict ridden.

The wager on resource nationalism, as a way toward making Russia great again, was marked by such a degree of competing and conflicting agendas that it caused much collateral damage both to energy policy and to economic development in general. Something similar may be said about potential ambitions to re-create a military superpower.

The host of problems detailed in relation to development of the Russian energy complex will pose serious limits to what Rudiger Ahrend has referred to as "pumping growth,"[56] and thus to the future availability of rents from energy assets. Admissions by military sources that a fifth of the defense budget gets stolen every year indicate that much of what does get allocated will not be used for the intended purpose.[57] And by all accounts, the quality of governance is deteriorating across the economy, suggesting that the prospects for modernization, inside or outside the energy complex, remain bleak at best.

Most important, speculation about what the future may bring must come to terms with the crucial question of deliberate agency by the president and his Petersburg entourage. Following the mobilization of mass protest from below that marked the winter of 2011–2012, the authority of the regime as a whole has suffered serious damage. And President Putin has himself exhibited suggestive signs that he is out of touch and no longer capable of firm leadership. His 2012 "state of the federation" address, on December 12, was an exercise in self-laudatory retrospection that was devoid of visions for the future. And his marathon press conference on December 20 showed a rambling president who repeatedly lost his temper and claimed to be unaware of the major problems of the day. For the first time ever, journalists could treat him with open sarcasm.[58]

The future of Russia will consequently be marked by a combination of weak prospects for continued growth in resource extraction, of endogenous institutional evolution toward degraded quality of governance, and of eroded regime authority. If Putin should succeed in remaining in power beyond 2018, Russia may see its role devolve into that of an increasingly backward and isolated former superpower, increasingly prone to lash out in defiance and denial. And even if a liberal candidate should succeed, against all odds, in winning the presidency, the prospects for successful intervention to turn the tide of increasing obsolescence and wasting of energy resources would not be good.

On the key question here—the reach of agency—it is fitting to end with one of the most frequently cited in a plethora of classic statements by Viktor Chernomyrdin, the last Soviet minister of gas and long the ultimate Kremlin insider: "We wanted for the best, but it turned out as always."[59]

Notes

1. Gustafson, *Wheel of Fortune*, pp. 4–5.
2. Rutland, "Russia as an Energy Superpower," p. 206.
3. World Bank, *Russian Economic Report, November 2004*.
4. Kuboniwa, "Hollowing Out Industrial Production." See also Kuboniwa, Tabata, and Ustinova, "How Large Is the Oil and Gas Sector of Russia?"
5. Gaddy and Ickes, "Russia After the Global Financial Crisis," pp. 282–287.
6. Ibid., p. 287.
7. Ahrend, "Can Russia Break the 'Resource Curse?'" p. 587.
8. Gaddy and Ickes, "Bear Traps," p. 7.
9. Hill and Gaddy, *The Siberian Curse*.
10. Ibid., p. 3.
11. Ibid.
12. For an attempt to measure the costs of the cold, see Hill and Gaddy, *The Siberian Curse*, chap. 3.
13. Gaddy and Ickes, "Bear Traps," p. 7.
14. Gaddy and Ickes, "Addiction and Withdrawal," p. 2.
15. Gaddy and Ickes, "Bear Traps," p. 118.
16. Ibid., pp. 79–80.
17. Ibid., p. 119.
18. See further Itoh, *Russia Looks East*, p. 37, n. 37.
19. President of Russia, "Dmitry Medvedev's Article 'Go Russia!'" September 10, 2009, http://eng.kremlin.ru/transcripts/298.
20. Gorham, "Medvedev's New Media Gambit."
21. "Medvedev Says 'Four I's Key' to Russia's Economic Program," *RIA Novosti*, February 15, 2008, http://en.ria.ru/russia/20080215/99286756.html.
22. Luke Harding, "Putin Anoints Medvedev As Successor," *The Guardian*, December 10, 2007, http://www.guardian.co.uk/world/2007/dec/10/russia.lukeharding.
23. Kochan and Abraham, *The Making of Modern Russia*, p. 126.
24. This parallel was suggested to me in conversation with Igor Torbakov, who first presented it in his article "Russia: Is Moscow Heading Toward the Time of Troubles?" *Eurasianet*, October 18, 2011, http://www.eurasianet.org/print/64333.
25. "Medvedev Backs Putin for Russian President," *RIA Novosti*, September 24, 2011, http://en.rian.ru/russia/20110924/167090260.html.

26. Thomas Grove and Gleb Bryanski, "Putin Sets Stage for Return As Russian President," *Reuters,* September 24, 2011, http://www.reuters.com/article/2011/09/24 /us-russia-idUSTRE78N0RH20110924.

27. Gustafson, *Wheel of Fortune,* p. 468.

28. According to the Russian Ministry of Interior, funds of more than 93 million rubles ($2.9 million) were embezzled during preparations for the APEC summit. "Over $2.9 Million Stolen During APEC Preparations," *RAPSI News,* November 8, 2012, http://rapsinews.com/anticorruption_news/20121108/265282902.html.

29. According to Deputy Prime Minister Dmitry Kozak, the cost of the Sochi Olympics would reach £32 billion, the most expensive Olympics cost ever and well above the original estimate of £12 billion. Critics like Boris Nemtsov claim that billions have been lost. London pulled off the summer Olympics with a budget of £9 billion. "Russia's 2014 Winter Olympics Are Dogged by Controversy," *The Guardian,* February 6, 2013, http://www.guardian.co.uk/sport/blog/2013/feb/06 /controversy-russia-sochi-winter-olympics.

30. Paul E. Richardson, "Siberia's Iron Road," *Russian Life,* May–June 2001, http://www.russianlife.com/paulerichardson/transsib.cfm.

31. Cooper, "Of BRICS and Brains," p. 261.

32. Ibid.

33. Blank, *The Material-Technical Foundations of Russian Military Power,* pp. 25–26.

34. Organization for Economic Cooperation and Development, *Economic Survey of the Russian Federation 2006,* pp. 26–27.

35. Gaddy, "The Russian Economy in the Year 2006," p. 45.

36. Sapir, "Russia's Economic Rebound," p. 19.

37. At the end of 1999, total Russian foreign debt stood at $178 billion. At the end of 2009, it had increased to $470 billion. Over the intervening decade, general government debt had been reduced, from $133 billion to $30 billion, or to less than 2 percent of GDP. Meanwhile, banks and corporations had increased their joint debt, from $29 billion to $425 billion. Numbers taken from Central Bank of Russia, "External Debt of the Russian Federation," http://www.cbr.ru/eng/statistics/print .aspx?file=credit_statistics/debt_e.htm&pid=svs&sid=ITM_38104.

38. Cited in Gaddy and Ickes, "Russia After the Global Financial Crisis," p. 288.

39. Dooley, Folkerts-Landau, and Garber, "The Revised Bretton Woods System."

40. The three countries that by the end of 2011 had the largest shares of accumulated investment into the Russian economy were Cyprus (22.5 percent), the Netherlands (14.1 percent), and Luxembourg (10.7 percent). Germany came in fourth (8.3 percent). Goskomstat, "Countries with the Largest Accumulated Investments in the Economy of Russia," http://www.gks.ru/bgd/regl/b12_06/Isswww.exe /Stg/d01/14-07.htm. The large share of the Netherlands is partly explained by the presence in that country of Gazprom Netherlands, which counts as a foreign source. The latter in particular calls for caution in talking about "foreign" direct investment in Russia.

41. In the first half of 2007, Rosneft and Gazprom purchased Yukos assets by allegedly securing foreign credits of, respectively, $25.1 billion and $5.8 billion; Tabata, "The Influence of High Oil Prices," p. 90, n. 29. Much of the heavy inflow of capital in 2007 could also be explained by Gazprom Netherlands investing to buy out Shell from Sakhalin. Viewed from a perspective of modernization and global integration, the latter should probably be counted with a negative sign.

42. US Department of State, "2012 Investment Climate Statement—Russia," June, http://www.state.gov/e/eb/rls/othr/ics/2012/191223.htm; Dan Murphy, "After Khodorkovsky Verdict, Russia's Medvedev Bemoans Business Climate," *Christian Science Monitor,* December 29, 2010, http://www.csmonitor.com/World/Europe /2010/1229/After-Khodorkovsky-verdict-Russia-s-Medvedev-bemoans-business -climate.

43. See Nove, *Was Stalin Really Necessary?*

44. Putin, *First Person,* p. 186.

45. Putin's view on Ukrainian statehood, for example, was made clear in an address to the NATO-Russia Council at the important April 2008 Bucharest summit: "Well, you understand, George [Bush], Ukraine is not even a state." Kuzio, "Poor Ukrainian-Russian Ties."

46. Service, *Stalin,* p. 273.

47. Jonathan Steele, "Putin Warns of Security Backlash," *The Guardian,* September 6, 2004, http://www.guardian.co.uk/world/2004/sep/06/chechnya.russia2.

48. For an English version of the article, see "Article by Prime Minister Vladimir Putin in *Rossiiskaya Gazeta,*" February 20, 2012, http://archive.premier .gov.ru/eng/events/news/18185. See also "Putin and the Army (Part III)," *Russian Defense Policy,* February 25, 2012, http://russiandefpolicy.wordpress.com/2012 /02/25/putin-and-the-army-part-iii.

49. Fortescue, "The Russian Law on Subsurface Resources," p. 179.

50. See Harley Balzer's articles "The Putin Thesis," "Vladimir Putin's Academic Writings," and "Vladimir Putin on Russian Energy Policy."

51. Gustafson, *Wheel of Fortune,* pp. 246–247.

52. Ibid., p. 249.

53. Ibid., pp. 249–252.

54. Ibid., p. 270.

55. Lindblom, *Politics and Markets,* p. 65.

56. As cited in Gaddy, "Perspectives on the Potential of Russian Oil," p. 346.

57. In an interview with *Rossiiskaya Gazeta* in May 2011, Sergei Fridinsky, Russia's chief military prosecutor, said that a fifth of the military hardware budget in Russia is stolen each year by corrupt officials and military contractors; see Isabel Gorst, "Russian Military Budget Sapped by Corruption," *Financial Times,* May 24, 2011, http://www.ft.com/intl/cms/s/0/961668be-8628-11e0-9e2c-00144feabdc0 .html#axzz2RH09hWnf. The subsequent corruption scandals surrounding the sacking of Defense Minister Anatoly Serdyukov suggest that the reality may be even more striking.

58. Tatiana Stanovaya, "Clueless in the Kremlin: Vladimir Putin's Press Conference," December 28, 2012, http://imrussia.org/en/politics/358-clueless-in-the -kremlin-vladimir-putins-press-conference.

59. In Russian, *Khoteli kak lutche, a poluchilos kak vsegda.* A collection of Chernomyrdin quotes may be found at http://www.dosuga.net/?type=marazm&seq =cherno&mk=on&num=.

Appendix 1:
Russian Economic Performance

1.1 Macroeconomic Indicators (percentage change)

	2003	2004	2005	2006	2007	2008	2009	2010	2011	2012
GDP	7.3	7.2	6.4	8.2	8.5	5.2	−7.8	4.5	4.3	3.4
Industrial production	8.9	8.0	5.1	6.3	6.8	0.6	−9.3	8.2	4.7	2.6
Capital investment	12.5	13.7	10.9	16.7	22.7	9.9	−15.7	6.0	8.3	6.7

Source: Bank of Finland Institute for Economies in Transition, Russia Statistics.

1.2 Federal Budget Performance (percentage of GDP)

	2003	2004	2005	2006	2007	2008	2009	2010	2011	2012
Revenues	19.5	20.1	23.7	23.4	23.6	21.8	18.8	18.7	20.9	21.0
Expenditures	17.8	15.8	16.3	16.0	18.1	17.8	24.7	22.7	20.1	21.0
Surplus	1.7	4.4	7.5	7.4	5.4	4.0	-5.9	-4.1	0.8	0.0

Source: Bank of Finland Institute for Economies in Transition, Russia Statistics.

1.3 Merchandise Trade and Current Account Surplus (US$ billions)

	2003	2004	2005	2006	2007	2008	2009	2010	2011	2012
Exports	135.9	183.2	240.0	297.5	346.5	466.3	297.2	392.7	515.4	528.0
Imports	76.1	97.4	123.8	163.2	223.1	288.7	183.9	245.7	318.6	335.7
Surplus	35.4	59.5	84.4	92.3	72.2	103.9	50.4	67.5	97.3	71.4

Source: Bank of Finland Institute for Economies in Transition, Russia Statistics.

1.4 Foreign Debt and Reserves (US$ billions, end of year)

	2003	2004	2005	2006	2007	2008	2009	2010	2011	2012
External debt	96.9	95.5	69.9	43.2	35.8	28.2	29.5	32.2	33.7	53.5
Stabilization Fund[a]	n/a	18.9	43.0	89.1	156.8	225.1	152.1	113.9	112.0	150.7
Reserve Fund	n/a	n/a	n/a	n/a	n/a	137.1	60.5	25.4	25.2	62.1
International reserves	76.9	124.5	182.2	303.7	478.8	426.3	439.5	479.4	498.6	537.6

Source: Bank of Finland Institute for Economies in Transition, Russia Statistics; Ministry of Finance of the Russian Federation; Bank of Russia.

Note: a. In 2008 the Stabilization Fund was split into the Reserve Fund and the National Welfare Fund.

Appendix 2:
Russian Oil
in Perspective

2.1 Proven Oil Reserves (thousand million barrels, end of year)

	1991	2001	2011	Ratio of Reserves to Production[a]
Venezuela	62.6	77.7	296.5	100+
Saudi Arabia	260.9	262.7	265.4	65.2
Canada	40.1	180.9	175.2	100+
Iran	92.9	99.1	151.2	95.8
Iraq	100.0	115.0	143.1	100+
Kuwait	96.5	96.5	101.5	97.0
Russia	n/a	73.0	88.2	23.5
Libya	22.8	36.0	47.1	100+
United States	32.1	30.4	30.9	10.8
China	15.5	15.4	14.7	9.9

Source: BP, *BP Statistical Review of World Energy, 2012.*
Note: a. The ratio of reserves to production indicates how many years existing reserves would last at 2011 production rates.

2.2 Oil Production (thousand barrels per day)

	2001	2006	2011	2011 Share of Total (%)
Saudi Arabia	9,158	10,775	11,161	13.2
Russia	6,989	9,656	10,280	12.8
United States	7,669	6,841	7,841	8.8
China	3,310	3,711	4,090	5.1
Canada	2,677	3,208	3,522	4.3
United Arab Emirates	2,551	3,149	3,322	3.8
Venezuela	3,142	2,940	2,720	3.5
Qatar	754	1,110	1,723	1.8

Source: BP, *BP Statistical Review of World Energy, 2012.*

Note: Production includes crude oil, shale oil, oil sands, and natural gas liquids (the liquid content of natural gas where this is recovered separately), and excludes liquid fuels from other sources such as biomass and coal derivatives.

Appendix 3:
Russian Gas
in Perspective

3.1 Proven Gas Reserves (trillion cubic meters, end of year)

	1991	2001	2011	Ratio of Reserves to Production[a]
Russia	n/a	42.4	44.6	73.5
Iran	19.8	26.1	33.1	100+
Qatar	6.4	25.8	25.0	100+
Turkmenistan	n/a	2.6	24.3	100+
United States	4.7	5.2	8.5	13.0
Saudi Arabia	5.2	6.5	8.2	82.1
Nigeria	3.4	4.6	5.1	100+
Canada	2.7	1.7	2.0	12.4
Azerbaijan	n/a	1.2	1.3	85.8

Source: BP, *BP Statistical Review of World Energy, 2012.*
Note: a. The ratio of reserves to production indicates how many years existing reserves would last at 2011 production rates.

3.2 Gas Production (billion cubic meters)

	2001	2006	2011	2011 Share of Total (%)
United States	555.5	524.0	651.3	20.0
Russia	526.2	595.2	607.0	18.5
Canada	186.5	188.4	160.5	4.9
Iran	66.0	108.6	151.8	4.6
Qatar	27.0	50.7	146.8	4.5
China	30.3	58.6	102.5	3.1
Norway	53.9	87.6	101.4	3.1
Saudi Arabia	53.7	73.5	99.2	3.0
Algeria	78.2	84.5	78.0	2.4
Indonesia	63.3	70.3	75.6	2.3
Malaysia	46.9	63.3	61.8	1.9
Turkmenistan	46.4	60.4	59.5	1.8
United Arab Emirates	44.9	49.0	51.7	1.6
Azerbaijan	5.0	6.1	14.8	0.5
Kuwait	10.5	12.5	13.0	0.4

Source: BP, *BP Statistical Review of World Energy, 2012.*
Note: Production excludes gas that is flared or recycled.

Appendix 4:
Developments of
Liquefied Natural Gas

4.1 LNG Exports (million tons)

	2002	2006	2010	2011
Qatar	13.9	22.9	57.5	75.5
Malaysia	15.3	21.0	23.1	25.0
Indonesia	22.9	22.2	23.6	21.4
Australia	7.5	14.5	19.1	19.2
Nigeria	8.1	12.5	18.1	18.7

Sources: International Energy Agency, Natural Gas Information 2003 and 2007; International Gas Union, World LNG Report 2010 and 2011.

4.2 LNG Imports (million tons)

	2002	2006	2010	2011
Japan	53.9	65.8	72.1	78.8
South Korea	17.2	24.4	32.0	35.8
United Kingdom	n/a	2.5	13.6	18.6
Spain	9.0	18.1	20.3	17.1
Taiwan	5.2	7.8	11.6	12.2
United States	4.8	12.3	8.9	5.9

Sources: US Energy Information Administration, World LNG Imports by Origin 2002 and 2006; International Gas Union, World LNG Report 2010 and 2011.

4.3 LNG Liquefaction Capacity (million tons)

	2000	2003	2006	2009	2012
Qatar	12.6	12.6	30.7	61.9	77.5
Indonesia	30.8	30.8	30.8	40.6	38.3
Malaysia	15.9	22.7	22.7	23.9	23.9

Source: "Global LNG Industry Heads Towards Supply Crunch," *Hydrocarbons Technology,* http://www.hydrocarbons-technology.com/features/feature50048/feature50048-2.html.

4.4 LNG Regasification Capacity (million tons)

	2000	2003	2006	2009	2012
United States	22.2	25.4	39.2	185.0	330.8
Japan	158.7	163.0	168.0	168.0	169.3
South Korea	35.9	46.1	54.1	84.6	84.6
Spain	10.6	19.4	35.7	44.6	53.9
United Kingdom	0.0	0.0	3.3	24.8	41.7
France	11.4	11.4	12.5	18.5	31.0

Source: "Global LNG Industry Heads Towards Supply Crunch," *Hydrocarbons Technology,* http://www.hydrocarbons-technology.com/features/feature50048/feature50048-3.html.

Appendix 5: Developments of Shale Gas

5.1 World Shale Gas Reserves (trillion cubic feet)

	Reserves in 2011
China	1,275
United States	862
Poland	187
France	180
Ukraine	42

Source: US Energy Information Administration, *World Shale Gas Resources.*

5.2 US Shale Gas Production

	1990	1995	2000	2005	2010	2011	2012	2015	2025	2035
Total gas production (in trillion cubic feet)	17.8	18.6	19.2	18.1	21.6	23.0	23.7	23.7[a]	26.3[a]	27.9[a]
Shale gas production (in trillion cubic feet)	0.2	0.2	0.3	0.8	5.0	6.8	7.7	8.2[a]	11.3[a]	13.6[a]
Shale gas production as percentage of total	1.1	1.5	1.7	4.2	23.1	29.8	32.4	34.8	42.8	48.8

Source: Source: US Energy Information Administration, *Annual Energy Outlook 2012.*
Note: a. Projections. According to the US Energy Information Administration, shale gas production in 2035 could range from 9.7 to 20.5 trillion cubic feet.

Appendix 6:
The European Gas Market

6.1 Sources of EU Natural Gas Supply (percentages of total)

	1994	1996	1998	2000	2002
Indigenous production[a]	63	72	69	66	67
Russia	19	17	19	19	19
Norway	9	n/a	n/a	n/a	n/a
Algeria	9	10	13	14	13
Others	0	1	0	1	2

	2004	2006	2008	2010	2012
Indigenous production[a]	59	38	37	35	33
Russia	24	23	23	22	23
Norway	n/a	16	18	19	22
Algeria	10	10	9	9	9
Others	7	13	5	15	15

Source: Eurogas, *Statistics 1994*, p. 6; Eurogas, *Statistics 1996*, p. 5; Eurogas, *Statistics 1998*, p. 5; Eurogas, *Statistics 2000*, p. 5; Eurogas, *Statistics 2002*, p. 5; Eurogas, *Statistics 2004*, p. 6; Eurogas, *Eurogas Members and EU27*, p. 7; Eurogas, *Eurogas Statistical Report* 2009, p. 7; Eurogas, *Eurogas Statistical Report 2011*, p. 8; Eurogas, *Eurogas Statistical Report* 2013, p. 6.

Notes: Some columns may not add to 100 due to rounding.

a. For 1994, indigenous production data are for Eurogas member countries; for 1996, 1998, 2000, 2002, and 2004, data are for EU member countries plus Norway and Switzerland; for 2006, 2008, 2010, and 2012, data are for EU member countries.

Appendix 7:
Existing Oil Pipelines

7.1 Existing Oil Pipelines

Name	Year of Completion	Origin	Destination	Transit Countries
Druzhba (Friendship)	1964	Russia	Germany, Czech Republic, Hungary[a]	Belarus, Poland, Ukraine, Slovakia
Baltic Pipeline System 1 (BPS-1)	2001	Russia	Russia	None
Caspian Pipeline Consortium (CPC)	2001	Kazakhstan	Russia	None
Baku-Tbilisi-Ceyhan (BTC)	2005	Azerbaijan	Turkey	Georgia
Eastern Siberia–Pacific Ocean (ESPO, Phase 1)	2009	Russia	China	None
Baltic Pipeline System 2 (BPS-2)	2011	Russia	Russia	None
Eastern Siberia–Pacific Ocean (ESPO, Phase 2)	2012	Russia	Pacific	None
Burgas-Alexandropoulos Pipeline (BAP)[b]	Incomplete	Bulgaria	Greece	None
Samsun-Ceyhan Pipeline (SCP)[c]	Incomplete	Turkey	Turkey	None

Notes: a. Deliveries through the Lithuanian and Latvian branches of the pipeline were stopped in 2003 and 2006, respectively.

b. The project was initiated in 2007 and should have been completed four years later, but the construction was put on hold due to environmental concerns raised by Bulgaria. In 2011, Bulgaria announced its intention to withdraw from the project, citing financial problems. The agreement was denounced by the Bulgarian parliament in spring 2013.

c. The pipeline was scheduled to become operational in 2012, but due to a pricing disagreement between Russia and Turkey the construction was put on hold. Turkey has threatened to freeze the project if the Turkish company Calik Holding refuses to replace Italy's ENI, which has been cooperating with Greek Cyprus.

Appendix 8:
Existing Gas Pipelines

8.1 Existing Gas Pipelines

Name	Year of Completion	Origin	Destination	Transit Countries
Bratstvo (Brotherhood)[a]	1967	Russia	Western, central, southeastern Europe	Ukraine
Finland Connector	1973	Russia	Finland	None
Northern Lights[b]	1985	Russia	Ukraine, Lithuania, Poland	Belarus
Yamal-Europe	1999	Russia	Germany	Belarus, Poland
Blue Stream	2002	Russia	Turkey	None
Baku-Tbilisi-Erzurum (BTE)/ South Caucasus	2006	Azerbaijan	Turkey	Georgia
Central Asia–China[c]	2010	Turkmenistan	China	Uzbekistan, Kazakhstan
Sakhalin-Khabarovsk-Vladivostok (SKV)	2011	Russia	Russia	None
Nord Stream[d]	2012	Russia	Germany	None

Notes: a. The main line of Bratstvo from 1967 goes to Slovakia, where it splits into one line to the Czech republic, Germany, France, and Switzerland; another goes to Austria, Italy, Hungary, and countries of the former Yugoslavia. A southern branch was added in 1974, taking gas to Romania, Bulgaria, and Turkey.

b. Northern Lights is a system of pipelines connecting Russia with European countries through Belarus.

c. The pipeline consists of two parallel lines, completed in 2009 and 2010. A third parallel line, in Uzbekistan, is scheduled to be completed in 2014.

d. Nord Stream has two lines, completed in 2011 and 2012.

237

Appendix 9: Planned Gas Pipelines

9.1 Planned Gas Pipelines

Name	Projected Year of Completion	Origin	Destination	Transit Countries
Galsi	2014	Algeria	Italy	None
South Stream[a]	2015	Russia	Italy, Austria, Greece	Bulgaria, Serbia, Hungary, Slovenia
Altai	2015	Russia	China	None
Trans-Saharan (NIGAL)	2015	Nigeria	Algeria	Niger
Nabucco	2017	Georgian-Turkish border or Iranian-Turkish border	Austria	Turkey, Bulgaria, Romania, Hungary
Trans-Anatolian Pipeline (TANAP)	2018	Azerbaijan	Turkey, then possibly EU	Georgia
Yamal-Europe 2[b]	2018–2019	Belarus	Slovakia, Hungary	Poland
Prikaspiiskoe (Pre-Caspian)[c]	Undetermined	Turkmenistan	Russia	Kazakhstan
Trans-Caspian Pipeline (TCP)[d]	Undetermined	Turkmenistan	Azerbaijan	None
Blue Stream II[e]	Undetermined	Russia	Undetermined	Turkey
Nord Stream II[f]	Undetermined	Russia	Undetermined	None

Notes: a. Possible branches to Croatia and Republika Srpska.

b. President Putin instructed Gazprom to revive this project in April 2013.

c. The Pre-Caspian pipeline is supposed to expand the Central Asia–Center (CAC) gas pipeline system. Although initially planned for 2012, the project has not made much progress.

d. Construction has been on hold due to unresolved disputes over the exploitation of oil and gas resources in the Caspian Sea.

e. Blue Stream II, proposed in 2002, was supposed to extend to Bulgaria, Serbia, Croatia, and Hungary. The idea was put on hold in 2007 when the high priority South Stream pipeline was proposed.

f. Nord Stream II would extend the existing connection between Russia and Germany by adding more lines. In addition, BP and Gazprom have been discussing the possibility of extending Nord Stream to the United Kingdom.

Acronyms

AAR	Alfa, Access, Renova (consortium of three Russian investment, financial, and industrial groups)
APEC	Asia-Pacific Economic Cooperation
BAP	Burgas-Alexandropoulos Pipeline (proposed oil pipeline between Bulgaria and Greece)
BP	British Petroleum
BPS	Baltic Pipeline System
BRIC	Brazil, Russia, India, and China
BTC	Baku-Tbilisi-Ceyhan (oil pipeline)
BTE	Baku-Tbilisi-Erzurum (gas pipeline)
CAC	Central Asia–Center (gas pipeline)
CIS	Commonwealth of Independent States
CNPC	China National Petroleum Corporation (China's largest oil and gas producer)
CPC	Caspian Pipeline Consortium
ESPO	Eastern Siberia–Pacific Ocean (oil pipeline)
ETG	EuralTransGas (energy-trading company registered in Hungary)
EU	European Union
GDP	gross domestic product
G7	Group of Seven
G8	Group of Eight
G-20	Group of 20
IMF	International Monetary Fund
LNG	liquefied natural gas
NATO	North Atlantic Treaty Organization
NIGAL	Trans-Saharan (proposed gas pipeline connecting Nigeria and Algeria)
OPEC	Organization of Petroleum Exporting Countries
SCP	Samsun-Ceyhan Pipeline (proposed oil pipeline across Turkey)

SKV   Sakhalin-Khabarovsk-Vladivostok (gas pipeline in Russia's Far
             East)
TANAP   Trans-Anatolian Pipeline (proposed pipeline from Azerbaijan to
             Turkey and further to Europe)
TCP   Trans-Caspian Pipeline (proposed gas pipeline between
             Turkmenistan and Azerbaijan)
TNK-BP   Tyumenskaya Neftyanaya Kompaniya–British Petroleum (Russian
             oil company founded in 2003 as a fifty-fifty joint venture
             between BP and the Russian consortium AAR; sold to Rosneft
             in 2012)
UGSS   Unified Gas Supply System (world's largest gas transmission
             system, owned and operated by Gazprom)

Bibliography

Adachi, Yuko. "Subsoil Law Reform in Russia Under the Putin Administration." *Europe-Asia Studies* 61, no. 8 (2009): 1393–1414.

Ahrari, Mohammed E. *The New Great Game in Muslim Central Asia.* Honolulu: University Press of the Pacific, 2002.

Ahrend, Rudiger. "Can Russia Break the 'Resource Curse'?" *Eurasian Geography and Economics* 46, no. 8 (2005): 584–609.

Alam, Shah. "Pipeline Politics in the Caspian Sea Basin." *Strategic Analysis* 26, no. 1 (2002). http://www.ciaonet.org/olj/sa/sa_jan02als01.html.

Alexeev, Michael, and Robert Conrad. "The Elusive Curse of Oil." *Review of Economics & Statistics* 91, no. 3 (2009): 586–598.

Amalrik, Andrei. *Will the Soviet Union Survive Until 1984?* New York: Harper and Row, 1970.

Auty, Richard M. *Sustaining Development in Mineral Economies: The Resource Curse Thesis.* London: Routledge, 1993.

Baev, Pavel K. "Russia Aspires to the Status of 'Energy Superpower.'" *Strategic Analysis* 31, no. 3 (2007): 447–465.

———. *Russian Energy Policy and Military Power: Putin's Quest for Greatness.* London: Routledge, 2008.

Balmaceda, Margarita M. "Background to the Russian-Ukrainian Gas Crisis: Clarifying Central Issues and Concepts." *Russian Analytical Digest* 53 (January 20, 2009). http://www.res.ethz.ch/analysis/rad/details.cfm?lng=en&id=95596.

———. *Energy Dependency, Politics, and Corruption in the Former Soviet Union: Russia's Power, Oligarchs' Profits, and Ukraine's Missing Energy Policy, 1995–2006.* London: Routledge, 2008.

———. "Intermediaries and the Ukrainian Domestic Dimension of the Gas Conflict." *Russian Analytical Digest* 53 (January 20, 2009). http://www.res.ethz.ch /analysis/rad/details.cfm?lng=en&id=95596.

———. "Russia's Central and Eastern European Energy Transit Corridor." In Pami Alto, ed., *Russia's Energy Policies: National, Interregional, and Global Levels.* Cheltenham: Elgar, 2012, pp. 136–155.

Balzer, Harley. "The Putin Thesis and Russian Energy Policy." *Post-Soviet Affairs* 21, no. 3 (2005): 210–225.

———. "Vladimir Putin on Russian Energy Policy." *In the National Interest,* November 2005. http://www.inthenationalinterest.com/Articles/November2005/November2005BalzerPFV.html.

———. "Vladimir Putin's Academic Writings and Natural Resource Policy." *Problems of Post-Communism* 53, no. 1 (2005): 48–54.

Bindemann, Kirsten. *Production-Sharing Agreements: An Economic Analysis.* Oxford: Oxford Institute for Energy Studies, 1999. http://www.oxfordenergy.org/pdfs/WPM25.pdf.

Blank, Stephen. "At a Dead End: Russian Policy and the Russian Far East." *Demokratizatsiya* 17, no. 2 (Spring 2009): 122–144.

———. "The 18th Brumaire of Vladimir Putin." In Uri Ra'anan, ed., *Flawed Succession: Russia's Power Transfer Crises.* Lanham: Lexington, 2006, pp. 133–170.

———. "Loans for Oil, the Russo-Chinese Deal, and Its Implications." *Northeast Asia Energy Focus* 6, no. 2 (Summer 2009): 19–29.

———. *The Material-Technical Foundations of Russian Military Power.* Ankara Paper no. 7. London: Cass, 2003.

———. "Russia's New Gas Deal with China: Background and Implications." *Northeast Asia Energy Focus* 6, no. 4 (Winter 2009): 16–29.

———. *Russo-Chinese Energy Relations: Politics in Command.* London: GMB, 2006.

———. "Turkmenistan and Central Asia After Niyazov." 2007. http://www.strategicstudiesinstitute.army.mil/pdffiles/pub791.pdf.

———. "The Turkmenistan-China Pipeline: What Are Its Implications?" *Northeast Asia Energy Focus* 7, no. 1 (Spring 2010): 25–35.

———. "Voodoo Economics: Notes on the Political Economy of Russian Defense." Paper presented to the 44th annual ASEEES Convention, New Orleans, November 15–18, 2012.

BP. *BP Energy Outlook 2030.* London, January 2012. http://www.bp.com/sectiongenericarticle800.do?categoryId=9037134&contentId=7068677.

———. *BP Statistical Review of World Energy, 2011.* London, June 2011. http://www.bp.com/liveassets/bp_internet/globalbp/globalbp_uk_english/reports_and_publications/statistical_energy_review_2011/STAGING/local_assets/pdf/statistical_review_of_world_energy_full_report_2011.pdf.

———. *BP Statistical Review of World Energy, 2012.* London, June 2012. http://www.bp.com/assets/bp_internet/globalbp/globalbp_uk_english/reports_and_publications/statistical_energy_review_2011/STAGING/local_assets/pdf/statistical_review_of_world_energy_full_report_2012.pdf.

Bradshaw, Michael. "A New Energy Age in Pacific Russia: Lessons from the Sakhalin Oil and Gas Projects." *Eurasian Geography and Economics* 51, no. 3 (2010): 330–359.

———. "Soviet Far Eastern Trade." In Allan Rodgers, ed., *The Soviet Far East: Geographical Perspectives on Development.* London: Routledge, 1990, pp. 239–268.

Bradshaw, Michael, and Andrew R. Bond. "Crisis amid Plenty Revisited: Comments on the Problematic Potential of Russian Oil." *Eurasian Geography and Economics* 45, no. 5 (2004): 352–358.

Braghiroli, Stefano, and Caterina Carta. "An Index of Friendliness Toward Russia: An Analysis of the Member States and the Member of the European Parliament's Positions." *Electronic Publications of the Pan European Institute*

(Turku School of Economics) no. 15 (2009). http://www.tse.fi/FI/yksikot/erillislaitokset/pei/Documents/Julkaisut/Braghiroli_and_Carta_1509_web.pdf.

Brown, Archie. *The Rise and Fall of Communism*. London: Vintage, 2010.

————. *Seven Years That Changed the World: Perestroika in Perspective*. Oxford: Oxford University Press, 2007.

Campbell, Robert W. *The Economics of Soviet Oil and Gas*. Baltimore: Johns Hopkins University Press, 1968.

Carrère d'Encausse, Hélène. *L'Empire éclaté*. Paris: Flammarion, 1978.

Closson, Stacy. "Russia's Key Customer: Europe." In Jeronim Perovic, Robert W. Orttung, and Andreas Wenger, eds., *Russian Energy Power and Foreign Relations: Implications for Conflict and Cooperation*. London: Routledge, 2009, pp. 89–108.

Considine, Jennifer I., and William A. Kerr. *The Russian Oil Economy*. Cheltenham: Elgar, 2002.

Cooper, Julian M. "Of BRICS and Brains: Comparing Russia with China, India, and Other Populous Emerging Economies." *Eurasian Geography and Economics* 47 no. 3 (2006): 255–284.

————. "The Russian Military-Industrial Complex: Current Problems and Future Prospects." In Pentti Forsström, ed., *Russia's Potential in the 21st Century*. Series 2, no. 14. Helsinki: National Defense College, 2001, pp. 43–56.

Corden, W. Max, and J. Peter Neary. "Booming Sector and De-Industrialisation in a Small Open Economy." *The Economic Journal* 92, no. 368 (December 1982): 825–848.

Dienes, Leslie. "Observations on the Problematic Potential of Russian Oil and the Complexities of Siberia." *Eurasian Geography and Economics* 45, no. 5 (2004): 319–345.

————. "Observations on the Russian Heartland." *Eurasian Geography and Economics* 45, no. 5 (2004): 156–163.

Dooley, Michael P., David Folkerts-Landau, and Peter Garber. "The Revised Bretton Woods System." *International Journal of Finance and Economics* 9, no. 4 (2004): 307–313.

Dusseault, David. "Russia's East and the Search for a New El Dorado: A Comparative Analysis of Russia's Kovytka, Sakhalin-2, and Chaiadinskoe Greenfield Projects." In Pami Alto, ed., *Russia's Energy Policies: National, Interregional, and Global Levels*. Cheltenham: Elgar, 2012, pp. 63–91.

Ellman, Michael, ed. *Russia's Oil and Natural Gas: Bonanza or Curse?* London: Anthem, 2006.

EU Commission. *An External Policy to Serve Europe's Energy Interests*. Brussels, 2006. http://ec.europa.eu/dgs/energy_transport/international/doc/paper_solana_sg_energy_en.pdf.

Eurogas. *Eurogas Members and EU27: Natural Gas Trends 2006*. http://www.eurogas.org/uploads/media/Statistics_2006_01.01.06.pdf.

————. *Eurogas Statistical Report 2009*. http://www.eurogas.org/uploads/media/Statistics_2008_01.01.08.pdf.

————. *Eurogas Statistical Report 2011*. http://www.eurogas.org/uploads/media/Statistics_2011_09.12.11.pdf.

————. *Eurogas Statistical Report 2013*. http://www.eurogas.org/uploads/media/Eurogas_Statistical_Report_2013.pdf

————. *Statistics 1994*. http://www.eurogas.org/uploads/media/STATISTICS_1994_01.01.94.pdf.

———. *Statistics 1996*. http://www.eurogas.org/uploads/media/STATISTICS_1996 _01.01.96.pdf.

———. *Statistics 1998*. http://www.eurogas.org/uploads/media/Statistics_1998 _01.01.98_01.pdf.

———. *Statistics 2000*. http://www.eurogas.org/uploads/media/STATISTICS_2000 _01.01.2000.pdf.

———. *Statistics 2002*. http://www.eurogas.org/uploads/media/STATISTICS_2002 _01.01.02.pdf.

———. *Statistics 2004*. http://www.eurogas.org/uploads/media/STATISTICS_2004 _01.01.04.pdf.

Fischer, Benjamin B. *A Cold War Conundrum: The 1983 Soviet War Scare*. CIA Library, posted March 19, 2007. https://www.cia.gov/library/center-for-the-study -of-intelligence/csi-publications/books-and-monographs/a-cold-war -conundrum/source.htm#HEADING1-08.

Fortescue, Stephen. "The Russian Law on Subsurface Resources: A Policy Marathon." *Post-Soviet Affairs* 25, no. 2 (2009): 160–184.

———. "The Russian Oligarchs and the Economic Crisis." *Russian Analytical Digest* 63 (July 7, 2009). http://se2.isn.ch/serviceengine/FileContent?serviceID =RESSpecNet&fileid=F89134E6-955D-B0A7-1240-AF0A136545AB&lng=en.

———. *Russia's Oil Barons and Metals Magnates: Oligarchs and the State in Transition*. New York: Palgrave Macmillan, 2006.

Fredholm, Michael. *Gazprom in Crisis: Putin's Quest for State Planning and Russia's Growing Natural Gas Deficit*. Russian Series no. 06/48. Zurich: Conflict Studies Research Centre, 2006. http://www.isn.ethz.ch/isn/Digital-Library /Publications/Detail/?ots591=0c54e3b3-1e9c-be1e-2c24-a6a8c7060233&lng =en&i =94459.

Freeland, Chrystia. *Sale of the Century: The Inside Story of the Second Russian Revolution*. Boston: Little, Brown, 2000.

Friedman, Thomas L. "The First Law of Petropolitics." *Foreign Policy* 154 (May–June 2006): 28–36.

Gaddy, Clifford G. "Perspectives on the Potential of Russian Oil." *Eurasian Geography and Economics* 45, no. 5 (2004): 346–351.

———. "The Russian Economy in the Year 2006." *Post-Soviet Affairs* 23, no. 1 (2006): 38–49.

Gaddy, Clifford G., and Barry W. Ickes. "Addiction and Withdrawal: Resource Rents and the Collapse of the Soviet Economy." 2006. http://econ.la.psu .edu/~bickes/addiction.pdf.

———. "Bear Traps: Can Russia Avoid the Pitfalls on the Road to Sustainable Economic Growth?" 2010. http://crifes.psu.edu/papers/bearcrifes.pdf.

———. "Resource Rents and the Russian Economy." *Eurasian Geography and Economics* 46, no. 8 (2005): 559–583.

———. "Russia After the Global Financial Crisis." *Eurasian Geography and Economics* 51, no. 3 (2010): 281–311.

———. "Russia's Virtual Economy." *Foreign Affairs* 77, no. 5 (September–October 1998): 53–67.

Gaidar, Yegor. *Collapse of an Empire: Lessons for Modern Russia*. Washington, DC: Brookings Institution, 2007.

Godzimirski, Jakub M. "The Northern Dimension of Russian Gas Strategy." *Russian Analytical Digest* 58 (April 21, 2009). http://www.isn.ethz.ch/isn/Digital -Library/Publications/Detail/?ots591=0C54E3B3-1E9C-BE1E-2C24-A6A

8C7060233&lng=en&grouppage582=82&size582=10&ord582=grp1&id =99249.

Goldman, Marshall I. *Petrostate: Putin, Power, and the New Russia.* Oxford: Oxford University Press, 2008.

————. *The Piratization of Russia: Russian Reform Goes Awry.* London: Routledge, 2003.

————. "The 'Russian Disease.'" *International Economy* 19, no. 3 (2005): 27–31.

Gorham, Michael. "Medvedev's New Media Gambit: The Language of Power in 140 Characters or Less." In Per-Arne Bodin, Stefan Hedlund, and Elena Namli, eds., *Power and Legitimacy: Challenges from Russia.* London: Routledge, 2012, pp. 199–219.

Götz, Roland. "The Southern Gas Corridor and Europe's Gas Supply." *Caucasus Analytical Digest* 3 (2009). http://www.res.ethz.ch/analysis/cad/details.cfm ?lng =en&id=96731.

Grace, John D. *Russian Oil Supply: Performance and Prospects.* Oxford: Oxford University Press, 2005.

Gustafson, Thane. *Crisis amid Plenty: The Politics of Soviet Energy Under Brezhnev and Gorbachev.* Princeton: Princeton University Press, 1989.

————. *Wheel of Fortune: The Battle for Oil and Power in Russia.* Cambridge: Belknap, 2012.

Hanson, Philip. "Observations on the Cost of the Yukos Affair to Russia." *Eurasian Geography and Economics* 46, no. 7 (2005): 481–494.

————. "The Resistible Rise of State Control in the Russian Oil Industry." *Eurasian Geography and Economics* 50, no. 1 (2009): 14–27.

————. "The Russian Economic Puzzle: Going Forwards, Backwards, or Sideways?" *International Affairs* 83, no. 5 (2007): 869–891.

Hedlund, Stefan. *Invisible Hands, Russian Experience, and Social Science: Approaches to Understanding Systemic Failure.* New York: Cambridge University Press, 2011.

————. "Russia and the IMF: A Sordid Tale of Moral Hazard." *Demokratizatsiya* 9, no. 1 (2001): 104–136.

————. *Russian Path Dependence.* London: Routledge, 2005.

————. *Russia's "Market" Economy: A Bad Case of Predatory Capitalism.* London: UCL, 1999.

Heinrich, Andreas. "Under the Kremlin's Thumb: Does Increased State Control in the Russian Gas Sector Endanger European Energy Security?" *Europe-Asia Studies* 60, no. 9 (2008): 1539–1574.

Henderson, James. *Domestic Gas Prices in Russia: Towards Export Netback?* NG no. 57. Oxford: Oxford Institute for Energy Studies, 2011. http://www.oxford energy.org/wpcms/wp-content/uploads/2011/11/NG_57.pdf.

————. *Non-Gazprom Gas Producers in Russia.* NG no. 45. Oxford: Oxford Institute for Energy Studies, 2010.

————. *The Pricing Debate over Russian Gas Exports to China.* NG no. 56. Oxford: Oxford Institute for Energy Studies, September 2011. http://www.oxford energy.org/wpcms/wp-content/uploads/2011/10/NG-561.pdf.

————. *Rosneft: On the Road to Global NOC Status?* WMP no. 44. Oxford: Oxford Institute for Energy Studies, January 2012. http://www.oxfordenergy.org /wpcms/wp-content/uploads/2012/01/WPM_44.pdf.

Hill, Fiona. *Energy Empire: Oil, Gas, and Russia's Revival.* London: Foreign Policy Centre, 2004. http://fpc.org.uk/fsblob/307.pdf.

————. "Russia: The 21st Century's Energy Superpower?" *Brookings Review* 20, no. 2 (2002): 28–31.

Hill, Fiona, and Clifford Gaddy. *The Siberian Curse: How Communist Planners Left Russia Out in the Cold.* Washington, DC: Brookings Institution, 2003.

Hoffman, David E. *The Oligarchs: Wealth and Power in the New Russia.* New York: PublicAffairs, 2011.

Holmes, Stephen. "Fragments of a Defunct State." *London Review of Books* 34, no. 1 (January 5, 2012). http://www.lrb.co.uk/v34/n01/stephen-holmes/fragments -of-a-defunct-state.

————. "Never Show Weakness: How Faking Autocracy Legitimates Putin's Hold on Power." In Per-Arne Bodin, Stefan Hedlund, and Elena Namli, eds., *Power and Legitimacy: Challenges from Russia.* London: Routledge, 2012, pp. 28–45.

International Energy Agency. *Natural Gas Information 2003.* Paris: Organization for Economic Cooperation and Development, 2003. http://www.oecd-ilibrary .org/content/book/nat_gas-2003-en.

————. *Natural Gas Information 2007.* Paris: Organization for Economic Cooperation and Development, 2007. http://www.oecd-ilibrary.org/energy/natural-gas -information-2007_nat_gas-2007-en.

————. *World Energy Outlook 2010.* Paris: Organization for Economic Cooperation and Development, 2010. http://www.worldenergyoutlook.org/media/weo website/2010/WEO2010_es_english.pdf.

International Gas Union. *World LNG Report 2010.* Vevey. http://www.igu.org /gas-knowhow/publications/igu-publications/IGU%20World%20LNG%20 Report%202010.pdf.

————. *World LNG Report 2011.* Vevey. http://www.igu.org/gas-knowhow /publications/igu-publications/LNG%20Report%202011.pdf.

Itoh, Shoichi. *The Pacific Pipeline at a Crossroads: Dream Project or Pipe Dream?* Report no. 73. Niigata: ERINA, 2007. http://www.erina.or.jp/en/Research/db /pdf2006/06050.pdf.

————. *Russia Looks East: Energy Markets and Geopolitics in Northeast Asia.* Washington, DC: Center for Strategic and International Studies, 2011. http://csis.org/files/publication/110721_Itoh_RussiaLooksEast_Web.pdf.

Jones Luong, Pauline, and Erika Weinthal. *Oil Is Not a Curse: Ownership Structure and Institutions in Soviet Successor States.* New York: Cambridge University Press, 2010.

Karl, Terry Lynn. *The Paradox of Plenty.* Berkeley: University of California Press, 1997.

Kivinen, Markku. "Public and Business Actors in Russia's Energy Policy." In Pami Alto, ed., *Russia's Energy Policies: National, Interregional, and Global Levels.* Cheltenham: Elgar, 2012, pp. 45–62.

Kjaernet, Heidi. "The Energy Dimension of Azerbaijani-Russian Relations: Maneuvering for Nagorno-Karabakh." *Russian Analytical Digest* 56 (March 3, 2009). http://www.isn.ethz.ch/isn/Digital-Library/Publications/Detail/?ots591 =0C54E3B3-1E9C-BE1E-2C24-A6A8C7060233&lng=en&grouppage582=82 &size582=10&ord582=grp1&id=97237.

Klebnikov, Paul. *Godfather of the Kremlin: Boris Berezovsky and the Looting of Russia.* New York: Harcourt, 2000.

Kleveman, Lutz. *The New Great Game: Blood and Oil in Central Asia.* New York: Atlantic Monthly, 2003.

Kochan, Lionel, and Richard Abraham. *The Making of Modern Russia.* Harmondsworth: Penguin, 1990.

Kotkin, Stephen. *Armageddon Averted: The Soviet Collapse, 1970–2000.* Washington, DC: Brookings Institution, 2001.

Kryukov, Valery, and Arild Moe. *Gazprom: Internal Structure, Management Principles, and Financial Flows.* London: Royal Institute of International Affairs, 1996.

Kuboniwa, Masaki. "Hollowing Out Industrial Production and Enlargement of Trade Sector in Russia's Marketization." Paper presented to the 34th annual AAASSS Convention, Pittsburgh, November 21–24, 2002.

Kuboniwa, Masaki, Shinichiro Tabata, and Nataliya Ustinova. "How Large Is the Oil and Gas Sector of Russia? A Research Report." *Eurasian Geography and Economics* 46, no. 1 (2005): 68–76.

Kuhn, Maximilian, and Frank Umbach. *Strategic Perspectives of Unconventional Gas: A Game Changer with Implication for the EU's Energy Security.* Strategy Paper 1, no. 1. London: EUCERS, May 2011. http://www.eucers.eu/wp-content /uploads/EUCERS_Strategy_Paper_1_Strategic_Perspectives_of _Unconventional_Gas.pdf.

Kupchinsky, Roman. "Gazprom's European Web."*Jamestown Foundation* (February 18, 2009). http://www.jamestown.org/single/?no_cache=1&tx_ttnews%5B swords%5D=8fd5893941d69d0be3f378576261ae3e&tx_ttnews%5Bany_of_the _words%5D=kupchinsky&tx_ttnews%5Bpointer%5D=2&tx_ttnews%5Btt_news %5D=34516&tx_ttnews%5BbackPid%5D=7&cHash=661619e74c6f4f12fbc2 74b66eec14d1.

———. "Russian Gas Flaring: A Political or Technical Problem?" *Eurasia Daily Monitor* 6, no. 211 (November 16, 2009). http://www.jamestown.org/single /?no_cache=1&tx_ttnews%5Btt_news%5D=35735.

Kuzio, Taras. "Poor Ukrainian-Russian Ties Reflect Yanukovych-Putin Relationship." *Eurasia Daily Monitor* 8, no. 180 (September 30, 2011). http://www .jamestown.org/single/?no_cache=1&tx_ttnews%5Btt_news%5D=38477.

Larsson, Robert L. *Nord Stream, Sweden, and Baltic Sea Security.* Stockholm: FOI, 2007. http://www.postimees.ee/foto/3/6/11846346f3bc3c25b19.pdf.

———. *Russia's Energy Policy: Security Dimensions and Russia's Reliability as an Energy Supplier.* Stockholm: FOI, 2006. http://storage.globalcitizen.net/data /topic/knowledge/uploads/20110731213514705.pdf.

Lavelle, Peter. "OPEC Dethroned, Putin's 'KremPEC' Arrives." *Future Briefs,* 2004. http://www.futurebrief.com/peterlavelleyukos002.asp.

Lavrov, Sergei. "The Rise of Asia and the Eastern Vector of Russia's Foreign Policy." *Russia in Global Affairs* 4, no. 3 (2006): 68–80.

Levine, Steve. *The Oil and the Glory: The Pursuit of Empire and Fortune on the Caspian Sea.* New York: Random, 2007.

Lindblom, Charles. *Politics and Markets: The World's Political-Economic Systems.* New York: Basic, 1997.

Lucas, Edward. *The New Cold War: How the Kremlin Menaces Both Russia and the West.* London: Bloomsbury, 2008.

Mendras, Marie. *Russian Politics: The Paradox of a Weak State.* New York: Columbia University Press, 2012.

Meulen, Evert Faber van der. "Gas Supply and EU-Russia Relations." *Europe-Asia Studies* 61, no. 5 (2009): 833–856.

Milov, Vladimir, Leonard L. Coburn, and Igor Danchenko. "Russia's Energy Policy, 1992–2005." *Eurasian Geography and Economics* 47, no. 3 (2006): 285–313.

Moe, Arild, and Valery Kryukov. "Oil Exploration in Russia: Prospects for Reforming a Crucial Sector." *Eurasian Geography and Economics* 51, no. 3 (2010): 312–329.

Naím, Moisés. "Russia's Oily Future: Overcoming Geology, Not Ideology, Will Become Moscow's Greatest Challenge." *Foreign Policy* 140 (January–February 2004): 95–96.

Nemtsov, Boris, and Vladimir Milov. "Putin and Gazprom: An Independent Expert Report." *European Energy Review,* June 3, 2009. http://www.european energyreview.eu/index.php?id=1066.

Nies, Susanne. *Oil and Gas Delivery to Europe: An Overview of Existing and Planned Infrastructures.* Paris: Institute Français Des Relations Internationales, 2011. http://www.ifri.org/files/Energie/OilandGas_Nies.pdf.

North, Douglass C. "Economic Performance Through Time." *American Economic Review* 84, no. 3 (1994): 359–368.

Nove, Alec. *Was Stalin Really Necessary? Some Problems of Soviet Political Economy.* London: Allen and Unwin, 1964.

Organization for Economic Cooperation and Development. *Economic Survey: Russian Federation 2004.* Paris, 2004.

————. *Economic Survey of the Russian Federation 2006.* Paris, 2006.

Orttung, Robert W. "Energy and State-Society Relations." In Jeronim Perovic, Robert W. Orttung, and Andreas Wenger, eds., *Russian Energy Power and Foreign Relations: Implications for Conflict and Cooperation.* London: Routledge, 2009, pp. 51–70.

Orttung, Robert W., and Indra Overland. "Russia and the Formation of a Gas Cartel." *Problems of Post-Communism* 58, no. 3 (2011): 53–66.

Pipes, Richard. "Flight from Freedom: What Russians Think and Want." *Foreign Affairs* 83, no. 3 (2004): 9–15.

————. *Russia Under the Old Regime.* New York: Scribner, 1974.

Pirani, Simon. *Elusive Potential: Natural Gas Consumption in the CIS and the Quest for Efficiency.* NG no. 53. Oxford: Oxford Institute for Energy Studies, July 2001. http://www.oxfordenergy.org/2011/07/elusive-potential-natural-gas -consumption-in-the-cis-and-the-quest-for-efficiency.

————. *Russian and CIS Gas Markets and Their Impact on Europe.* Oxford: Oxford Institute for Energy Studies, 2009.

————. "The Russo-Ukrainian Gas Dispute, 2009." *Russian Analytical Digest* 53 (January 20, 2009). http://www.res.ethz.ch/analysis/rad/details.cfm?lng=en&id =95596.

————. "Turkmenistan: An Exporter in Transition." In Simon Pirani, ed., *Russian and CIS Gas Markets and Their Impact on Europe.* Oxford: Oxford Institute for Energy Studies, 2009.

Pleines, Heiko. "Developing Russia's Oil and Gas Industry: What Role for the State?" In Jeronim Perovic, Robert W. Orttung, and Andreas Wenger, eds., *Russian Energy Power and Foreign Relations: Implications for Conflict and Cooperation.* London: Routledge, 2009, pp. 71–86.

Poussenkova, Nina. "The Global Expansion of Russia's Energy Giants." *Journal of International Affairs* 63, no. 2 (2010): 103–124.

————. *Lord of the Rigs: Rosneft as a Mirror of Russia's Evolution.* Houston: Japan Petroleum Center and James A. Baker III Institute for Public Policy at Rice University, 2007. http://www.carnegieendowment.org/publications/index.cfm ?fa =view&id=19049&prog=zru.

Putin, Vladimir. *First Person: An Astonishingly Frank Self-Portrait by Russia's President.* New York: PublicAffairs, 2000.

Rahr, Alexander. "Strategic Neighbourhood: EU-Europe Versus EU-East." *CIS Barometer* 36 (September 2004). http://www.ssoar.info/ssoar/bitstream/handle /document/13088/ssoar-2004-rahr-strategic_neighbourhood_eu-europe_versus _eu-east.pdf?sequence=1.

Riley, Alan. "Commission v. Gazprom: The Antitrust Clash of the Decade?" Policy Brief no. 285. Brussels: Centre for European Policy Studies, October 2012. http://www.ceps.eu/book/commission-v-gazprom-antitrust-clash-decade.

Robbins, Lionel. *The Theory of Economic Policy in English Classical Political Economy.* London: Macmillan, 1952.

Roland, Gérard. *Transition and Economics: Politics, Markets, and Firms.* Cambridge: Massachusetts Institute of Technology Press, 2000.

Rose, Richard. "Living in an Anti-Modern Society." *East European Constitutional Review* 8, nos. 1–2 (1999): 62–70.

Rosefielde, Steven. *Russia in the 21st Century: The Prodigal Superpower.* New York: Cambridge University Press, 2005.

Ross, Michael L. "The Political Economy of the Resource Curse." *World Politics* 51, no. 2 (1999): 297–322.

Rutland, Peter. "Putin's Economic Record: Is the Oil Boom Sustainable?" *Europe-Asia Studies* 60, no. 6 (2008): 1051–1072.

———. "Russia as an Energy Superpower." *New Political Economy* 13, no. 2 (2008): 203–210.

———. "Russia's Economic Role in Asia: Towards Deeper Integration." In Ashley J. Tellis and Michael Wills, eds., *Strategic Asia 2006–07: Trade, Interdependence, and Security.* Seattle: National Bureau for Asian Research, 2006, pp. 173–204.

Rutledge, Ian. *The Sakhalin II PSA: A Production "Non-Sharing" Agreement— Analysis of Revenue Distribution.* Prague: CEE Bankwatch Network, 2004. http://www.bothends.info/mfi/dos3-SakhalinPSA.pdf.

Sachs, Jeffrey D., and Andrew W. Warner. "The Curse of Natural Resources." *European Economic Review* 94, no. 4 (2001): 827–838.

———. *Natural Resource Abundance and Economic Growth.* Working Paper no. 5398. Cambridge, MA: National Bureau of Economic Research, December 1995. http://www.nber.org/papers/w5398.pdf?new_window=1.

Sagers, Matthew J. "Developments in Russian Gas Production Since 1998: Russia's Evolving Gas Supply Strategy." *Eurasian Geography and Economics* 48, no. 6 (2007): 651–698.

Saivetz, Carol R. "Perspectives on the Caspian Sea Dilemma: Russian Policies Since the Soviet Demise." *Eurasian Geography and Economics* 44, no. 8 (2003): 588–606.

———. "Russia: An Energy Superpower?" Cambridge: Massachusetts Institute of Technology, Center for International Studies, December 2007. http://web.mit.edu/cis/editorspick_saivetz07_audit.html.

Sapir, Jacques. "Russia's Economic Rebound: Lessons and Future Directions." *Post-Soviet Affairs* 18, no. 1 (2002): 1–30.

Service, Robert. *Stalin: A Biography.* New York: Macmillan, 2004.

Smith, Keith C. *Russia and European Energy Security: Divide and Dominate.* Washington, DC: Center for Strategic and International Studies, 2008.

———. *Russian Energy Politics in the Baltic States, Poland, and Ukraine: A New Stealth Imperialism.* Washington, DC: Center for Strategic and International Studies, 2004.

———. *Security Implications of Russian Energy Policies.* Policy Brief no. 90. Brussels: Centre for European Policy Studies, January 2006. http://www.ceps.eu/book/security-implications-russian-energy-policies.

Smith Stegen, Karen. "Deconstructing the 'Energy Weapon': Russia's Threat to Europe as Case Study." *Energy Policy* 39 (2011): 6505–6513.

Socor, Vladimir. "BP's Appraisal Doubles the Proven Reserves of Turkmenistan Gas." *Eurasia Daily Monitor* 9, no. 137 (July 19, 2012). http://www.jamestown.org/single/?no_cache=1&tx_ttnews%5Btt_news%5D=39649&tx_ttnews%5BbackPid%5D=587.

———. "Gazprom, Turkey Revive and Reconfigure Blue Steam Two." *Eurasia Daily Monitor* 6, no. 154 (August 11, 2009). http://www.jamestown.org/programs/edm/single/?tx_ttnews%5Btt_news%5D=35394&tx_ttnews%5BbackPid%5D=485&no_cache=1.

———. "New Gas Trader to Boost Turkmenistan-Ukraine Transit." *Eurasia Daily Monitor* 1, no. 64 (August 1, 2004). http://www.jamestown.org/single/?no_cache=1&tx_ttnews[tt_news]=26693.

———. "Russia Completing Baltic Pipeline System Construction, Reducing Druzhba Flow." *Eurasia Daily Monitor* 9, no. 39 (February 24, 2012). http://www.jamestown.org/programs/edm/single/?tx_ttnews%5Btt_news%5D=39055&tx_ttnews%5BbackPid%5D=27&cHash=1ff31e16f1e8c1184ad3f44528505278.

———. "Russia to Increase Purchase Prices for Central Asian Gas." *Eurasia Daily Monitor* 5, no. 50 (March 17, 2008). http://www.jamestown.org/single/?no_cache=1&tx_ttnews%5Btt_news%5D=33464.

———. "Samsun-Ceyhan Pipeline Project Designed to Divert Kazakhstani Oil." *Eurasia Daily Monitor* 6, no. 195 (October 23, 2009). http://www.jamestown.org/programs/edm/single/?tx_ttnews%5Btt_news%5D=35645&tx_ttnews%5BbackPid%5D=485&no_cache=1.

———. "Sochi Agreements and Aftermath Deflate South Stream Hype." *Eurasia Daily Monitor* 6, no. 101 (May 27, 2009). http://www.jamestown.org/single/?no cache=1&tx_ttnews%5Btt_news%5D=35043.

———. "Three Central Asian Countries Inaugurate Gas Export Pipeline to China." *Eurasia Daily Monitor* 6, no. 230 (December 15, 2009). http://www.jamestown.org/single/?no_cache=1&tx_ttnews%5Btt_news%5D=35838.

Soto, Hernando de. *The Mystery of Capital: Why Capitalism Triumphs in the West and Fails Everywhere Else.* New York: Basic, 2000.

Spechler, Dina Rome, and Martin C. Spechler. "A Reassessment of the Burden of Eastern Europe on the USSR." *Europe-Asia Studies* 61, no. 9 (2009): 1645–1657.

Stent, Angela. "An Energy Superpower? Russia and Europe." In Kurt M. Campbell and Jonathon Price, eds., *The Global Politics of Energy.* Washington, DC: Aspen Institute, 2008, pp. 76–95.

Stern, Jonathan. *The Future of Russian Gas and Gazprom.* Oxford: Oxford Institute for Energy Studies, 2005.

———. *The Russian Natural Gas "Bubble."* London: Royal Institute of International Affairs, 1995.

Stern, Jonathan, and Howard Rogers. *The Transition to Hub-Based Gas Pricing in Continental Europe.* NG no. 49. Oxford: Oxford Institute for Energy Studies, March 2011. http://www.oxfordenergy.org/wpcms/wp-content/uploads/2011/03/NG49.pdf.

Sutela, Pekka. "Forecasting the Russian Economy for 2010–2012." *Russian Analytical Digest* 88 (November 29, 2010). http://www.isn.ethz.ch/isn/Digital-Library/Publications/Detail/?ots591=0c54e3b3-1e9c-be1e-2c24-a6a8c7060233&lng=en&id=124640.

―――. "Russia's Response to the Global Financial Crisis." *Policy Outlook,* July 29, 2010. http://www.carnegieendowment.org/publications/index.cfm?fa=view &id=41305.

Tabata, Shinichiro, ed. *Dependent on Oil and Gas: Russia's Integration into the World Economy.* Slavic Eurasian Studies no. 11. Hokkaido: Slavic Research Center, 2006.

―――. "The Great Russian Depression of the 1990s: Observations on Causes and Implications." *Post-Soviet Geography and Economics* 41, no. 6 (2000): 389–398.

―――. "The Influence of High Oil Prices on the Russian Economy: A Comparison with Saudi Arabia." *Eurasian Geography and Economics* 50, no. 1 (2009): 75–92.

―――. "Price Differences, Taxes, and the Stabilization Fund." In Michael Ellman, ed., *Russia's Oil and Natural Gas: Bonanza or Curse?* London: Anthem, 2006, pp. 35–53.

―――. "The Russian Stabilization Fund and Its Successor: Implications for Inflation." *Eurasian Geography and Economics* 48, no. 6 (2007): 699–712.

Tikhomirov, Vladimir. "Capital Flight from Post-Soviet Russia." *Europe-Asia Studies* 49, no. 4 (1997): 591–615.

Tocqueville, Alexis de. *The Old Regime and the Revolution.* New York: Harper and Brothers, 1856; repr. Mineola, NY: Dover, 2010.

Tolf, Robert W. *The Russian Rockefellers: The Saga of the Nobel Family and the Russian Oil Industry.* Stanford: Hoover Institution, 1976.

Tompson, William. "Putting Yukos in Perspective." *Post-Soviet Affairs* 21, no. 2 (2005): 159–181.

Torbakov, Igor. "Europe Rejects Gazprom's Ultimatum." *Eurasia Daily Monitor* 3, no. 78 (April 21, 2006). http://www.jamestown.org/single/?no_cache=1&tx _ttnews[tt_news]=31609.

―――. "Yukos Bankruptcy: The Big Picture." *Eurasia Daily Monitor* 3, no. 151 (August 4, 2006). http://www.jamestown.org/single/?no_cache=1&tx_ttnews %5Btt_news%5D=31949.

Torjesen, Stina. "Russia and Kazakhstan: A Special Relationship." *Russian Analytical Digest* 56 (March 3, 2009). http://www.css.ethz.ch/publications/pdfs/RAD -56-6-8.pdf.

Treisman, Daniel. "Is Russia Cursed by Oil?" *Journal of International Affairs* 63, no. 2 (2010): 85–102.

―――. *"Loans for Shares" Revisited.* Working Paper no. 15819. Cambridge, MA: National Bureau of Economic Research, 2010. http://www.nber.org/papers /w15819.

Trenin, Dmitry. "Russia Reborn: Reimaging Moscow's Foreign Policy." *Foreign Affairs* 88, no. 6 (2009): 64–78.

―――. *Russia's Strategic Choices.* Carnegie Policy Brief no. 50. Washington, DC: Carnegie Endowment for International Peace, May 2007. http://www.carnegie endowment.org/publications/index.cfm?fa=view&id=19366.

US Energy Information Administration. *Annual Energy Outlook 2012.* Washington, DC, June 2012. http://www.eia.gov/forecasts/aeo/pdf/0383(2012).pdf.

―――. *World LNG Imports by Origin 2002.* Washington, DC, November 2004. http://www.eia.gov/countries/otherpages/LNGimp2002.cfm.

―――. *World LNG Imports by Origin 2006.* Washington, DC, November 2007. http://www.eia.gov/countries/otherpages/LNGimp2006.cfm.

―――. *World Shale Gas Resources.* Washington, DC, April 2011. http://www .marcellus.psu.edu/resources/PDFs/WorldShaleGas_USEIA.pdf.

Vatansever, Adnan. *Russia's Oil Exports: Economic Rationale Versus Strategic Gains.* Carnegie Paper no. 116. Washington, DC: Carnegie Endowment for International Peace, December 2010. http://www.carnegieendowment.org/files /russia_oil_exports.pdf.

World Bank. *Russian Economic Report, November 2004.* Washington, DC, 2004. http://siteresources.worldbank.org/INTRUSSIANFEDERATION/Resources /305499-1245838520910/6238985-1251964834794/RER_9_eng.pdf.

Yergin, Daniel. "Global Markets Feel the Force of North America's 'Shale Gale.'" In *World Energy Insight 2010.* London: World Energy Council, 2010. http://www.worldenergy.org/documents/wec_combined.pdf.

———. *The Prize: The Epic Quest for Oil, Money, and Power.* London: Simon and Schuster, 1991.

Zarakhovich, Yuri. "Putin Resolves Protest in Pikalevo." *Eurasia Daily Monitor* 6, no. 110 (June 9, 2009). http://www.jamestown.org/single/?no_cache=1&tx _ttnews %5Btt_news%5D=35097.

Index

255

About the Book

The sudden arrival of massive energy wealth during Putin's long reign has turned Russia's focus to resources, with some good and some very bad results. Considering why the good—a windfall of money to pay debts and put the country's finances in order—has been so overshadowed by the bad—resource dependence, reliance on rents, and unbridled corruption— Stefan Hedlund explores the many dimensions of Russia's energy policies and politics.

Stefan Hedlund is professor of Russian studies at Uppsala University. His recent publications include *Invisible Hands, Russian Experience, and Social Science: Approaches to Understanding Systemic Failure* and *Russian Path Dependence*.